COMMERCIAL DISPUTES

MARITIME AND TRANSPORT LAW LIBRARY

Ship Building, Sale and Finance
Edited by Barış Soyer and Andrew Tettenborn

The Modern Law of Marine Insurance
Volume 4
Edited by D. Rhidian Thomas

Air Cargo Insurance
Malcom A. Clarke and George Leloudas

Offshore Oil and Gas Installations Security
An International Perspective
Mikhail Kashubsky

International Trade and Carriage of Goods
Edited by Barış Soyer and Andrew Tettenborn

Maritime Law and Practice in China
Liang Zhao and Lianjun Li

Maritime Cross-Border Insolvency
Lia Athanassiou

The Law of Yachts and Yachting
Second Edition
Edited by Filippo Lorenzon and Richard Coles

Maritime Liabilities in a Global and Regional Context
Edited by Barış Soyer and Andrew Tettenborn

New Technologies, Artificial Intelligence and Shipping Law in the 21st Century
Edited by Barış Soyer and Andrew Tettenborn

The Law of Wreck
Nicholas Gaskell and Craig Forrest

Codification of Maritime Law
Challenges, Possibilities and Experience
Edited by Zuzanna Pepłowska-Dąbrowska and Justyna Nawrot

Transport Documents in Carriage Of Goods by Sea
International Law and Practice
By Caslav Pejovic

Maritime Law
Fifth Edition
Edited by Yvonne Baatz

Ship Operations: New Risks, Liabilities and Technologies in the Maritime Sector
Edited by Barış Soyer and Andrew Tettenborn

Maritime Safety in Europe
Edited by Justyna Nawrot and Zuzanna Pepłowska-Dąbrowska

Fresh Produce Shipping
Damages and Compensation
Rex C. Tester

Freeports and Free Zones
Operations and Regulation in the Global Economy
Mark Rowbotham

Disruptive Technologies, Climate Change and Shipping
Edited by Barış Soyer and Andrew Tettenborn

Responsibility and Accountability in Maritime Law
The Criminalisation of the Ship's Master
Simon Daniels

Cartner on the International Law of the Shipmaster
On the New Command at Sea
Second Edition
John A C Cartner

Illegal Charters and Aviation Law
Alena Soloveva

Commercial and Maritime Law in China and Europe
Shengnan Jia and Lijun Zhao

Offshore Floating Production
Legal and Commercial Risk Management
Stuart Beadnall, Simon Moore and Max Lemanski

The Modern Law of Marine Insurance
Volume Five
Edited by D. Rhidian Thomas

Merchant Ship's Seaworthiness: Law and Practice
Xiankai Zhan & Pengfei Zhang

Inland Waterway Transport
The European Legal Framework
Massimiliano Grimaldi

Unmanned Ships and the Law
Bulent Sozer

Damages, Recoveries and Remedies in Shipping Law
Edited by Barış Soyer

Commercial Disputes
Resolution and Jurisdiction
Edited by Barış Soyer

COMMERCIAL DISPUTES

RESOLUTION AND JURISDICTION

EDITED BY

BARIŞ SOYER

CONSULTING EDITORS:

GEORGE LELOUDAS AND
ANDREW TETTENBORN

informa law
from Routledge

First published 2025
by Informa Law from Routledge
4 Park Square, Milton Park, Abingdon, Oxon OX14 4RN

and by Informa Law from Routledge
605 Third Avenue, New York, NY 10158

Informa Law from Routledge is an imprint of the Taylor & Francis Group, an informa business

British Library Cataloguing-in-Publication Data
A catalogue record for this book is available from the British Library

Library of Congress Cataloging-in-Publication Data
Names: Soyer, Barış, editor.
Title: Commercial disputes : resolution and jurisdiction / edited by Barış Soyer ; consulting editors, George Leloudas & Andrew Tettenborn.
Description: Abingdon, Oxon [UK] ; New York, NY : Routledge, 2025. | Series: Maritime and transport law library | Includes bibliographical references and index.
Identifiers: LCCN 2024030610 (print) | LCCN 2024030611 (ebook) | ISBN 9781032726199 (hardback) | ISBN 9781032726229 (paperback) | ISBN 9781032726243 (ebook)
Subjects: LCSH: Arbitration and award—England. | Arbitration and award—Wales. | Arbitration and award—European Union countries. | Arbitration and award. | Dispute resolution (Law) | International commercial arbitration.
Classification: LCC KD7645 .C66 2025 (print) | LCC KD7645 (ebook) | DDC 347/.09—dc23/eng/20240714
LC record available at https://lccn.loc.gov/2024030610
LC ebook record available at https://lccn.loc.gov/2024030611

ISBN: 978-1-032-72619-9 (hbk)
ISBN: 978-1-032-72622-9 (pbk)
ISBN: 978-1-032-72624-3 (ebk)

DOI: 10.4324/9781032726243

Typeset in Times New Roman
by Apex CoVantage, LLC

This book is dedicated to the memory of our friend and colleague **Professor Dr. Iur. Bűlent Sözer.** We lost Bűlent following a short period of illness in December 2023. He was a well-educated and kind person with a brilliant work ethic and served as a visiting fellow of the Institute of International Shipping and Trade Law for a decade. He passed away shortly after publishing a monograph on autonomous ships – a project that he started working on whilst at Swansea in 2019.

BRIEF CONTENTS

DETAILED CONTENTS

BIOGRAPHIES OF EDITORS

George Leloudas
Professor of Law
Institute of International Shipping and Trade Law, Swansea University

Professor Leloudas is a graduate of the National and Kapodistrian University of Athens, and holds LLM degrees in commercial law from the University of Bristol, and in air and space law from the McGill Institute of Air and Space Law. He also completed his PhD in air law with emphasis on liability and insurance at Cambridge University.

His principal teaching and research interest is the carriage of passengers and goods by air, road and sea, but his interests extend to multimodal transport, insurance law, the regulation of autonomous transport systems, including cyber risks and artificial intelligence, and arbitration law. He has published two monographs, the first one on *Risk and Liability in Air Law* and the second one on *Air Cargo Insurance* with Professor Malcolm Clarke of Cambridge University. He is also the General Editor of the preeminent air law publication, *Shawcross and Beaumont on Air Law*, and has numerous peer-reviewed publications and grants in the areas of private (international) law and regulation.

Before joining the Institute, he worked as a solicitor at Gates and Partners in London for several years where he advised airlines and their insurers on liability and regulatory matters. He was also an assistant to the legal counsel of the International Union of Aviation Insurers (IUAI) providing support in relation to the replacement of the Rome Convention on Surface Damage with the 2009 Montreal Conventions. He is an instructor at the Training and Development Institute of the International Air Transport Association (IATA) where he teaches international air law for lawyers and legal professionals, law of aviation insurance, and air cargo liability law.

Barış Soyer
Professor of Commercial and Maritime Law
Director of the Institute of International Shipping and Trade Law, Swansea University

Professor Soyer directs the Institute of International Shipping and Trade Law at Swansea University, and is a member of the British Maritime Law Association and British Insurance Law Association. He is the author of *Warranties in Marine Insurance* (2001), *Marine Insurance Fraud* (2014), and many articles published in journals such as *Cambridge Law Journal*, *Law Quarterly Review*, *Edinburg Law Review*, *Lloyd's Maritime & Commercial Law Quarterly*, the *Journal of Business Law*, the *Torts Law Journal*, and the *Journal of Contract Law*. *Warranties in Marine Insurance* won the Cavendish Book Prize 2001 and was awarded the British Insurance Law Association Charitable Trust Book Prize in 2002 for its contribution to insurance literature. *Marine Insurance Fraud* also won the latter prize in 2015.

He has also edited large numbers of collections of essays on commercial, maritime, and insurance law. In addition, he sits on the editorial boards of the *Journal of International Maritime Law, Shipping and Trade Law* and editorial committee of the *Lloyd's Maritime and Commercial Law Quarterly (International Maritime and Commercial Law Yearbook)*. He currently teaches Charterparties: Law and Practice and Marine Insurance on the LLM Programme at Swansea.

Andrew Tettenborn
Professor of Commercial Law
Institute of International Shipping and Trade Law, Swansea University

Professor Tettenborn has been attached to the IISTL at Swansea Law School since 2010, teaching international trade, banking, and admiralty. He has also taught at the universities of Cambridge, Exeter, and Geneva, and held visiting positions in Europe, Australia, and the United States. He acts as General Editor of *Marsden's Collisions at Sea* and *Clerk & Lindsell on Torts*, and also of the leading student textbook on commercial law (*Sealy & Hooley's Text, Cases and Materials*); and jointly with Professor Francis Rose authored *Admiralty Claims*.

He has authored numerous articles on commercial law and obligations, sits on the editorial boards of *Lloyd's Maritime & Commercial Law Quarterly* and the *Journal of International Maritime Law*, and has advised government departments and the Law Commission.

BIOGRAPHIES OF CONTRIBUTORS

Masood Ahmed
Associate Professor
University of Leicester

Masood read law at the University of Cambridge (Sidney Sussex College). His research focuses on civil procedure, civil justice systems and reform, alternative dispute resolution (ADR), and international commercial arbitration, and research has been published in leading international academic journals. He has been involved in various major civil justice reform projects in England & Wales and has advised His Majesty's Courts & Tribunal Service (HMCTS), Ministry of Justice, and the Law Society of England & Wales. He served two terms as a member of the Civil Procedure Rule Committee and was involved in the implementation of the Online Civil Money Claims (OCMC) system, reforms to the court rules on open justice and enhancing the role of ADR within the civil court process. He is currently a member of the Main Working Party of the Civil Justice Council (CJC) which is advising the Master of the Rolls on a major review of the pre-action protocols. He is a commentator of *The White Book* (the leading text on the English Civil Procedure Rules), the ADR and Case Note editor of the *Civil Justice Quarterly*, and an editor of the *Journal of Personal Injury Law*. He is a Research Fellow on the "Affordable Access to Justice" project at the Erasmus University (Netherlands) and one of the lead researchers on the European Law Institute (ELI) project "Ditigitalisation of the Civil Courts".

Simon Baughen
Professor of Shipping Law
Institute of International Shipping and Trade Law, Swansea University

Professor Simon Baughen was appointed to the Institute of International Shipping and Trade Law as a professor in September 2013. He had previously been a reader at the University of Bristol Law School where he had worked since joining academia in 1989. He studied law at Oxford and practised in maritime law from 1979 to 1988. His research interests lie mainly in the field of shipping law in which he has written extensively over the last 30 years. He is the author of *Shipping* Law, now in its eighth edition, and took over authorship of *Summerskill on Laytime* in 2013 for its fifth edition which is now in its seventh edition. He also researches in the environmental and human rights law implications of the activities of multinational corporations in the developing world. He has produced two books on this topic: *International Trade and the Protection of the Environment* (2007) and *Human Rights and Corporate Wrongs. Closing the Governance Gap?* (2015).

Ruth Hosking
Barrister
Quadrant Chambers

Ruth's practice encompasses the broad range of general commercial litigation and arbitration. Her particular areas of specialism include shipping, civil fraud, private international law, and commodities. She undertakes drafting and advisory work in all areas of her practice and regularly appears in court and in arbitration, both as sole counsel and as a junior. She also accepts appointments as an arbitrator (both as sole and as part of a panel). She has appeared in the House of Lords, Court of Appeal, High Court, and has represented clients in a variety of international and trade arbitrations (including ICC, LCIA, LMAA, GAFTA, and FOSFA). She has been involved in a number of high profile cases, including "*The Achilleas*", a leading case on the contractual principles of remoteness of damage and "*The Atlantik Confidence*", the first case in which an English Court has determined that a person was barred from relying on the limits provided by the Limitation Convention.

She has a client-friendly approach to litigation and is happy to advise on urgent matters out of hours and at short notice. She adopts a collaborative approach to litigation, involving clients, experts and her instructing solicitors in progressing cases to trial or arbitration. She is ranked as a "Leading Junior" in the latest editions of Chambers UK and The Legal 500. In 2018, she was shortlisted for the Legal 500 Shipping Junior of the Year. In 2022, she was awarded Shipping Junior of the Year at Chambers UK Bar Awards and was shortlisted for Junior of the Year at the Legal 500 Awards.

Prior to coming to the bar, she studied for an LLM in commercial and corporate law specialising in restitution, corporate insolvency, conflict of laws, and marine insurance at UCL; and was a visiting law tutor at King's College London teaching tort (including economic torts) from 2001 to 2002.

John A. Kimbell KC
Barrister
Quadrant Chambers

John A. Kimbell KC specialises in all aspects of aviation, shipping, and insurance law. In addition to his work in the High Court, he represents a wide range of clients in commercial arbitration (LMAA, GMAA, ICC, LCIA, and DIS). He also acts as a commercial arbitrator in London and Hamburg (LMAA, LCIA, ICC, GMAA) and as a commercial mediator. Since 2018, he has sat in the High Court (Chancery, IPEC, LCCC, and QBD) as a Deputy High Court Judge and in the Crown Court in England as a Recorder.

In the aviation field he has handled a wide range of disputes arising from carriage by air, aircraft sale, aviation hull and indemnity insurance, and leasing disputes (in the UK and abroad). He has recently appeared for lessors in *Olympic Council of Asia v Novans Jets LLP* [2023] EWHC 276 (Comm); [2021] EWHC 1063 (Comm) and *Aviamport SA v South American Aircraft Leasing* SA (2021) Comm Ct. He specialises in advising clients in multi-jurisdictional disputes with foreign law aspects. He was retained in relation to the loss of Egyptair Flight 804 and Air France Flight 447 and the shooting down of Malaysian Air MH17. He has extensive experience in dealing with claims arising from helicopter and aircraft crashes (including military aircraft). He recently appeared in *Akulinina v IFly* SA [2022] EWHC 166 (QB), concerning jurisdiction under the Montreal Convention. He is currently representing the lessors of a fleet in a war risks insurance claim arising from the conflict in Ukraine.

His shipping work encompasses both "wet" collision and other Admiralty Court matters and "dry" bill of lading, charterparty, shipbuilding, and marine insurance disputes. He regularly appears in the Commercial and Admiralty Court as well as in maritime (LMAA) arbitrations. He is chair of the Admiralty Bar Group (www.admiraltybar.org). He is an editor of both the leading works on admiralty law and practice: *Marsden on Collisions at Sea* (15th edition, 2022) and *Admiralty Jurisdiction & Practice* (5th edition, 2017) both of which are regularly cited in court. He is also the joint author of the shipping chapter in *Palmer on Bailment* (3rd edition, 2009) and *Foreign Currency: Claims, Judgments and Damages* (2016).

In relation to insurance disputes, he represented the indemnity insurers in the case of *Woodford v AIG Europe Ltd* [2018] EWHC 358 (QB) and in January 2023 the carrier liability insurers in the Supreme Court in *JTI Polska v Mark-Trans-Sped* (2021) UKSC 0144. He has also been instructed as an independent expert by the marine insurers in the scuttling and anti-suit injunction case, *The Alexandros* T C-590/21, which is currently before the European Court and for the war risks insurers in the case of *Norwegian Hull Club v Horizon* in Hamburg.

He is fluent in German and accepts instructions in that language. Since 2001, he has been qualified to practice as a lawyer (*Rechtsanwalt*) in Germany. John is recommended in the current editions of The Legal 500 and Chambers UK as a leading silk in the fields of aviation, shipping, and travel.

Aygün Mammadzada
Lecturer
Institute of International Shipping and Trade Law, Swansea University

Aygun holds an LLB, LLM in International Business Law and a PhD in Law. She is a Lecturer in Law at Swansea University Hillary Rodham Clinton School of Law and acted as the managing editor of *Global Constitutionalism* published by the Cambridge University Press. Her primary research focuses on international business, trade and maritime law, commercial conflict of laws, intellectual property law, dispute resolution, including arbitration and litigation, as well as digitalisation, legal innovation, and technology. Her doctoral research on "Enhancing Party Autonomy under the Hague Convention on Choice of Court Agreements 2005: Comparative Analysis with the EU Brussels Recast Regulation 2012 and New York Arbitration Convention 1958" was fully funded by the University of Southampton.

During her academic career she has held various research fellowships at different institutions in Europe as a visiting scholar. She is a qualified lawyer in the Azerbaijan Republic and prior to her PhD research, she worked as a lawyer at the Ministry of Education of Azerbaijan Republic, International Project and Legal Officer of the Ministry on the Twinning Project and Erasmus+ Exchange Program of the European Commission and also practiced law at several law firms in Azerbaijan.

Karen Maxwell
Barrister
Twenty Essex, London

Karen practises in commercial law and international trade, with a particular focus on arbitration and shipping. After being called to the Bar, she practised at Twenty Essex where she established a commercial law practice. She then spent time at Practical Law, establishing and leading Practical Law Arbitration. Following the acquisition of PLC by Thomson Reuters, she was appointed head of Current Awareness, with responsibility for updates published in Lawtel, Westlaw and Practical Law. She returned to resume her practice at Twenty Essex in 2016.

She is regularly instructed to advise and appear in shipping, shipbuilding, and arbitration disputes. She has particular expertise in arbitration law and procedural issues relating to arbitration, including award challenges, appointments and arbitrator challenges, costs and enforcement. She is also increasingly appointed as an arbitrator (sole, party-appointed, and chair) in commercial and maritime disputes, and has conducted hearings and drafted awards in numerous cases.

She writes and lectures widely on arbitration, private international law and shipping topics. She is the co-author of *London Maritime Arbitration*, the fourth edition of which was published in 2017.

Francesco Munari
Professor of EU law
University of Genoa Law School, Partner at Deloitte Legal

Professor Francesco Munari is a tenured professor of EU law at the University of Genoa, where he teaches maritime law and transnational law of the environment. He is also partner at Deloitte Legal and is the head of practice in international and EU law as well as ports, shipping, and transport. His practice comprises EU and international law, antitrust and regulated markets, transport and transport infrastructures, in particular ports and airports, maritime law, environmental law. He has substantial experience also in commercial and corporate matters, where he acts also as litigator and arbitrator.

He serves as a member of the board of CIDOIE (Interuniversity Centre on Law concerning International Economic Organizations), SIDIUE (the Italian Society of International and EU Law); CIELI (Italian Centre of Excellency for Logistics and Transport), EMLO (European Maritime Law Organization), SIPOTRA (Italian Society of Transport Policy), and AIDIM (Italian Association of Maritime Law).

Marta Pertegás Sender
Director of M-EPLI (Maastricht European Private Law Institute)
Maastricht University

Marta Pertegás Sender holds professorial positions at the Faculties of Law of Maastricht University (The Netherlands) and the University of Antwerp (Belgium). Since 2019, she is a Visiting Professor at the University of Johannesburg (South Africa) and since 2021, an Adjunct Professor at IE Madrid (Spain).

She has extensively researched, lectured and published on international dispute resolution, the private international Law of the European Union, and the work of the Hague Conference on Private International Law (HCCH). In her former capacity of HCCH diplomat-lawyer, she worked on legislative projects in the area of international civil procedure and commercial law, including the adoption of the 2015 Hague Principles on Choice of Law in International Commercial Contracts, the entry into force of the 2005 Choice of Court Convention and preparatory work on the 2019 Judgments Convention. She has also contributed to legislative projects of the European Union and other intergovernmental organisations, such as the United Nations Commission on International Trade Law (UNCITRAL), the International Institute for the Unification of Private Law (UNIDROIT), and the World Intellectual Property Organization (WIPO).

At Maastricht University, she currently serves as one of the two Directors of M-EPLI (Maastricht European Private Law Institute) and she is a member of the Executive Board of the Dutch Branch of the International Law Association since 2015. She obtained her law degree from the University of Barcelona and her LL.M. and Ph.D. from the K.U. Leuven.

Richard Sarll
Barrister
7 King's Bench Walk, London

Richard Sarll specialises in disputes relating to commercial and admiralty law. He is a co-author of *Carver on Charterparties*, now in its second edition, in which he authored the chapter on the termination of charters. He is also a co-editor of *Lowndes & Rudolf*, 15th edition, the leading textbook on general average and the York-Antwerp Rules. He has, for a number of years, sat on the Admiralty Court Users Committee, as well as the General Average Sub-Committee of the Association of Average Adjusters, of which he is an associate member by examination. Since 2023, he has been an External Member of the Institute of Maritime Law, Southampton. His reported cases include *The Longchamp*, a much-discussed general average case which reached the Supreme Court.

David Steward
President, Arbitrator
London Maritime Arbitrators Association (LMAA)

A graduate in law from the University of Cambridge, David Steward qualified as a solicitor and practised for over 30 years with an international law firm in the City of

London, dealing with a wide range of maritime and offshore energy matters. Among other things, he handled disputes under charterparties and bills of lading, as well as contracts for shipbuilding and repair, ship sale and purchase, offshore construction, drilling, and other offshore services. He also drafted and negotiated contracts of these types. His experience extends from commercial ships, superyachts, and military vessels to floating production units and drilling rigs. In April 2011, he became wholly independent of his former firm and is a full-time arbitrator with Arbitrators at 10 Fleet Street. He was elected President of the LMAA in 2021. David has experience of institutional arbitration (ICC and LCIA) as well as ad hoc. He regularly sits as sole arbitrator or on a tribunal of two or three.

Daniel Wand
Barrister
4 King's Bench Walk

Daniel is a barrister in London. He has an established court and advisory practice which encompasses civil and commercial litigation, aviation, marine and construction disputes, property and trusts, and public law and human rights. A significant proportion of his work has an international or cross-border element. Daniel holds a PhD from the University of Leeds as well as LLM and LLB degrees from the University of Sheffield. He is a contributing editor to *Shawcross and Beaumont: Air Law*.

Patricia Živković
Associate Director of the Centre for Private International Law
University of Aberdeen

Dr Patricia Živković is an academic specialising in international commercial arbitration. She joined the School of Law at the University of Aberdeen in 2019, where she teaches courses on international commercial arbitration, negotiation skills, and technology and law. She is also currently the Associate Director of the Centre for Private International Law. She previously worked as an arbitration lawyer in Croatia, and she actively promoted the use of alternative dispute resolution mechanisms as a co-founder of the Young Croatian Arbitration Practitioners, which is an association for younger members of the arbitration community in Croatia. In addition, she has extensive experience coaching students for the Willem C. Vis International Commercial Arbitration Moot Court and she served as an associate editor of the Kluwer Arbitration Blog. She also has in-house experience in the IT industry, having previously held the position of head of the Legal Department. While working in-house, Dr Živković gained experience in negotiation as a lead legal negotiator by negotiating licence and service contracts, and disputes arising from the existing contracts. She is a member of the Committee of the Northern Chapter of the Scottish Branch of the CIArb, and the Scottish Universities Dispute Resolution Network. She is also a Co-Editor-in-Chief of the Journal for Strategic Management and Negotiation.

She received her undergraduate degree in 2011 from the Faculty of Law at the University of Zagreb and went on to earn an LL.M. degree in international business law in 2012, followed by a PhD in 2016 from the Central European University in

Budapest/New York. She is a researcher in the fields of international commercial law, international dispute resolution, and regulation of AI systems and biometric data, with her work focused on addressing legal issues in international dispute resolution (with a special focus on costs and applicable laws in international commercial arbitration), as well as exploring the challenges and opportunities presented by the rapid development of AI-based technologies (particularly in the collection and processing of biometric data).

FOREWORD

This excellent collection of chapters on commercial disputes, particularly maritime disputes, is the product of the Institute of International Shipping and Trade Law's (IISTL) 18th International Colloquium in 2023, and aims to smooth out at least some of the wrinkles currently seen in the path of dispute resolution. Barış Soyer, Professor of Commercial and Maritime Law at Swansea University, has brought together a distinguished group of specialists and consulting editors who explain some of the current issues.

Arbitration, as might be expected in maritime cases, looms large, making up the first part of the book. Issues such as jurisdiction, court supervision, and forms of order need no introduction, but knowledge of how they actually work remains vital for any commercial specialist. Besides these, recent developments are catered for in an important discussion of digitisation in ADR, and an unexpected but highly informative chapter on ADR in passenger claims.

The other two parts of the book concentrate on the transnational side of commerce. Part 2 deals with jurisdiction, both in the EU (still vital for UK lawyers, as modified by Brexit) and outside it. Coverage includes specialist areas of anti-suit relief, two chapters on enforcement of judgments in the EU, and interesting tours of both the 2005 Hague Convention on exclusive jurisdiction agreements and the 2019 Hague Convention on the Recognition and Enforcement of Foreign Judgments in Civil or Commercial Matters – this has now been signed by the UK which is the first step to ratification which is expected in due course and fills a Brexit gap. There is a rare but original examination of the jurisdictional rules applying to general average.

These lead on in a nicely seamless transition to three final chapters on choice of law in contracts, the challenges and limitations of choice of law clauses, and finally something not to be forgotten about, the applicable law in international commercial arbitration.

These are subjects which cover a broad field of interest. The Swansea IISTL's colloquiums have now been going for over 20 years attracting many of the leading players in the field, with consistently impressive results. This book carries on that notable tradition and is greatly to be welcomed.

Sir William Blair
3 Verulam Buildings
London

FOREWORD

PREFACE

Commercial disputes are always complex and time-consuming. In practice, their most complex and time-consuming aspect often concerns not the law, but the process of dispute resolution and the working out of remedies. Hence this book, which comes at a very opportune time, since we now know the rough shape of the post-Brexit jurisdiction landscape. Many now believe that this creates not so much to a threat to England & Wales as a jurisdiction of choice, as a serious opportunity. The demise of the Brussels system, UK accession of the Hague Convention on Choice of Court Agreements 2005, and the now near-certainty of its accession to the Hague Judgments Convention of 2019 could well give London an edge it has not enjoyed for some time.

As regards other forms of dispute resolution, the statistics have already confirmed that Brexit has not had much impact: London remains a firm favourite forum for arbitration and other forms of resolution. But this does not mean that arbitration law is not subject to its own pressures for change. There is a growing realisation that existing procedural rules relating to arbitration need a fair amount of rejigging, and that arbitration law as a whole needs to take measures to accommodate the solving of at least some commercial disputes by AI. In addition, there is a growing interest in developing an even more user-friendly approach to ADR. We have aimed to focus on these issues.

The book falls neatly into three parts. The first part considers contemporary matters concerning arbitration and ADR. Contributions home in on likely emerging issues on arbitration law reform and unresolved questions, plus the impact of digitalisation on dispute resolution. Secondly, we devote a whole section to jurisdiction issues, and to more general and procedural issues affecting recovery. Significant developments (national and international) have taken place in this area in recent years; and the academics and practitioners who wrote this book have taken full advantage of this. In the final part, we look at how far issues related to choice of law can have a significant impact on the outcome of a commercial dispute.

The contributions to this book first saw the light of day as papers delivered at the 18th International Colloquium organised by Swansea Law School's Institute of International Shipping and Trade Law (IISTL) in September 2023. We are enormously grateful to many for making possible the Colloquium and the book that grew from it. Our colleagues Ms Angela Nicholas and Ms Xinge LI were indispensable in providing the essential unsung backup without which these international events just cannot happen. Our publishers, Informa Law, again provided us with their unstinting support as they had with the previous events. Comments of participants to the event helped our contributors to develop their papers further in the weeks following the event.

George Leloudas
Barış Soyer
Andrew Tettenborn
May 2024, Swansea, Wales

TABLE OF CASES

France

India

International (ICC arbitrations)

People's Republic of China

Singapore

Spain

Sweden

United Kingdom

United States

TABLE OF LEGISLATION

Directives

Regulations

PART 1

ARBITRATION AND OTHER DISPUTE RESOLUTION MECHANISMS

CHAPTER 1

"*Indisputably Due*". An Express Power for Summary Procedures in London Maritime Arbitration?

*David Steward**

I Introduction

There is a longstanding tradition of resolving maritime disputes in London. These include not only disputes relating to the carriage of goods by sea, but also (for example) ship sale and purchase, shipbuilding, yachts and superyachts, offshore energy operations, and international trade. I believe that there are two main reasons why London arbitration is still the preferred method of dispute resolution for the maritime sector. The first is the body of expertise and experience, not only in London, but also elsewhere in the UK. The second is the very effective way that the Arbitration Act 1996 works together with the LMAA Terms and Procedures.[1]

Following the 25th anniversary of the Act, the Law Commission of England and Wales have reviewed it. They have taken the view that the Act still works very well and there is no need for extensive reform, but they have made some proposals. These include an express provision for summary procedures. In September 2023, the Law Commission published its final report and a draft bill,[2] and the draft bill contains a new s 39A which will be deliberated as part of this contribution.

II Law Commissions Proposal on Summary Judgments

I will start my evaluation by making a reference to the first paper of the Law Commission on the subject.[3] The Law Commission proposed a non-mandatory provision, giving arbitrators the power to adopt a summary procedure to decide issues which have no real prospect of success and no other compelling reason to continue to a full hearing.[4] They contemplated that the summary procedure to be adopted should be a matter for

---

* **Arbitrator, Arbitrators at 10 Fleet Street; President, the London Maritime Arbitrators Association (LMAA).** I am grateful to my fellow arbitrator, James Clanchy, for his helpful and expert contribution to my preparation for this paper. Any errors are entirely mine. The views expressed in this paper are those of the author and do not necessarily represent those of Arbitrators at 10 Fleet Street or the LMAA.

1 The Terms and Procedures are available on the LMAA's website: www.lmaa.london.

2 Law Commission: *Review of the Arbitration Act 1996: Final report and Bill* (Law Com No 413, September 2023). The Arbitration Bill, based closely on the recommendation of the Law Commission, was introduced into Parliament on 21 November 2023.

3 Law Commission: *Review of the Arbitration Act 1996* (Law Com No 257, September 2022).

4 This latter test has been dropped and does not appear in the Bill: see Law Commission: *Review of the Arbitration Act 1996: Final report and Bill* (Law Com No 413, September 2023), at para 6.48.

DOI: 10.4324/9781032726243-2

the arbitral tribunal, in the circumstances of the case, in consultation with the parties, and that the Act should stipulate the threshold for success. They said that a summary procedure ought to be adopted only on the application of one of the parties, rather than on the tribunal's own initiative, partly to preserve party autonomy, but also, in their words, "to guard against excessive procedural zeal" by arbitrators.[5]

The Commission acknowledged that tribunals probably already had powers which were compatible with adopting a summary procedure in an appropriate case. They noted also that there was some support in case law and among authors for the view that a summary procedure could be compatible with an arbitrator's duty of fairness.[6] So why has an express power been included in the draft bill?

The Commission suggest that a provision to this effect will "reassure arbitrators": they have been told how its explicit recognition might "combat 'due process paranoia'". There is apparently a perception that some arbitrators shy away from adopting a summary procedure "for fear that their award will be challenged, under section 68, for the serious irregularity of failing to comply with their duty under section 33".[7]

My impression is that the pressure for summary procedures comes mainly, though not exclusively, from the banking sector. I can understand, for example, that a bank might favour a summary process where it considers that a defaulting borrower has no real defence. I will discuss in this contribution why in my experience there has not been a great deal of pressure from the maritime sector for summary procedures, and whether their introduction will be likely to make much difference in practice for maritime arbitration.

It is important to set the scene. There is a perceived division between maritime arbitration and so-called international arbitration, mainly in the eyes of those who practise the latter. Although maritime arbitration is almost entirely international, it is often excluded from that wider category, most of which is institutional.

The LMAA considered the Commission's proposals as to summary procedures and expressed reservations. Their paper was excellent, but we were concerned that an express power might encourage skirmishing and satellite applications, creating a risk of additional cost and delay.

The Commission say that this would be a "world-leading development";[8] but will it really make much difference to maritime arbitration? That question has led me to reflect on how we currently deal with unmeritorious claims and defences. By this, I mean: how do we determine whether a party is right to say that a claim or defence has no merit? It is not for us to pre-judge that question.

We have to be careful about terminology here. There are various uses of the term "summary procedure". Rule 39(1) of the Stockholm Chamber of Commerce Rules refers to deciding issues "by way of summary procedure, without necessarily undertaking

5 Law Commission: *Review of the Arbitration Act 1996* (Law Com No 257, September 2022), at para 6.23.

6 See, for example, the judgment of Mr Justice Blair in *Travis Coal Restructured Holdings LLC v Essar Global Fund Ltd* [2014] EWHC 2510 (Comm), [2014] 2 Lloyd's Rep 494.

7 Law Commission: *Review of the Arbitration Act 1996* (Law Com No 257, September 2022), at paras 6.21–6.22.

8 Ibid. at para 6.10.

every procedural step that might otherwise be adopted for the arbitration". For the purposes of an article in 2018, David Ryan and Kanaga Dharmananda SC said:

> Summary disposition in arbitration is often defined by reference to similar procedures in litigation. It includes decisions on the merits which consider only limited evidence. Here, "summary disposition" is taken to include any form of deciding issues on "an expedited, summary basis" using "more limited information and evidence". Given the desire to maintain balance between fairness and lowering the time and cost of arbitration, any procedure to shorten proceedings will be considered relevant as a summary disposition.[9]

I will describe later the definition adopted by the Law Commission.

When I describe the practices of maritime arbitrators, we could get into a nice semantic discussion about whether or not they are using summary procedures at all. My point is not only about summary disposition in any strict sense. As far as I know, maritime tribunals rarely – if ever – adopt a procedure akin to summary judgment: if at all, only in the very clearest of cases. But they frequently employ their existing powers to achieve a prompt resolution. Whether or not their techniques are strictly summary in nature, they use several, individually or in combination: principally, separating out issues for determination, expediting proceedings, and deciding issues on written submissions and documents alone.

I include in this not only Full and Aspiring Full Members of the LMAA, but also others who arbitrate on LMAA Terms and Procedures, such as barristers and former judges.

Against that background, the key provisions of the Arbitration Act 1996 are as follows.

1. section 33: the general duty of the tribunal to act fairly and impartially, giving each party a reasonable opportunity of putting his case and dealing with that of his opponent, and to provide a fair means for the resolution of the matters falling to be determined;
2. section 34: the tribunal's power to decide all procedural and evidential matters, subject to the right of the parties to agree any matter;
3. section 30: the tribunal's competence to rule on its own jurisdiction;
4. section 47: the tribunal's power to make more than one award at different times on different aspects of the matters to be determined: in particular, an award relating to an issue affecting the whole claim, or to a part only of the claims or cross-claims.

In the LMAA Terms 2021, paragraph 15 reads as follows, so far as relevant:

> (a) It shall be for the tribunal to decide all procedural and evidential matters, but the tribunal will where appropriate have regard to any agreement reached by the parties on such matters. The normal procedure to be adopted is set out in the Second Schedule, subject to the tribunal having power at any time to vary that procedure.

9 "Summary Disposal in Arbitration: Still Fair or Agreed to be Fair", 35 Journal of International Arbitration (2018), pp 31–57.

(b) In the absence of agreement it shall be for the tribunal to decide whether and to what extent there should be oral or written evidence or submissions in the arbitration. The parties should however attempt to agree at an early stage whether the arbitration is to be on documents alone (i.e. without any oral hearing) or whether there is to be such a hearing.

Subject to the duties in s 33, there are already useful tools here for arbitrators to use in managing unmeritorious claims and defences. In my experience, maritime arbitrators in London have no hesitation in using them where appropriate. The Second Schedule to the LMAA Terms sets out the normal, but not invariable, procedure. Paragraph 4 provides expressly that the usual time for service of a defence, 28 days, can be abridged in exceptional cases. It refers, by way of example, to applications for interim or partial final awards for sums which are said to be indisputably due and owing.

Expedited and streamlined procedures are common – and arbitrators are accustomed to adopting them, by reference to s 34 – for the types of dispute that frequently arise in the maritime sector. For example, a party may want clarity as to its rights and duties while a ship is at sea or in port. This has been particularly significant recently for ships trapped in Ukraine. In other cases, a delivery date under a shipbuilding contract may be approaching, with the parties divided on issues as to the final contract price payable on delivery, extension of the delivery date, or the state of completeness of the ship.

At a recent seminar, I heard a US lawyer describing how in an investment dispute, a tribunal refused to "bifurcate" the case and hear first an issue as to its jurisdiction. Apparently, this led to a long procedure and ultimately a 300-page award, in which the case was rejected for lack of jurisdiction. In maritime cases, a challenge to jurisdiction will usually be dealt with in an award on other issues if it is closely bound up with those issues, for example where there is a dispute as to the existence of a contract containing the relevant arbitration agreement. Otherwise, subject to the agreement of the parties, it is common for a tribunal to deal with jurisdiction before proceeding to consider the merits. This does not necessarily entail any curtailment of evidence or submissions, but it reflects a willingness of arbitrators to expedite the resolution of issues.

A large proportion of LMAA arbitrations are resolved by refence to written submissions and documents alone. Our statistics for 2022 reveal that, of an estimated total of 420 awards published during that year on LMAA Terms and Procedures, only 93 were made after hearings. This does not mean that the majority of LMAA arbitrations concern small amounts: it is to some extent a reflection of the willingness of parties in the maritime sector to adopt streamlined procedures, or the willingness of tribunals to be robust in not allowing oral hearings where they are not justified.

There are defined procedures for small and intermediate claims which the parties can choose to adopt, either in their arbitration agreement or after a dispute has arisen. Even where the full Terms apply and there is to be an oral hearing or hearings, some issues are determined on written submissions along the way. These are not necessarily "preliminary issues" as that term is usually understood: they may not be determinative of the entire dispute, or determined by reference to agreed facts. Rather, they may be taken at an early stage in the interests of efficiency and cost-effectiveness. Whether or not issues are separated out in this way, or dealt with together, arbitrators might fix a short timetable for submissions and an early hearing.

I would not say that we never see hopeless claims or defences, but I suspect that we see fewer than in other sectors. This may be because there are gatekeepers in maritime arbitration, such as claims handlers in defence clubs, other insurers, experienced solicitors and barristers, all of whom can cast a cool eye over the case. We do not often find ourselves dealing with issues about default of borrowers, as in the banking sector, but you might say that a similar concern for shipowners is payment of hire under time charters. They often ask for a quick award for hire which has been withheld. In this respect, we take our lead from the judgment of Mr Justice Robert Goff in *SL Sethia Liners Ltd v Naviagro Maritime Corporation* (*The Kostas Melas*).[10] I note in passing that in *The Kostas Melas*, Owners gave notice of their application for a first award on a Thursday and it was heard by the arbitrators on the following Wednesday.

The case deals with the principles relating to two key matters: the law of equitable set-off and the power of arbitrators to make what was described as an "interim" award. (We now avoid the use of that word, in case it is taken to imply that the award is not final.) A charterer may exercise an equitable set-off of claims against hire if they "arise out of the same transaction or are closely connected with it". A claim must "go directly to impeach the plaintiff's demands, that is, [be] so closely connected with his demands that it would be manifestly unjust to allow him to enforce them without taking into account the cross-claim".[11]

Mr Justice Robert Goff described the commercial considerations underlying this sort of award:

> Nowadays, particularly when interest rates are high and business concerns are short of cash, cash flow has become a matter of considerable, sometimes crucial, importance. Owners of ships on time charter have therefore sought the assistance of maritime arbitrators to ensure prompt payment of hire payable under time charters, when this is withheld in circumstances which are under dispute. Sometimes owners can have recourse to the power, usually conferred under time charters, to withdraw the vessel when hire is not promptly paid; but circumstances may be such that it is not practicable to exercise this power, for example, where the market is unfavourable, or where the ship is loading or laden with cargo in circumstances where it is not practicable to withdraw the ship. So owners have turned to arbitrators for assistance; and the maritime arbitrators in the City of London have responded to that need by making, when they consider it appropriate so to do, prompt interim awards in respect of the minimum sums which they hold to be due by way of hire.[12]

Noting that the court should not fetter their power unnecessarily, the judge cautioned that arbitrators must still act fairly. He held that a party who claims to exercise a right of deduction can be called upon at very short notice to satisfy a tribunal that he is exercising his right in good faith and upon reasonable grounds:

> If he cannot do so, an award may be made against him, excluding his right to deduction from the hire payment in question – though leaving it open to him to pursue his cross-claim

10 [1981] 1 Lloyd's Rep 18.

11 *Federal Commerce & Navigation Co. Ltd. v Molena Alpha Inc. (The Nanfri)*, [1978] 2 Lloyd's Rep 132 (CA).

12 [1981] 1 Lloyd's Rep 18 at 26.

> as such, or even, if for example he can subsequently satisfy a tribunal on better evidence that he is entitled to do so, to exercise his right of deduction in respect of the same cross-claim against a subsequent payment.[13]

As to making a first award, arbitrators cannot award a minimum sum without deciding that it is due and owing. If they did so, it would change the parties' economic positions without deciding any matter in dispute and generally, arbitrators have no power to order such a change. A *Kostas Melas*–type award is not provisional in nature, but neither does it necessarily dispose of the whole case, because the charterers may still pursue their counterclaims. Nevertheless, it is a means of dealing promptly with an unmeritorious attempt to withhold payment of sums which are indisputably due.

It is becoming increasingly common to see terms in time charters which require payment of hire without deduction, set-off or withholding.

There may also be partial final awards for freight under voyage charterparties, on the basis that there can be no set-off of a claim for damages against freight.[14]

III An Evaluation on the Proposed Section 39A

That brings us to the Bill. Section 39A sets out the power to make an award on a summary basis as follows.

> (1) Unless the parties otherwise agree, the arbitral tribunal may, on an application made by a party to the proceedings (upon notice to the other parties), make an award on a summary basis in relation to a claim, or a particular issue arising in a claim, if the tribunal considers that –
>
> (a) a party has no real prospect of succeeding on the claim or issue, or
>
> (b) a party has no real prospect of succeeding in the defence of the claim or issue.[15]
>
> It then defines what is meant by this:
>
> (2) For the purposes of subsection (1), an arbitral tribunal makes an award "on a summary basis" in relation to a claim or issue if the tribunal has exercised its power under section 34(1) (to decide all procedural and evidential matters) with a view to expediting the proceedings on the claim or issue.[16]
>
> There must be consultation with the parties:
>
> (3) Before exercising its power under section 34(1) as mentioned in subsection (2), an arbitral tribunal must afford the parties a reasonable opportunity to make representations to the tribunal.[17]

My understanding is that s 39A is intended to be permissive in nature. In other words, the intention is that a tribunal should be able to use its powers under s 34 to expedite

13 Ibid. at 27.

14 See *Aries Tanker Corp v Total Transport (The Aries)* [1977] 1 Lloyd's Rep 334 (HL).

15 See Law Commission: *Review of the Arbitration Act 1996: Final report and Bill* (Law Com No 413, September 2023), at p 179: the draft of s 39A in this document differed from the wording in s 7 of the final Bill, in that it used the words "or in relation to the issue".

16 Ibid.

17 Ibid.

proceedings if it considers, following an application on notice, that a claim or issue, or the defence thereof, has no real prospect of success. There is no reason to think that s 39A will circumscribe the power to expedite in other circumstances. Also, the provision is non-mandatory, so the parties can agree otherwise, either expressly or by adopting the terms or rules of an association or institution.

In my experience, the term "due process paranoia" is rarely used in maritime arbitration. It seems to be more current in the wider category of so-called international arbitration. This is certainly not because maritime arbitrators pay insufficient regard to the need for due process. Their awards are rarely challenged in court, and even more rarely is any challenge successful. Rather, maritime arbitrators are experienced and familiar with the commercial expectations of parties in the sector, and they are given confidence by the express provisions of the LMAA Terms, operating in conjunction with the Arbitration Act. Of course, any power is potentially useful, and I am confident that maritime tribunals will give proper consideration to any application under the new s 39A. In my view, however, the likelihood is that in most cases, they will continue to use their powers as before, on the basis that these enable them to resolve issues promptly and fairly. It remains to be seen whether this legislation will provide any "comfort" more widely in international arbitration. Arbitrators will still have to give both parties a reasonable opportunity of putting their cases. They will also have to consult with the parties on the form of the summary procedure and consider the defined threshold. The question is whether those arbitrators who are said to "shy away" from summary procedures will be emboldened by an express provision for a power which probably they already have.

In [illegible] the term [illegible] process [illegible] rarely used [illegible] [illegible] [illegible] of [illegible] [illegible]. [illegible] [illegible] [illegible] [illegible] [illegible] [illegible] and [illegible] [illegible] the [illegible] [illegible] [illegible] [illegible] [illegible] [illegible] [illegible] the [illegible].

CHAPTER 2

Interim Orders and Emergency Arbitrators in Maritime Arbitration

*Karen Maxwell**

I What Are Interim Orders?

Just like parties to litigation, parties to London maritime arbitration often need to take steps to protect their position or maintain the status quo until the arbitration is completed and an award published. Interim orders may take many forms. For example, a claimant or counterclaimant may seek a freezing order to restrain the removal or dissipation of assets against which they may wish to enforce an award. Suppose a dispute concerns goods or other property which is likely to deteriorate during the arbitration, or in respect of which storage charges are accruing. In that case, a party may wish to seek an order requiring the preservation or sale of that property. Similarly, if there is a risk of evidence being destroyed or lost, orders requiring the preservation of evidence may also be sought. In some cases, more wide-ranging interim orders – notably anti-suit or anti-arbitration injunctions – may be required to protect the integrity of the arbitral process.

In summary, interim relief generally takes the form of a temporary order "holding the ring" until the underlying issues are finally determined and ruled upon in a final award. Unlike a final award, an interim order is usually provisional in nature and is subject to later adjustment or setting aside by the tribunal. Interim orders form an important plank of the supportive procedural structure within which an arbitral reference can function efficiently and effectively, leading to an enforceable award. In principle, interim orders can be made by both a tribunal and a national court, and the importance of interim relief is reflected in the fact that most institutional rules[1] and national legislation make express provision for the grant of interim orders.

II The Framework of the Arbitration Act 1996

One of the fundamental principles underpinning the 1996 Act is that of party autonomy. It follows from this fundamental principle that the English court should exercise a limited and supportive function, intervening only as provided by the Act

* **Barrister and arbitrator, Twenty Essex.**
1 See ICC Rules of Arbitration 2021 art 28(1); LCIA Arbitration Rules 2020 art 25.1; UNCITRAL Arbitration Rules 2021 art 26; HKIAC 2018 Administered Arbitration Rules art 23; SIAC Rules 2016 art 24.

DOI: 10.4324/9781032726243-3

or as permitted by the parties' arbitration agreement.[2] Of course, in practice, some functions are better suited to a court than a tribunal. For example, a court can make orders against third parties who are not bound by the arbitration agreement and can impose effective sanctions (such as sanctions for contempt of court) if orders are breached. Such measures are not available to arbitrators, who derive their power from the agreement between the parties. Nevertheless, the starting point under the Act is that the parties have agreed to arbitrate and that their agreement should be respected and enforced by limiting court intervention.

Under the 1996 Act, both the tribunal and the English court may have the power to assist the parties by granting interim relief in appropriate cases. In some instances, the Act confers and precisely delineates the scope of the tribunal's and court's respective powers to grant interim relief. For example, in relation to property which is the subject of the arbitration, both the tribunal (s 38(4)) and the court (s 44(2)) have the power to make orders for inspection, photographing, preservation, custody, or detention of the property. However, those powers are not identical in scope: the tribunal's power under s 38(4) is limited to property owned by or in the possession of a party to the arbitration, whereas the court's power extends to third parties. The court also has an additional power, under s 44(2), to authorise any person to enter premises in the possession or control of a party to the arbitration. These differences in the scope of the tribunal's and court's powers reflect the practical inability of an arbitral tribunal to make orders binding on third parties.[3]

Outside those specific and closely defined statutory powers, the effect of s 39(1) of the Act[4] is that a tribunal is empowered to grant interim orders only if the parties have so agreed. Such an agreement would usually be contained in institutional rules but could (more unusually) be included in the arbitration clause. Where there is no such agreement (as is frequently the case in maritime arbitration in the UK), the parties must turn to the court for assistance.

The court's powers to grant interim relief are contained in s 44 of the Act, which confers on the court "the same power of making orders . . . as it has for the purposes of and in relation to court proceedings" in respect of several matters, including "the granting of an interim injunction".[5] It is apparent from this wording that the broad intention of the section is to import, into the arbitral context, the powers that a court would have in the context of litigation. However, the exercise of these parallel s 44 powers requires the applicant to satisfy stringent requirements, designed to restrict the court's role and ensure that the dispute's centre of gravity remains with the tribunal. These restrictions were seen as a central aspect of "the redefinition of the relationship between arbitration and the Court"[6] ushered in by the Act. As

2 Section 1; see Departmental Advisory Committee on Arbitration Law, *Report on the Arbitration Bill* (February 1996) paras 18–22 ("DAC Report").

3 See also the powers in relation to preservation of evidence conferred on the tribunal and court, respectively, by ss 38(6) and 44(2).

4 "The parties are free to agree that the tribunal shall have power to order on a provisional basis any relief which it would have power to grant in a final award".

5 Sections 44(1), (2)(e).

6 DAC Report, note 2, para 214.

further discussed later, the meaning and scope of these statutory requirements have given rise to difficulties in practice, some of which are now addressed in proposed legislative amendments. The restrictions imposed by s 44 also raise some tricky questions about the relationship between s 44 and the court's parallel power to grant injunctive relief (under s 37 of the Senior Courts Act 1981). In general, the court has declined to exercise its jurisdiction under s 37 in cases where the requirements of s 44 have not been met: absent very clear agreement to that effect, s 37 cannot be used to circumvent the s 44 restrictions.[7]

The shared and overlapping nature of the supportive functions of the tribunal and court inevitably means that there are grey areas at the intersection between the court's and tribunal's areas of competence. The difficulties of delineating the respective competence of the court and tribunal become even more acute in cases where the parties' arbitration agreement provides for emergency arbitration. Emergency arbitration is a relatively recent phenomenon (and certainly would not have been in the contemplation of the drafters of the 1996 Act when they designed s 44). Still, it has been enthusiastically embraced by arbitral institutions. In broad outline, emergency arbitration involves the urgent appointment of an independent emergency arbitrator tasked with swiftly determining applications for provisional interim relief. Any interim order made by the emergency arbitrator is subject to later review, adjustment, or setting aside by the tribunal once appointed. For example, under the LCIA Arbitration Rules (2020), art 9B sets out a procedure for the appointment of an emergency arbitrator ("a temporary sole arbitrator to conduct emergency proceedings pending the formation or expedited formation of the Arbitral Tribunal"). The power is engaged "in the case of emergency at any time prior to the formation or expedited formation of the Arbitral Tribunal" and the LCIA Court determines applications for appointment. The emergency arbitrator must decide on the emergency relief claim as soon as possible but no later than 14 days following the appointment (though the LCIA Court is empowered to extend this deadline). When the tribunal is appointed, it may confirm, vary, discharge, or revoke any order made by the Emergency Arbitrator or issue an additional order.

Emergency arbitration is not referred to in the UK Act for the simple reason that emergency arbitration did not exist at the time the Act was drafted. This is not the case in other jurisdictions, where in recent years, rafts of legislation to support and give effect to emergency arbitration have been enacted. For example, in Singapore, the International Commercial Arbitration Act 1994 was amended in 2012 to extend the definition of "arbitral tribunal" for the purposes of the Act to include an emergency arbitrator. The Hong Kong Arbitration Ordinance confers power on the court to enter judgment in the terms of an order made by an emergency arbitrator. In the UK, as further discussed later, issues have arisen in practice in connection with the relationship between the developing mechanisms for emergency arbitrations, and the requirements of s 44 and have led to several proposed amendments.

7 See, for example, *Sabmiller Africa v East African Breweries* [2009] EWCA Civ 1564, [2010] 2 Lloyd's Rep 422; *Enercon GmbH v Enercon (India) Ltd* [2012] EWHC 689 (Comm), [2012] 1 Lloyd's Rep 519 [68].

III Maritime Arbitration in the UK: The LMAA Terms and LCIA Rules

Turning from legislation to institutional provisions: the vast majority of maritime arbitration in the UK is conducted pursuant to the LMAA (London Maritime Arbitrators Association) Terms. However, the LCIA also deals with some maritime disputes, particularly shipbuilding disputes. The two institutions adopt diametrically opposed approaches to granting tribunal-granted interim orders and emergency arbitration.

The LMAA is an association of practising arbitrators, not an administering institution, and its arbitration rules (the LMAA Terms) apply by agreement between the parties (or by virtue of an LMAA arbitrator accepting appointment on the basis that LMAA Terms will apply). Notably, the LMAA Terms do not include any agreement entitling the tribunal to grant interim orders nor for the appointment of an emergency arbitrator. In LMAA arbitrations, therefore, a party wishing to claim interim relief must apply to the court by bringing itself within s 44 of the Act.

By contrast, the LCIA Arbitration Rules are more closely aligned with the approach of other international arbitration institutions. Emergency arbitration provisions were introduced into the LCIA Arbitration Rules in 2014, and under art 25.1 of the LCIA Arbitration Rules (2020), the tribunal has the power to order provisional relief. As further discussed later, it was in the context of LCIA arbitration that the potential issues arising from the relationship between s 44 and the emergency arbitration provision were first addressed by the English court.

IV Court or Tribunal: Pros and Cons

Pausing there, it is perhaps worth considering why the LMAA has turned its face against introducing provisions enabling a tribunal to grant interim orders or providing for emergency arbitration. The starting point is that LMAA arbitrations are seated in London, with easy access to the Commercial Court. The Court has vast expertise in dealing with freezing orders (one of the most commonly sought interim orders) and interim orders generally and can offer very short notice hearings, if necessary, by telephone or via virtual platforms. In short, the Court offers a high-quality, efficient, and user-friendly service, familiar to those involved in the shipping industry. It would be difficult for the LMAA to provide a cost-effective competing mechanism.

Furthermore, there are unavoidable practical issues relating to tribunal-granted interim relief. In many cases, interim relief is required early in proceedings, before the tribunal has been fully constituted. In practice, even emergency arbitration can sometimes be too slow and unwieldy a procedure for the applicant. There are now examples in the case law of parties applying to court under s 44 pending the emergency arbitrator's decision.[8]

8 For example, *Shapoorji Pallonji & Co v Yumn Ltd* [2021] EWHC 862 (Comm), [2021] 2 Lloyd's Rep 59, a case which raises the further interesting question of whether the court should decline to grant an order if to do so would be inconsistent with the (slightly different) approach to such relief that the emergency arbitrator would probably adopt in due course.

Even after the tribunal is constituted, arbitrators are often uncomfortable about granting "without notice" relief, which may be required in the case of interim orders, in particular freezing injunctions. Due process concerns on the part of arbitrators (and emergency arbitrators) mean that it will often be more straightforward to apply to court. Applications for freezing injunctions, for example, are almost invariably made to court rather than to the tribunal. There is a longstanding but slightly arid debate about whether the parties could ever confer power on a tribunal to grant an interim freezing injunction.[9] In practice, the issue is unlikely to arise because a tribunal-granted freezing injunction could never be as effective as a court-ordered injunction, not least because of the inability of the tribunal to bind third parties such as banks. Most parties will, therefore, prefer to seek injunctive relief from the court.

Most importantly, there are practical issues around enforcing tribunal-granted interim injunctions. It is far from clear whether an interim injunction granted by a tribunal would constitute an "award" for the purposes of enforcement under the New York Convention. Some jurisdictions have passed legislation which purports to characterise a provisional award granted by an emergency arbitrator as an "award" within the New York Convention: however, such legislation would not, of course, bind the enforcing courts of other jurisdictions. Nor would breach of a tribunal-ordered interim injunction give rise to sanctions for contempt of court. In addition, and as noted earlier, a tribunal's injunction will bind only the parties to the arbitration. Unlike a court order, it will have no effect on third parties, including, in particular, banks holding assets caught by a freezing injunction. This is a significant limitation on the practical utility of tribunal-granted relief.

Finally and more generally, the LMAA is not an administering institution[10] and has in general adopted a cautious approach to rule changes.[11] It appears to have concluded that adequate support is available via the tried-and-tested court route. The LMAA's rising caseload[12] suggests that it has probably made the right call as far as its users are concerned.

V Freezing Injunctions

One of the most significant and powerful procedural tools available to a claimant (or counterclaimant) is the "freezing order" or "freezing injunction". A freezing injunction does not secure a claim but restrains a party from dissipating or removing assets that might otherwise be available for enforcement. Freezing injunctions may extend to assets held outside the jurisdiction (a "worldwide" injunction) and are a highly effective tool in aid of enforcement. The court will often also grant ancillary orders requiring,

9 *Kastner v Jason* [2004] EWHC 592 (Ch), [2004] EWCA Civ 1599.

10 The LMAA Terms (2021) provide for the President of the LMAA to make default appointments in certain situations, but the LMAA itself does not perform any supportive, supervisory, or administrative role.

11 See, for example, the Explanatory Note accompanying the 2017 version of the Terms, which explains the "light touch" approach underlying the formulation of the terms and (in relation to amendments) the view that any amendments should be made incrementally: "if it ain't broke, don't fix it". https://lmaa.london/wp-content/uploads/2020/08/Note-on-LMAA-2017-Terms.pdf, accessed 23 November 2023.

12 "LMAA arbitration: a strong showing in 2022". https://lmaa.london/london-retains-its-crown-in-international-maritime-arbitration/, accessed 15 July 2024.

for example, disclosure of assets. The purpose of all such orders is to prevent the defendant or respondent from frustrating the enforcement of an award or judgment by dissipating, moving, or hiding assets. As such, the availability of freezing injunctions is an important aspect of the support provided to arbitration by English law.

In some cases, assets held by third parties may be potentially vulnerable to enforcement proceedings. This may happen where, for example, a group of companies moves assets around the companies within the group in order to protect the award debtor from enforcement. Sophisticated and complex corporate structures enable such manoeuvring, which is not unusual. In *TSB Private Bank International SA v Chabra*,[13] the court held that it had the power to grant a freezing injunction against a third party, against whom there was no cause of action, and that it would permit the joinder of that third party for those purposes. The circumstances in which such relief is available are carefully defined, and the courts have emphasised that the jurisdiction is to be exercised cautiously.[14] There must be good reason to suppose that assets held in the name of a defendant against whom the claimant asserts no cause of action (the "NCAD"[15]) would be amenable to some process, ultimately enforceable by the court, by which the assets would be available to satisfy a judgment against a defendant against whom the claimant asserts a cause of action (the "CAD"). For these purposes, "good reason to suppose" is equivalent to "good arguable case" – i.e. the judge must consider that it is more than barely arguable, but it need not be a case with more than a 50% chance of success. Furthermore, the court must be satisfied that it is just and convenient to exercise the jurisdiction, which is exceptional and to be exercised "with caution". A good example of assets falling within the *Chabra* jurisdiction would be where there is good reason to suppose that the assets held by the NCAD are, in truth, assets of the CAD. Establishing substantial control by the CAD over the NCAD assets may be relevant but will not necessarily justify a freezing order: the test, ultimately, is whether there is good reason to suppose that the assets would be amenable to enforcement of a judgment obtained against the CAD.

VI Proposed Amendments to the Arbitration Act 1996

In 2022, the Law Commission commenced a consultation on review of the Arbitration Act 1996. In general, it was felt that the Act works well in practice and has enhanced the development of arbitration in this jurisdiction. However, the Act has never been reviewed or amended since it came into force more than 25 years ago. The Law Commission's first consultation paper on reviewing the Arbitration Act 1996[16] was published in

---

13 [1992] 1 WLR 231.

14 See, for example, *Lakatamia Shipping Co Ltd v Su* [2014] EWCA Civ 636, [2015] 1 WLR 291; *Yukos Capital Sarl v OJSC Rosneft Oil Co* [2010] EWHC 784 (Comm), [2011] 1 All ER (Comm) 172; *Linsen International Ltd v Humpuss Sea Transport Pte Ltd* [2011] EWHC 2339 (Comm), [2011] 2 Lloyd's Rep 663.

15 The Privy Council has subsequently confirmed, in *Broad Idea International Ltd v Convoy Collateral Ltd* [2021] UKPC 24, that there was no reason in principle why the court's jurisdiction to grant an injunction was limited to cases where a claimant could establish a cause of action against the defendant. The court's equitable jurisdiction to grant an injunction against a party subject to its personal jurisdiction existed whenever it was just and equitable to grant relief.

16 Law Commission, *Review of the Arbitration Act 1996 – A consultation paper* (Consultation Paper 257, 2022) ("Law Commission Arbitration Act 1996 Consultation Paper").

September 2022 and made several wide-ranging proposals. The final report and draft bill were published in September 2023 and were included in the King's Speech 2023[17] and was introduced to Parliament. Following the 2024 General Election, the Bill was included in the July 2024 King's Speech and was re-introduced to Parliament on 18 July 2024. The bill covers several areas of arbitration law, including some of the issues that have emerged in practice in connection with interim orders and emergency arbitration. It proposes amendments (principally to s 44 of the Act) to address those concerns.

Before examining the proposals and bill further, it is perhaps worth noting that the Law Commission's terms of reference in conducting its review of the Act required it to determine whether the Act:

> continues to promote the UK as a leading destination for commercial arbitration . . . the Commission and the Department recognise the value of arbitration to the UK economy, and resolve that the review should be conducted in a manner which aims to enhance the competitiveness of the UK as a global centre for dispute resolution and the attractiveness of English and Welsh law as the law of choice for international commerce.[18]

Accordingly, the review involved close consultation with users of arbitration (both legal practitioners and commercial parties) with a view to ensuring that the current "system" meets their needs and that the UK can maintain its competitive edge, against the background in particular of the increasing popularity of other arbitral seats, in particular, Singapore.

A Section 44

As noted earlier, s 44 of the Act (headed "court powers exercisable in support of arbitral proceedings") confers power on the court to grant interim relief, including injunctions. It provides:

> (1) Unless otherwise agreed by the parties, the court has for the purposes of and in relation to arbitral proceedings the same power of making orders about the matters listed below as it has for the purposes of and in relation to legal proceedings.
>
> (2) Those matters are –
>
> (a) the taking of the evidence of witnesses;
>
> (b) the preservation of evidence;
>
> (c) making orders relating to property which is the subject of the proceedings or as to which any question arises in the proceedings –
>
> (i) for the inspection, photographing, preservation, custody or detention of the property, or
>
> (ii) ordering that samples be taken from, or any observation be made of or experiment conducted upon, the property;
>
> and for that purpose authorising any person to enter any premises in the possession or control of a party to the arbitration;

17 British Prime Minister's Office, *The King's Speech 2023: background briefing notes*. www.gov.uk/government/publications/the-kings-speech-2023-background-briefing-notes, accessed 23 November 2023.

18 Law Commission Arbitration Act 1996 Consultation Paper, note 16, appendix 1: Terms of reference.

(d) the sale of any goods the subject of the proceedings;
(e) the granting of an interim injunction or the appointment of a receiver.

(3) If the case is one of urgency, the court may, on the application of a party or proposed party to the arbitral proceedings, make such orders as it thinks necessary for the purpose of preserving evidence or assets.

(4) If the case is not one of urgency, the court shall act only on the application of a party to the arbitral proceedings (upon notice to the other parties and to the tribunal) made with the permission of the tribunal or the agreement in writing of the other parties.

(5) In any case the court shall act only if or to the extent that the arbitral tribunal, and any arbitral or other institution or person vested by the parties with power in that regard, has no power or is unable for the time being to act effectively.

(6) If the court so orders, an order made by it under this section shall cease to have effect in whole or in part on the order of the tribunal or of any such arbitral or other institution or person having power to act in relation to the subject-matter of the order.

(7) The leave of the court is required for any appeal from a decision of the court under this section.

The wording of s 44 (which has been described as one of the most difficult provisions of the Act[19]) has given rise to several difficulties in relation to the dividing line between the powers of the courts and the tribunal. The key "problem areas" relate, specifically, to the ability to make orders against third parties and the effect (if any) of emergency arbitrator provisions on the court's s 44 powers.

Section 44 is a non-mandatory provision – i.e. it can be excluded by the parties' agreement (neither the LMAA Terms nor the LCIA Rules contain any such exclusion). The legislative technique adopted in s 44 is to confer on the court "the same power of making orders" in respect of a number of specified matters "as [the court] has for the purposes of and in relation to legal proceedings".[20] In other words, the intention was to align court and arbitration, at least as far as the scope of the power to grant interim orders is concerned.

However, additional limits on the court's powers of intervention are set out in subsections (3) to (5). Different criteria apply, depending on whether the case is one of "urgency". In an urgent case, the court may "make such orders as it thinks necessary for the purpose of preserving evidence or assets".[21] Otherwise, the court may intervene only if the application is made with the tribunal's permission or the agreement in writing of the other parties to the arbitration. In all cases, subsection (5) imposes an overarching restriction: the court is entitled to act

19 R. Merkin & L. Flannery, *Merkin and Flannery on the Arbitration Act 1996* (6th Edn, Informa Law 2020), para 44.1 (Merkin & Flannery).

20 Section 44(1).

21 The term "assets" is not defined in the Act but has been interpreted broadly and includes a cause of action: *Cetelem SA v Roust Holdings Ltd* [2005] 2 Lloyd's Rep 494 (CA). This allows the section to be interpreted as encompassing freezing injunctions, which at least in most cases (though cf *Broad Idea*, note 15) are granted to preserve an asset in the form of a cause of action.

> only if or to the extent that the arbitral tribunal, and any arbitral or other institution or person vested by the parties with power in that regard, has no power or is unable for the time being to act effectively.

These limits on the court's power share the same central purpose: they are intended to reflect party autonomy and prevent the court from usurping the tribunal's role. As noted earlier, although the court's more general power under s 37 of the Senior Courts Act 1981 does not impose similar limitations, s 37 cannot be used to sidestep the s 44 requirements. It is immediately apparent, however, that the limitation imposed by subsection (5) ("arbitral tribunal . . . has no power or is unable for the time being to act effectively") overlaps substantially with the question of whether a case is "urgent".[22] If a tribunal cannot act effectively, the court's intervention becomes more urgent – and vice versa. It is equally clear that the question of whether a tribunal can act "effectively" or whether a case is "urgent" involves an element of judgment and, to that extent, overlaps with the more general question of whether it is just and equitable for the court to intervene.

It will be noted that, under subsection (7), the leave of "the court" is required for any appeal from an order made under s 44. "The court" is defined in the Act as the first instance court,[23] with the consequence that (by contrast with the usual position) the Court of Appeal has no power to grant leave to appeal. In effect, the subsection cuts down the usual rights of appeal by requiring permission to be obtained from the first instance court and removing the Court of Appeal's power to do so.

B Section 44: Proposed Reforms

i Third Parties

The Law Commission proposed a number of reforms to s 44. The most significant relates to the court's power to make orders against third parties – i.e. those who are not a party to the arbitration or the arbitration agreement. Over recent years, the question of whether s 44 extends to third parties has generated a significant debate. There are conflicting first-instance decisions on the question of whether s 44 empowers the court to make orders against a third party.[24] Teasing out the ratio of these decisions is not always straightforward, not least because many of them were principally concerned

22 As is clear from the DAC report, note 2, paras 214–216.

23 *Inco Europe Ltd v First Choice Distribution* [2000] 1 WLR 586; *Virdee v Virdi* [2003] EWCA Civ 41; *Henry Boot Construction (UK) Ltd v Malmaison Hotel (Manchester) Ltd* [2001] QB 388.

24 Early decisions tended towards the view that s 44 allowed orders against third parties, though most of these decisions concerned service out and so the issue was not fully argued: see e.g. *Unicargo v Flotec Maritime S de RL (The Cienvik)* [1996] 2 Lloyd's Rep 395; *Vale do Rio Doce Navegacao SA v Shanghai Bao Steel Ocean Shipping Co Ltd* [2000] 2 Lloyd's Rep 1 (both pre-1996 Act cases which supported the view that it was sufficiently arguable that service out against third parties was available under CPR 62.5); *BNP Paribas SA v OJSC Russian Machines* [2012] 1 Lloyd's Rep 61 (in which Blair J held that there was a good arguable case that s 33 did apply to claims against non-parties); *Western Bulk Shipowning III A/S v Carbofer Maritime Trading APS (The Western Moscow)* [2012] 2 Lloyd's Rep 163 (an application for a *Chabra* order, in which Christopher Clarke J indicated that he inclined to the view that service out against a third party was permissible); *Public Joint Stock Co Vseukrainskyi Aktsionernyi Bank v Maksimov* [2013] EWHC 3203 (Comm), [2013] All ER (D) 140 (Aug) (another *Chabra* case in which Blair J held that there was power to order service out against a non-party). The authorities are reviewed in detail in *Cruz City 1* and *DTEK*.

with analysing the service out provisions of the CPR. However, more recently, the Commercial Court has reached a broad consensus that s 44 does not, in general terms, extend to third parties: see, in particular, *DTEK Trading SA v Morozov*[25] in which the court followed the (*obiter*) approach of Males J (as he then was) in *Cruz City 1 Mauritius Holdings v Unitech Ltd.*[26]

In *Cruz City 1*, an award creditor (which had already secured a worldwide freezing injunction and the appointment of receivers over the assets of the award debtor) applied for a freezing injunction in respect of assets held by the award debtor's subsidiaries – a so-called *Chabra* order. The subsidiaries challenged the court's jurisdiction to allow service of proceedings on them. Males J (as he then was) held that the court had no such jurisdiction under the applicable CPR provisions. In so deciding, he indicated (*obiter*) that the better view was that s 44 did not confer any power on the court to make orders against non-parties. He gave three main reasons for that view. Firstly, the provision's wording suggested that it was not intended to apply to third parties. His reasoning at [48] focuses closely on the wording of s 44 as follows:

> "(i) The section is expressed by the opening words of subsection (1) to be subject to contrary agreement between the parties, which must mean the parties to the arbitration agreement. While it would theoretically be possible that the availability of remedies against non-parties should depend on the parties' agreement, it seems much more likely that Parliament contemplated an agreement between the parties to the arbitration as to the powers which one party could invite the court to exercise against the other.
>
> (ii) Subsection (4) provides that, except in cases of urgency, the court can only act on an application made with the permission of the arbitral tribunal or the agreement in writing of "the other parties" – which clearly means the other parties to the arbitration. It is possible, I suppose, that Parliament intended to empower arbitrators to give permission for an application to be made against a non-party, but that seems surprising in view of the consensual nature of arbitration and the fact that arbitrators generally have no jurisdiction over non-parties. It would be surprising too if the arbitrators were empowered to give such permission without hearing from the non-party, although to allow a non-party even this limited standing to make submissions to the arbitrators (for which purpose it would generally need to know something about the arbitral proceedings) seems hard to reconcile with the private and confidential nature of arbitration.
>
> (iii) Subsection (5) provides that the court shall act only if the arbitrators have no power or are unable for the time being to act effectively. But that will always be the case where an order is sought against a non-party.
>
> (iv) Similarly, subsection (6), which allows the court to hand back to the arbitral tribunal the "power to act in relation to the subject matter of the order", can have no application to an order made against a non-party.
>
> (v) The effect of subsection (7) is that there can be no appeal from any order under section 44 unless the first instance court gives permission. It would be surprising if in the exceptional case of an order against a non-party, backed up by the sanction

25 [2017] EWHC 94 (Comm), [2017] 1 Lloyd's Rep 126.

26 [2014] EWHC 3704 (Comm), [2015] 1 Lloyd's Rep 191.

of contempt proceedings, the non-party's right of appeal was limited in this way. A non-party has not agreed to the finality and promptness of decision making which are meant to be the hallmarks of arbitration and which provide the rationale for curtailing a party's rights of appeal.

(vi) None of these indications is conclusive, but together they suggest, to my mind, that the section is simply not concerned with applications against non-parties."

Secondly, Males J noted that s 44 applies regardless of whether the seat of the arbitration was England and Wales and suggested that it would be surprising if Parliament had intended the court to have the power to make potentially wide-ranging orders against third parties worldwide. Thirdly, Males J observed that there was nothing in the DAC Report suggesting an intention to apply the powers under s 44 to third parties.

Males J's *obiter* observations, which were essentially based on a fine-textured analysis of the detailed wording of s 44, attracted some criticism from commentators who favoured a more purposive approach to statutory interpretation.[27] They reasoned that the overriding intention of s 44 (as evidenced by the terms of s 44(1)) was to transpose, to the arbitration context, the powers that were available in litigation. *Chabra* had been decided a few years before the Act came into force: had Parliament intended to exclude *Chabra* orders from s 44, one might have expected to see express provision to that effect. And in any event, some of the potentially available s 44 orders (in particular orders for the taking of the evidence of witnesses) necessarily involved third parties. Nevertheless, Males J's reasoning was adopted by Sara Cockerill QC (as she then was) in *DTEK*, now the leading case on the question of the scope of s 44. *DTEK* was concerned with an application under s 44(2)(b) of the 1996 Act for the preservation of evidence (in that case, a settlement agreement concluded with the third party). The judge acknowledged that the basic intention of s 44 was to entitle the court to exercise the same powers in support of arbitration as it would have in court proceedings, and accepted that the inability to make orders against third parties was a matter of concern. Nevertheless, like Males J, she felt constrained by the wording of s 44 to hold that such relief was not available.[28] The decision in *DTEK* was subsequently followed by Moulder J in *Trans-Oil International SA v Savoy Trading LP*.[29]

One further twist was provided by the Court of Appeal's decision in *A v C*.[30] This case can be seen as a partial retreat, or perhaps as laying the ground for a partial retreat, from the Commercial Court consensus: the Court of Appeal held that orders for the taking of evidence by deposition could be made against third parties under s 44(2)(a) ("taking the evidence of witnesses") in support of a New York seated arbitration. Perhaps more importantly, the Court also left open the question of whether any of

27 See, for example, Merkin & Flannery, note 19.
28 See [36]–[56].
29 [2020] EWHC 57 (Comm) [36]–[45].
30 [2020] EWCA Civ 409, [2020] 1 WLR 3504.

the other sub-paragraphs of s 44(2) might extend to third parties.[31] That means that there is, in the current state of the authorities, some uncertainty about the scope and application of s 44. (In passing, there is also an anomaly arising in connection with the rules governing depositions in support of foreign court proceedings: as the Court of Appeal accepted, in the context of court proceedings, the English court would not have the power to order such a deposition without an incoming letter of request, whereas s 44 (which applies to foreign-seated arbitrations) imposes no such requirement.)

The Commercial Court's restrictive interpretation of s 44 has potentially far-reaching consequences. It would preclude, for example, the making of *Chabra* freezing orders against third parties holding assets which are, in reality, the assets of the party to the arbitration and which might, therefore, be available for enforcement. Although the bar for granting a *Chabra* order is set relatively high, such orders would nevertheless provide an extremely potent weapon for claimants and award creditors.

Having reviewed the authorities, the Law Commission's starting point was that s 44 could not be interpreted on a "one-size-fits-all" basis. Adopting a broader and more purposive approach to statutory construction, the Law Commission noted that the intention was to import the law on various matters, as that law would apply in domestic legal proceedings. Furthermore, in the Law Commission's view, the wording of s 44 did not require any blanket exclusion of orders against third parties. Nevertheless, recognising the lack of certainty arising from the current state of the authorities, the Law Commission recommended (and the bill provides) that s 44 should be clarified to make clear that orders against third parties are, in principle, available against third parties to the same extent that they would be in court proceedings. Of course, in many cases, the claimant will be unable to satisfy the stringent conditions for the grant of *Chabra* relief. Still, in principle, such relief should be available under s 44 in support of arbitration as it is in court proceedings. Such a clarification is to be welcomed: it reflects better the overall purpose of s 44. It will also enhance the competitiveness of UK seated arbitration in circumstances where other leading jurisdictions (including Hong Kong and Singapore) allow freezing injunctions to be made against third parties in the context of arbitration.

As adjuncts to that reform, the Law Commission proposed that third parties' rights of appeal regarding orders made against them should be unlimited – i.e. third parties would not be caught by the restrictions on appeal under s 44(7) that apply to parties to the arbitration – and the bill includes provision to this effect. This is logical: third parties have not agreed to arbitrate, and there would appear to be no reason why their rights of appeal against orders made against them, notwithstanding their non-involvement in any arbitration, should be circumscribed in the same way as parties who have signed up to arbitration as a dispute resolution process. It will also be necessary to review and update the CPR service out provisions to ensure that they reflect the (clarified) scope of s 44.

31 Ibid. [57] (Males LJ).

ii Emergency Arbitrators

As noted earlier, the proliferation of emergency arbitrator schemes has led many jurisdictions to introduce a supportive legislative framework within which a consensual emergency arbitration mechanism can operate effectively. There is some anecdotal evidence and empirical research suggesting that the availability of emergency arbitration and the ability to enforce emergency arbitrator decisions may be an increasingly significant factor in party choice.[32] However, such evidence must be viewed against the background that applications for emergency arbitration are still made in only a very small proportion of arbitrations – and even if an application is made, it is, in most cases, refused.[33] The proportion of LCIA arbitrations in which parties apply for the appointment of an emergency arbitrator appears to be particularly low (applications for an appointment of an emergency arbitrator were made in less than 1% of cases in 2022, and all applications were refused).[34] The reasons for this are unclear but are possibly connected with the availability of the expedited tribunal formation procedure contained in art 9A of the LCIA Rules (2020) and (more generally) the availability of freezing injunctions and other interim relief from the Commercial Court.

Against that background, and perhaps mindful of the expertise that institutions have built up in connection with emergency arbitration, the Law Commission has not recommended the introduction of legislative provisions applying the Act generally to emergency arbitration, or for the administration of emergency arbitration, or for the enforcement of emergency arbitrators' awards or decisions. The Law Commission has taken the view that emergency arbitrator regimes are best administered by arbitral institutions rather than the courts. Nevertheless, emergency arbitration is a concept recognised by English law, and some minor "tweaks" have been suggested to enhance its effectiveness.

The first area considered by the Law Commission relates to the wording of s 44(5), which stipulates that the court may intervene "only if or to the extent that the arbitral tribunal, and any arbitral or other institution or person vested by the parties with power in that regard, has no power or is unable for the time being to act effectively". This wording raises the question of whether the existence of emergency arbitrator provisions in institutional rules means that there is an institution or other person with power and ability to act effectively, at least in non-urgent cases. This issue was touched on but not decided in *Gerald Metals v Timis.*[35] That case concerned an LCIA arbitration in which the claimant had applied to the LCIA for the appointment of an emergency arbitrator for the purposes of obtaining a freezing injunction restraining the respondent from dissipating assets. The respondent subsequently offered undertakings, in light of which the LCIA decided that the case was no longer urgent and declined to appoint an

32 See, for example, QMUL and White & Case, *2021 International Arbitration Survey: Adapting arbitration to a changing world* 8. https://arbitration.qmul.ac.uk/media/arbitration/docs/LON0320037-QMUL-International-Arbitration-Survey-2021_19_WEB.pdf, accessed 23 November 2023.

33 ICC Arbitration and ADR Commission, *Report on Emergency arbitrator proceedings* (2019). https://iccwbo.org/wp-content/uploads/sites/3/2019/03/icc-arbitration-adr-commission-report-on-emergency-arbitrator-proceedings.pdf, accessed 23 November 2023.

34 LCIA, *Annual Casework Report 2022* 24. www.lcia.org/News/lcia-news-annual-report-on-2022-updates-on-the-lcia-court-and.aspx, accessed 23 November 2023.

35 [2016] EWHC 2327 (Ch), [2016] All ER (D) 31 (Oct).

emergency arbitrator. The claimant then applied to the court for a freezing injunction under s 44, which was refused because subsection (5) was not satisfied.

The decision was widely discussed and was interpreted by some commentators as indicating that the mere existence of an emergency arbitration mechanism in institutional rules might preclude the court from intervening because an applicant under s 44 would be unable to establish that the tribunal or other institution or body had no power to act effectively. The Law Commission disagreed with this interpretation of *Gerald Metals* but nevertheless originally recommended that the offending wording should be removed from s 44(5). It reasoned that the "urgency" and "necessity" requirements imposed by subsection (3) already encompassed and required consideration of the question of whether any tribunal or other body or person is empowered to act effectively. The additional wording in s 44(5) was, therefore, of symbolic value only.

These observations prompted some strong feedback during the second consultation period, in the light of which the Law Commission abandoned this recommendation. It accepted the view of most consultees that s 44(5) continues to discharge an important function of underlining the respective roles of the court and arbitrator, and ultimately agreed that it should be retained for that reason. As a result, the effect of subsection (5) is still "at large" and will have to be ruled on by the court when the issue arises for decision.

In addition, however, the Law Commission proposed that the court should be empowered to enforce the peremptory orders of emergency arbitrators. Section 41 of the Act confers power on the tribunal to make peremptory orders in certain circumstances and s 42 provides that, unless otherwise agreed, the court "may make an order requiring a party to comply with a peremptory order". The bill amends these provisions by extending them to emergency arbitrators, in effect making the orders of emergency arbitrators equally enforceable and effective.

The Law Commission further proposed that an emergency arbitrator should be empowered to give permission for a s 44 application (as an arbitrator is entitled to under s 44(4)). Given that even emergency arbitration can take weeks rather than days, this will no doubt prove to be a useful power in very urgent cases or perhaps in cases where orders against third parties are sought.

VII Conclusion

One of the stated aims of the Law Commission's review of the Act was to maintain the competitiveness of the UK as an arbitral seat. In general, the Law Commission has concluded that the Act is working well in practice and that no root and branch reform is required. However, the reforms it has suggested concerning interim relief, as embodied in the bill passing through Parliament, are to be welcomed. The proposed amendments to s 44 reflect the purpose of the Act and will allow arbitrating parties the full range of interim remedies available to litigants. The minor amendments relating to emergency arbitrators are a pragmatic response to a still-developing area of arbitration and are likely to enhance the effectiveness of emergency arbitration in those cases where the parties have opted for it.

CHAPTER 3

The Court's Oversight of Arbitration and Challenging Jurisdiction

*Ruth Hosking**

I Introduction

Until comparatively recently, the English courts tended to be jealous of arbitration and to regard arbitrators as rivals to be kept in their place. In the 1856 case of *Scott v Avery*,[1] Campbell LJ advanced the theory that this arose from a desire by the judges to get cases into Westminster Hall. The traditional position was still being pursued in 1922: for instance, Scrutton LJ was indignant in *Czarnikow v Roth, Schmidt & Co*,[2] at the suggestion that the parties to an arbitration might, by agreement, put their chosen arbitrator beyond judicial scrutiny: "There must be no Alsatia[3] in England where the King's writ does not run".

Judicial attitudes to arbitration began to change in the mid-20th century, and the Commercial Court began to support the autonomy of the arbitration process. However, the courts remained heavily involved in supervising arbitrations through the "case stated" procedure: an arbitrator, who was presumed likely to make an error of law, could be required to state a case on a question of law for the court's opinion. In fact, by the 1970s, the right to appeal on points of law was almost automatic. Attitudes have changed since then and there have been significant developments in the law of arbitration: the Court's powers in relation to arbitrations are now relatively limited both in relation to appeals on points of law and more widely.

The UK Government asked the Law Commission to review the Arbitration Act 1996 (AA 96) to determine whether there might be any amendments to the Act to ensure that it is fit for purpose and that it continues to promote the UK as a leading destination for commercial arbitrations. To that end:

1. The Law Commission published its first consultation paper on 22 September 2022. It addressed a shortlist of topics and asked consultees whether any other topic beyond the shortlisted topics needed to be considered. The response date was 15 December 2022.
2. The Law Commission published its second consultation paper on 27 March 2023, which included some recommendations concerning the proper

* **Barrister, Quadrant Chambers**.

1 (1856) 5 HLC 811.

2 [1922] KB 478, 488 (CA).

3 The ancient name for Alsace, an area around Whitefriars in London in the 17th century which was a sanctuary for criminals and debtors.

DOI: 10.4324/9781032726243-4

law of the arbitration agreement and revisited s 67 AA 1996 and discrimination. The response date was 22 May 2023.

3 The Law Commission published its final report on 6 September 2023.

This paper considers the issue of the Court's oversight of arbitration and challenges to jurisdiction under three headings: (I) Historical Background, (II) The Current Regime, and (III) The Law Commission's Proposals.

II Historical Background

It was common practice in medieval England[4] for disputes and quarrels to be submitted by the parties to the decision of one or more arbitrators selected by the parties who would secure the arbitration by executing private conditional bonds.[5]

The earliest recorded examples of commercial cases having been settled in London stretch back to the 7th century. William the Conqueror granted a charter to the inhabitants of the City of London that they should enjoy the same law as they had done under Edward the Confessor. Henry I issued the great charter of 1132 confirming the old legal customs of London and allowing citizens to appoint whom they wished of themselves to "keep the pleas of the Crown".

In the 13th century, regular trade between England and Spain began, and the merchants of Barcelona had their own banks in London. Records from as early as 1303 indicate Catalonians being appointed as London arbitrators.[6] In the 14th century, there was provision for "quality" arbitrations. The Statute of Staples 1353 provided for the determination of disputes concerning the quality of wool sold or the method of packing by six assessors, four aliens and two English, whose decision would be binding on the Court.

Merchant guilds of the City of London began to spring up, such as the Mercer's (the wool exporters' guild), the Goldsmiths, and the Vintner's. Some established arbitration tribunals to hear disputes between their members. In the 15th century, the Courts, for the first time, affirmed the need for finality and certainty in awards.[7] During the Tudor and Stuart reigns, that centralist organ of government, the Court of Star Chamber, began to develop jurisdiction to hear commercial cases, but still sent cases involving freight and average to arbitration by merchants.[8] During the latter half of the 16th century, however, it was clear that the tribunals that gave the merchants the most satisfaction were not the Courts of the land but those in which they had a hand.[9] An observer wrote at the time: "what a ridiculous thing is it, that judges in Chancery must determine of merchants' negotiations, transacted in foreign parts, which they understood no better than do the seats they sit on".[10]

---

4 See Sir William Searle Holdsworth, *History of English Law* (Sweet & Maxwell 1972) vol XIV 187 ("Holdsworth").

5 A.W. Brian Simpson, *A Brief History of the Common Law of Contract* (Clarendon 1975).

6 Frederick Sandborn, *Origins of Early English Maritime Commercial Law* (Century Co 1930) 268.

7 Anon YB 8 Edw IV, fl.11, 9 (1468).

8 Dasent's cases, 1549–1589.

9 Holdsworth, note 4, vol V 149.

10 William Cole, *A Rod for the Lawyers* (Printed for Giles Calvert 1659) iv, 323.

In the 17th century, there was an increase in the number of commercial arbitrations in London and the passing of the first English Arbitration Act by William III: the Arbitration Act of 1698,[11] which formally recognised that it was lawful for merchants to submit disputes to arbitration. During the 18th and 19th centuries, there was a gradual but inexorable extension of judicial control over arbitration and awards, for instance, the Common Law Procedure Act 1854. The first edition of Russell on the *Law of Arbitration* was published in 1837. The number and type of disputes involving shipping, commodities, and finance grew and grew. The traditional Courts were not regarded as up to the task.

The Arbitration Act of 1889[12] codified practice relating to arbitration and enabled the arbitrator to state his award in the form of a "special case", enabling the Court "to adjudicate on any point of law arising in the reference". In addition to the development of arbitration, a new court, namely the Commercial Court, was established to deal with disputes involving shipping, commodities, and finance. The catalyst for establishing the Commercial Court can be traced back to a case before Mr Justice Lawrance J called *Rose v Bank of Australasia*.[13] Lord Justice Mackinnon famously later recorded:[14]

> The Judge knew as much about the principles of general average as a Hindoo about figure skating. He listened with a semblance of interest . . ., reserved judgment and forgot all about the case. After a long delay he was somehow reminded that he ought to give judgment. This he did – in favour of the plaintiff. To his horror Gorrell Barnes QC then rose and said he had failed to deal with a very important point. Not having the least idea what the point was, he pulled himself together and said: "Oh Yes; I meant to say that having considered that I think the adjusters took the right view, and in that respect also I think the claim as made out by them ought to succeed". The defendants went off the Court of Appeal [who] reversed Lawrance J. As appears in [1894] A.C. 687, the House of Lords restored the judgment of Lawrance J.

This led to the resolution of the Queen's Bench Division judges in 1894 that a Commercial Court should be constituted and led to the appointment of Mr Justice Mathew as the first Commercial Judge. Lord Parker wrote in 1959 of the Commercial Court and London arbitration:[15]

> The two systems ought indeed to be properly regarded as co-ordinate rather than rival. Many disputes, like questions as to quality, are clearly more suitable for arbitration. No question of law is involved, and an arbitrator in the trade can, by handling the sample, determine the dispute in a moment without the necessity of hearing advocates, and without the procedure and trappings of a court of law. At the other extreme, a dispute depending solely or mainly on the construction of an exemption clause in a commercial contract is more suitable to be determined by the Commercial Court. That is not to say

11 9 & 10 Will III c 15. See also *Consuetudo, vel Lex Mecatoria* (c 1670).

12 Lord Bramwell drafted a fully comprehensive Arbitration Bill but the government fell before it was enacted. Subsequently, a modified version was introduced in the form of the Arbitration Act 1889.

13 [1894] AC 684. Counsel included Gorrell Barnes QC and Sir Thomas Edward Scrutton.

14 Reproduced in Hew R Dundas, "Appeals on Questions of Law: Section 69 Revitalised" (2003) 69(3) Arbitration 172–183; see also C.K. Allen, "The Origins of the Commercial Court" (1944) 60 LQR 324–325.

15 See, generally, Lord Parker of Waddington, "1959 Lionel Cohen Lecture" at the Law Faculty of the Hebrew University of Jerusalem. https://en.law.huji.ac.il/book/lionel-cohen-annual-lecture-series, last accessed 12 January 2024.

> that an experienced arbitrator, be he lay or legal, might not arrive at a correct decision, but such a case . . . will, no doubt ultimately come to the courts and that being so it might as well come there at once thereby avoiding considerable delay.

The regime under which decisions of arbitrators were brought before the High Court was radically altered by the Arbitration Act 1979. Section 1(4) of that Act provided that the High Court should not grant leave to appeal unless, having regard to all the circumstances, the determination of the question of law concerned could substantially affect the rights of one or more of the parties. The Act itself would not have brought about such a change; it was the court's approach to the discretion given to them under the Act that achieved this.

In 1982 the House of Lords in *The Nema*[16] gave guidance on the circumstances in which permission to appeal to the High Court from the decision of an arbitrator should be given:

1. In one-off cases, leave to appeal was only granted if the decision was obviously wrong.
2. In cases of general importance, permission to appeal was granted if there was a substantial likelihood that the arbitrator(s) got it wrong.

This decision involved reversing the approach taken by Mr Justice Robert Goff in the Commercial Court when it fell to him to make the initial interpretation of s 1(4) of the 1979 Act. Three years after the *Nema*, Lord Diplock in *The Antaios*[17] revisited the issue of permission to appeal and held that in arbitrations which turned on the construction of a standard term, leave should not be given unless the judge considered that a strong *prima facie* case had been made out that the arbitrator had been wrong in his construction. Lord Diplock believed that this applied even in circumstances where there were judicial statements (but not decisions) in other reported High Court cases, which suggested that upon a question of the construction of that standard term, there may be two schools of thought among commercial judges.

The objective of the 1996 Act was to improve and clarify the major elements of English arbitration law. During the consultative process, which led to enacting the 1996 Act, various commentators questioned whether the right to appeal an arbitration award on a point of law should be abolished entirely. Lord Saville, who became Chairman of the Departmental Advisory Committee in the autumn of 1994, said in a speech delivered on 4 November 1996 in London:[18]

> Another feature of our existing law which has caused disquiet abroad and which many regard as detracting from arbitrating here is the ability to seek leave to appeal to the Court from the substantive award of the arbitral tribunal. What is said is that to allow an appeal of this kind is to frustrate the agreement of the parties to resolve their disputes by arbitration, since the result of a successful appeal is to substitute a court resolution for an arbitral resolution.

---

16 *Pioneer Shipping Ltd v BTP Tioxide Ltd (The Nema)* [1982] AC 724 (HL).

17 *Antaios Compania Naviera SA v Salen Rederierna AB (The Antaios)* [1985] AC 191 (HL) 203–204.

18 Saville LJ, "The Arbitration Act 1996 and its Effect on International Arbitration in England" (1997) 63 Arbitration 104, 108, col. 1.

The Committee decided against recommending the abolition of any right of appeal on the substantive merits of the dispute, preferring further to limit the right to appeal. Lord Saville explained the rationale behind that decision in these terms:[19]

> it is well arguable that this limited right of appeal can properly be described as supportive of the arbitral process. Where the parties have agreed that their dispute will be resolved in accordance with English law, and the tribunal then purports to reach an answer which is not in accordance with English law, it can be said with some force that unless the Courts correct this error, the tribunal itself will have failed to carry out the bargain of the parties.

It is fair to say that such an argument has not always been met with universal approval.[20]

III The Current Regime – The Arbitration Act 1996

The 1996 Act is divided into mandatory and non-mandatory provisions.[21] Save for the mandatory sections, party autonomy is key; the parties are free to choose what happens in the event of a particular occurrence (often determined by any institutional rules the parties have agreed to apply).

The court's oversight of arbitration can be divided into three main categories:

1 challenges and appeals (ss 67, 68 & 69 AA 1996);
2 evidence and assets (s 44 AA 1996);
3 additional powers (ss 18, 24, 32, 42, 43 & 45 AA 1996).

This chapter focuses on the first and briefly deals with the third. Karen Maxwell deals with the second in Chapter 2.

A Challenges and Appeals

i Challenging Jurisdiction

The substantive jurisdiction of an arbitral tribunal is determined by determining (1) whether there is a valid arbitration agreement, (2) whether the arbitral tribunal is properly constituted, and (3) what matters have been submitted to arbitration in accordance with the arbitration agreement.[22]

Suppose a party participates in arbitral proceedings but objects to the tribunal's jurisdiction. In that case, they must raise their objection promptly or risk losing the

19 Ibid., 108, col. 2. See also Departmental Advisory Committee on Arbitration Law, *Report on the Arbitration Bill* (February 1996) para 285 ("DAC report").

20 For instance, see Roger Holmes, Michael O'Reilly, "Appeals from Arbitral Awards: Should Section 69 be Repealed?" (2003) 69 Arbitration 1, 6.

21 Arbitration Act 1996, s 4. The mandatory provisions are listed in Schedule 1 and have effect notwithstanding any agreement to the contrary. The mandatory provisions are ss 9 to 13, 24, 26(1), 28, 29, 31 to 33, 37(2), 40, 43, 56, 60, 66 to 68, and 72 to 75.

22 This is the definition of substantive jurisdiction in the Arbitration Act 1996, s 82 (which refers to s 30) and also appears in s 72.

right to object later on.[23] Having raised their objection, the participating party has three options:

1 Under s 30 AA 1996, the tribunal is itself competent to rule on whether it has jurisdiction.
2 Under s 32 AA 1996, the objecting party can apply to the court under s 32 (on which see further detail below under the Miscellaneous heading).
3 The objecting party can invoke s 67 AA 1996 (which is dealt with in detail later).

These three options for challenge can be combined and are not mutually exclusive – i.e. it can object and then apply to the court under s 32 or it can object and then challenge any award under s 67.

If a party objecting to the tribunal's jurisdiction does not participate, they can apply to the court to question whether the tribunal has jurisdiction as provided for in s 72(1). They can also challenge any award under s 67 AA 1996 or resist enforcement of any arbitral award under s 66(3) on the basis that the tribunal lacked jurisdiction to make the award.

ii Section 67: Challenging the Award: Substantive Jurisdiction[24]

A party to arbitral proceedings may (upon notice to the other parties and to the tribunal) apply to the court either (1) challenging any award of the tribunal as to its substantive jurisdiction or (2) for an order declaring an award made by the tribunal on the merits to be of no effect, in whole or in part, because the tribunal did not have substantive jurisdiction.

A party may lose the right to object (s 73 AA 1996) and the right to apply is subject to restrictions in ss 70(2) & (3) AA 1996. The Court may (1) confirm the award, (2) vary the award, or (3) set aside the award in whole or in part.

A challenge to the award for want of jurisdiction must be supported by evidence of the facts said to give rise to the absence of substantive jurisdiction.[25] Under CPR rules 3.3(4) and/or 23.8(c), the Court has the power to dismiss any claim without a hearing. It is likely to do so where the nature of the challenge or the evidence filed in support of it leads the Court to consider that the claim has no real prospect of success.

Any hearing of an application under s 67 AA 1996 by the court will be conducted on a *de novo* basis – i.e. it will consider the matter afresh, as if for the first time. Put another way, the court is exercising original rather than appellate jurisdiction. This is not explicit in the wording of s 67, but in *Dallah v Pakistan (Dallah)*,[26] the Supreme Court said that in such cases, the court will make an independent assessment of the

23 Arbitration Act 1996, ss 31(1) to (3) and 73(1).

24 This is a mandatory provision and cannot be contracted out of.

25 Commercial Court of England and Wales, *Commercial Court Guide* (11th Edn 2023), para O8.4 ("Commercial Court Guide").

26 [2010] UKSC 46, [2011] AC 763 [26], [96] and [159]–[160]. However, *Dallah* was concerned with the operation of s 103 AA 1996, and thus, the comments in relation to s 67 are not part of the binding decision. Moreover, *Dallah* was a case where the party that objected to jurisdiction did not participate in the arbitral proceedings, so a s 67 challenge would be *de novo* even on the Law Commission's initial proposals (details of which are given later).

matter. The tribunal's decision carries no weight, and the court can fully re-examine the facts, regardless of how fully they were explored by the tribunal when it determined its own jurisdiction.

iii Section 68: Challenging the Award: Serious Irregularity[27]

A party to arbitral proceedings may, upon notice to the other parties and to the tribunal, apply to the court challenging an award in the proceedings on the grounds of serious irregularity affecting the tribunal, the proceedings, or the award.

Section 68(2) AA 1996 defines serious irregularity as one or more of the following kinds which the court considers has caused or will cause substantial injustice to the applicant:

1 failure by the tribunal to comply with section 33 (general duty of tribunal);
2 the tribunal exceeding its powers (other than exceeding its substantive jurisdiction);
3 failure by the tribunal to conduct the proceedings in accordance with the procedure agreed by the parties;
4 failure by the tribunal to deal with all the issues that were put to it;
5 any arbitral or other institution or person vested by the parties with powers in relation to the proceedings or the award exceeding its powers;
6 uncertainty or ambiguity as to the effect of the award;
7 any irregularity in the conduct of the proceedings or in the award which is admitted by the tribunal or by any arbitral or other institution or person vested by the parties with powers in relation to the proceedings or the award.

If there is shown to be a serious irregularity affecting the tribunal, the proceedings or the award, the court may (1) remit the award to the tribunal, in whole or in part, for reconsideration, (2) set aside the award in whole or in part, or (3) declare the award to be of no effect, in whole or in part.

A challenge to the award for serious irregularity must be supported by evidence of the circumstances on which the claimant relies as giving rise to the irregularity complained of and the nature of the injustice which has been or will be caused to the claimant.[28] Under CPR rules 3.3(4) and/or 23.8(c), the Court has the power to dismiss any claim without a hearing. It is likely to do so where the nature of the challenge or the evidence filed in support of it leads the Court to consider that the claim has no real prospect of success.

Where the court makes an order dismissing a s 68 claim without a hearing pursuant to para O8.6 of the Commercial Court Guide, the applicant has the right to apply to the Court to set aside the order and seek directions for the application hearing. If such an application is made and dismissed after a hearing, the Court may consider whether awarding costs on an indemnity basis is appropriate.[29]

27 This is a mandatory provision and cannot be contracted out of.
28 Commercial Court Guide, note 25, para O8.4.
29 Ibid., para O8.8.

iv Section 69: Appeal on Point of Law

Unless otherwise agreed by the parties, a party to arbitral proceedings may, upon notice to the other parties and to the tribunal, appeal to the court on a question of law arising out of an award made in the arbitration.

An appeal cannot be brought without the parties' agreement or the court's leave. Permission to appeal will only be granted where the court is satisfied that:

1 The determination of the question will substantially affect the rights of one or more of the parties;
2 That the question is one which the tribunal was asked to determine;
3 That, on the basis of the award:
   a the decision of the tribunal on the question was obviously wrong; or
   b the question is one of general public importance and the decision of the tribunal is at least open to serious doubt; and
4 That, despite the agreement of the parties to resolve the matter by arbitration, it is just and proper in all the circumstances for the court to determine the question.

There are strict court rules as to what evidence can and cannot be filed in support of a s 69 AA 1996 application.[30] The Court will usually determine applications for permission to appeal on a point of law without an oral hearing but may direct otherwise.[31]

An agreement to dispense with reasons for the tribunal's award shall be considered an agreement to exclude the court's jurisdiction under s 69 AA 1996.[32] Many of the arbitral institutional rules exclude the right to appeal on a point of law.[33]

B Additional Court Powers

i Section 18: Failure of Appointment Procedure

If, or to the extent that, there is no agreement between the parties as to what is to happen in the event of a failure of the procedure for the appointment of the arbitral tribunal, then a party to an arbitration agreement may (upon notice to the other parties) apply to the court to exercise its powers under s 18 AA 1996.

If such an application is made, the Court has the power to:

1 give directions as to the making of any necessary appointments;
2 direct that the tribunal shall be constituted by such appointments (or any one or more of them) as have been made;
3 revoke any appointments already made;
4 make any necessary appointments itself.

30 See Ministry of Justice, *CPR – Rules and Directions* (2023) Practice Direction 62, para 12.1ff. See also O8.1 of the Commercial Court Guide, note 25, para 08.1 for further requirements of s 69 appeal.

31 See Ministry of Justice, *CPR – Rules and Directions* (2023) Practice Direction 62, para 12.12.

32 See Arbitration Act 1996, s 69(1).

33 See, for example, rule 26.8 LCIA Rules and art 35(6) ICC Rules.

ii Section 24: Power of Court to Remove Arbitrator

A party to arbitral proceedings may (upon notice to other parties and all arbitrators) apply to the court to remove an arbitrator on a number of grounds, including that (1) they do not possess the qualifications required by the arbitration agreement; (2) they have justifiable doubts as to impartiality; or (3) they have justifiable doubts as to capacity (mental or physical) to conduct the arbitration. The Court shall not exercise its power under s 24 where the parties vest an arbitral or other institution with the power to remove an arbitrator unless satisfied that the applicant has exhausted all available recourse to that route.

iii Section 32: Court to Determine Preliminary Point of Jurisdiction

On the application of a party to arbitral proceedings (upon notice to the other parties), the court may determine any question as to the tribunal's substantive jurisdiction. The court can only exercise its power under s 32 with either (1) the agreement of the parties to the arbitration or (2) with the permission of the tribunal and being satisfied that (i) the determination of the question will likely produce substantial savings in costs, (ii) that the application was made without delay, and (iii) that there is good reason why the court should decide the matter.

iv Section 42: Enforcement of Peremptory Orders of Tribunal

Unless otherwise agreed by the parties, the court may make an order requiring a party to comply with a peremptory order made by the tribunal. Such an application to the court may be made (1) by the tribunal, (2) by a party to the arbitration with the permission of the tribunal, or (3) where the parties have agreed that the powers of the court under this section shall be available. The court may not act unless it is satisfied that the applicant has exhausted any available arbitral process in respect of failure to comply with the tribunal's order.

v Section 43: Securing the Attendance of Witnesses

A party to arbitral proceedings may use the same court procedures as are available in relation to legal proceedings to secure the attendance before the tribunal of a witness in order to give oral testimony or to produce documents or other material evidence. The court can only exercise this power with the tribunal's permission or the agreement of all parties to the arbitration. This power can only be used when the witness is in the UK and the arbitral proceedings are conducted in England and Wales.

vi Section 45: Determination of Preliminary Point of Law

Unless otherwise agreed by the parties, the court may, on the application of a party to arbitral proceedings (and on notice to other parties), determine any question of law arising in the course of proceedings in which the court is satisfied affects the rights of one or more of the parties. The court can only exercise this power with either (1) the agreement of all parties or (2) with the tribunal's permission and being satisfied that the determination of the question is likely to produce substantial savings in costs and the application was made without delay.

Two recent examples of s 45 AA 1996 being utilised are *The Eternal Bliss*[34] (a case about whether demurrage was liquidated damages for all the consequences of a charterer's failure to load or unload within the laytime allowed) and *The Thorco Lineage*[35] (a case about the interpretation of "goods lost or damaged" at the end of the Hague-Visby Rules Article IV r. 5(a)).

IV The Law Commission's Proposals

A Other Stakeholder Suggestions Relating to the Court's Oversight of Arbitration Not Shortlisted by the Law Commission for Review

In their First Report, the Law Commission set out other suggestions from stakeholders about possible areas for review and considered them all. Those dealing with the Court's oversight of arbitration are set out herein.

i Section 32: Court to Determine the Preliminary Point of Jurisdiction
There was a suggestion that the Act should clarify the relationship between s 32 and s 72 (saving for rights of person who takes no part in proceedings). In *Armada Ship Management v Schiste Oil and Gas Nigeria Ltd*,[36] the court held that, where one party was not participating, an application under s 32 would *likely* be inappropriate where s 72 is engaged. That was also the view of the Departmental Advisory Committee in 1996 ("DAC Report").[37] The Law Commission agreed with this position and stated that an amendment to the Act, which makes a s 32 application never appropriate where s 72 was engaged, might be rash. They thought it was a matter best left to development through the courts.[38]

However, the Law Commission raised a different potential amendment to s 32 in their First Consultation Paper, namely whether, if s 67 AA 1996 is limited, in some circumstances, to an appeal rather than a rehearing, the same limitation should apply to s 32.[39] Some consultees suggested that an application for a preliminary determination under s 32 should be available as of right. However, the responses received by the Law Commission did not suggest widespread support for that approach.[40]

ii Section 42: Enforcement of Peremptory Orders of Tribunal
There was a suggestion that the Act should stipulate that the court shall order compliance with a peremptory order unless persuaded otherwise, and the default should be enforcing the tribunal order. The Law Commission considered that rather

34 [2020] EWHC 2373 (Comm), [2020] 2 Lloyd's Rep. 419 (first instance) and [2021] EWCA Civ 1712, [2022] 1 Lloyd's Rep.12 (CA). Permission to Appeal to the Supreme was granted, but the case was settled prior to before the Supreme Court hearing.

35 [2023] EWHC 26 (Comm), [2023] 2 All ER (Comm) 427.

36 [2021] EWHC 1094 (Comm), [2022] 1 All ER (Comm) 1091.

37 DAC report, note 19, para 141.

38 Law Commission, *Review of the Arbitration Act 1996 – A consultation paper* (Consultation Paper 257, 2022) paras 11.67–11.69 ("First Consultation Paper").

39 Ibid., Question 23.

40 Law Commission, *Review of the Arbitration Act 1996 – Second consultation paper* (Consultation Paper 258, 2023) para 3.81 ("Second Consultation Paper").

than have a default rule in favour of the court rubber-stamping the peremptory order, the current position was correct – i.e. the court has an unfettered discretion whether to lend weight of state coercion to a tribunal's peremptory order.[41]

iii Section 43: Securing the Attendance of Witnesses

There were two stakeholder suggestions in relation to this section, namely:

1 whether the Act should clarify whether s 43 applies regardless of the seat of the arbitration;
2 whether the Act should clarify that it suffices for the witness to be within the UK temporarily and that attendance could be via video link and in person.

As to those two suggestions, the Law Commission opined that:

1 Section 43(3)(b) requires the arbitration to be conducted in England and Wales and that relates to venue, not seat which is made clear in s 2(3) AA 1996. Together, s 43(3)(a) and (b) are concerned with ensuring that the court has geographical reach over the witness when requiring their attendance and that the Act is sufficiently clear.
2 Section 43 already allows for these possibilities; the specifics will vary from case to case and are best addressed by the courts.[42]

iv Section 68: Challenging the Award: Serious Irregularity

There was a suggestion that the Act should clarify whether remission of the award is to the same tribunal. The Law Commission noted that s 68(3) was couched in terms of remission of the award to "the" tribunal and that, in normal language, that would be the tribunal referred to in s 68(1). They were not persuaded that there was a need for legislative reform.

v Section 69: Appeal on Point of Law

There were two stakeholder suggestions in relation to s 69, namely:

1 that the remedy should only be available to domestic (not international) arbitrations;
2 the Act should stipulate that there was no right to an oral hearing to reconsider the grant or refusal of leave to appeal on a point of law.

Concerning the first, the Law Commission opined that the DAC was not attracted to the idea of separate regimes for domestic and international arbitrations. The Law Commission equally saw no convincing reason to treat domestic and international arbitrations separately.

Concerning the second, the Law Commission noted that s 69(5) provides that the court shall determine an application for leave to appeal without a hearing unless it appears to the court that a hearing is required. It is, therefore, at the discretion of

41 First Consultation Paper, note 38, paras 11.180–11.181.
42 Ibid., paras 11.82–11.85.

the court. They further note that if an application under s 69 is dismissed without a hearing, the only option is to appeal, as a matter of statute, whether under ss 67 and 68, there can be an oral re-hearing, as a matter of court rules as well as an appeal under statute. In their view, the suggested reform is already the position under the Act.[43]

B Section 67 – Challenge to Jurisdiction

i First Consultation Paper

In the First Consultation Paper, the Law Commission considered whether an application under s 67 should, by default, be limited to a review of the tribunal's decision such that the Court would not ordinarily receive oral evidence or new evidence which was not before the tribunal. However, the court could draw any inference of fact it considered justified on the evidence. In that way, the application under s 67 would mirror an appeal in court proceedings.[44] In allowing a *de novo* hearing England is not unique. Countries which have adopted the UNCITRAL Model Law tend to conduct *de novo* hearings including Canada, Australia, and Hong Kong.[45]

As noted by the Law Commission, the principal objection to reform appears to be theoretical. The DAC Report stated that "[c]learly the tribunal cannot be the final arbiter of a question of jurisdiction, for this would provide a classic case of pulling oneself up by one's own bootstraps".[46] However, the Law Commission was not persuaded by the theoretical objections to reform and in the First Consultation Paper, provisionally proposed that:

1 where a party has participated in arbitral proceedings and has objected to the jurisdiction of the arbitral tribunal; and
2 the tribunal has ruled on its jurisdiction in an award,

then any subsequent challenge under s 67 should be by way of an appeal and not a rehearing.

ii Responses to the First Consultation Paper

Consultees expressed strong views on the topic on both sides of the debate. Among the proposal's supporters were solicitors' firms Bryan Cave Leighton Paisner LLP and Clifford Chance LLP. In contrast, for example, Pinsent Masons LLP and Brick Court Chambers were against the proposal, the latter stating:[47]

> [A] de novo review of the tribunal's jurisdiction is justified as a matter of principle. It is an essential procedural safeguard, which is necessary to ensure that the parties have in fact consented to arbitration. . . . This is particularly so given that a jurisdictional challenge may turn on questions of fact as well as questions of law. Because the arbitral tribunal cannot be the final arbiter of its own jurisdiction, it follows that both the tribunal's findings of fact and its holdings of law in relation to jurisdiction must be open to challenge before the Court. The

43 Ibid., paras 11.142–11.148.
44 Ibid., para 8.23.
45 Ibid., para 8.28 and notes 23–26.
46 DAC Report, note 19, para 143.
47 Second Consultation Paper, note 40, para 3.21.

> Court could not discharge that function if it were to be confined by statute to carrying out an "appellate review" of the decision of the tribunal, rather than undertaking a full hearing.

Other suggestions from consultees included:

1 that if there were concerns about the amount of evidence that a party seeks to put before the court on a s 67 rehearing, the court itself can sensibly limit that evidence through its case management powers;[48]
2 that the proposal undermined the principle of competence;[49]
3 that the language of appeal was unhelpful because an appeal can be by way of review or rehearing.

iii Second Consultation Paper

The Law Commission was not persuaded that limiting evidence by case management powers was the answer. They noted that if a challenge under s 67 is a full rehearing, then the parties should be free to introduce whatever evidence they wish. It would be difficult for the court to label a challenge under s 67 as a full rehearing while also limiting evidence or criticising a party by reference to what happened in a previous hearing "all the more so when that previous hearing resulted in an award supposedly of no legal or evidential value".[50]

The Law Commission accepted that it was better not to focus on the label of appeal, review, or rehearing but instead on the practical constraints to a challenge under s 67. Those practical constraints were:

1 New arguments should not usually be raised at the court hearing.
2 New evidence should not usually be raised at the court hearing.
3 Oral evidence should not ordinarily be reheard by the court, unless perhaps in exceptional circumstances.
4 Courts should give deference to the decision of the tribunal – i.e. the decision of the tribunal should be afforded some legal and evidential value.

The Law Commission concluded that their preferred approach was for their proposals to be adopted in rules of court rather than by way of amendments to the legislation or simply allowing case law to develop.

iv Final Report and Bill

The Law Commission published its Final Report and Bill on the Review of the Arbitration Act on 6 September 2023. On the question of whether a challenge should be a review or a rehearing, the Law Commission noted that there had been strong views expressed on both sides of the debate but that there had been consistent support in favour of reform, by two-thirds majority responding to the first consultation paper and three-quarters responding to the second consultation paper.[51]

48 Ibid., para 3.46.
49 Ibid., para 3.54.
50 Ibid., paras 3.51 and 3.53.
51 Law Commission, *Review of the Arbitration Act 1996: Final report and Bill* (Law Com No 413, 2023) para 9.51.

The Law Commission noted[52] that the judges from the Business and Property Courts in London stated in their response that *Dallah* left no doubt that s 67 was a full rehearing. They said that it might be appropriate to limit new evidence or oral evidence but that it might be necessary to allow such evidence in some cases, for example, where there were no transcripts of the evidence before the tribunal or the tribunal had excluded evidence that a party wished to adduce. They continued to express concern that anything other than a full rehearing might preclude an issue estoppel from arising.

When considering the principal objection to their proposal – i.e. that, if an arbitral tribunal has no jurisdiction, then its ruling should have no weight at all and therefore should be no deference, the Law Commission opined:

1 The objection assumes that the tribunal has no jurisdiction. If, instead, the tribunal does have jurisdiction, then the objection falls away as the tribunal's ruling was proper.
2 It is only an objection which avails the arbitral respondent; an arbitral claimant can hardly complain that the tribunal should have rejected their claim.

The second point does not convince me. Just because a claimant has commenced arbitration in respect of a claim, it does not (notwithstanding the *Fiona Trust*[53] presumption of a one-stop shop) automatically follow that the arbitral tribunal has jurisdiction over all disputes between the parties. They may therefore wish to object to the tribunal taking jurisdiction in respect of, for example, a counterclaim made by an arbitral respondent.

The Law Commission stated that their proposal struck a balance so that challenges before the court are allowed; but there are limits to the arguments and evidence which can be presented. Having previously considered that the court's existing case management powers would have been sufficient the position changed in the Final Report.

The Law Commission's recommendation 11 was to introduce legislation to confer the power to make rules of court so that in any challenge under s 67 by a party who has taken part in the arbitral proceedings (1) the court will not entertain any new grounds of objection, or any new evidence unless even with reasonable diligence it could not have been put before the tribunal and (2) evidence will not be reheard, save in the interests of justice.

Clause 11 of the draft Bill accordingly provides for new paragraphs (3A) and (3B) to be inserted into s 67. They provide as follows:[54]

> (3A) Rules of court about the procedure to be followed on an application under this section may, in particular, include provision within subsection (3B) in relation to a case where the application –

52 Ibid., para 9.46.

53 *Premium Nafta Products Limited v Fili Shipping Company Limited* [2007] UKHL 40. The *Fiona Trust* doctrine presumes that rational businessmen are likely to have intended that the same court or tribunal will decide any disputes arising between them, unless they use clear language indicating otherwise.

54 These provisions became (3B) and (3C) in the version of the Bill that was introduced into Parliament.

(a) relates to an objection as to the arbitral tribunal's substantive jurisdiction on which the tribunal has already ruled, and
(b) is made by a party that took part in the arbitral proceedings.

(3B) Provision is within this subsection if it provides that –

(a) a ground for the objection that was not raised before the arbitral tribunal must not be raised before the court unless the applicant shows that, at the time the applicant took part in the proceedings, the applicant did not know and could not with reasonable diligence have discovered the ground;
(b) evidence that was not heard by the tribunal must not be heard by the court unless the applicant shows that, at the time the applicant took part in the proceedings, the applicant could not with reasonable diligence have put the evidence before the tribunal;
(c) evidence that was heard by the tribunal must not be reheard by the court, unless the court considers it necessary in the interests of justice.

Whilst I understand the desire to reach a balance, I remain concerned about the Law Commission's recommendations for the following reasons:

1 In cases where the Tribunal have found they have jurisdiction and it is challenged, there does seem to me to be a theoretical problem with only considering if they are wrong (whether by way of review or appeal) for the reasons given by, among others, Brick Court Chambers in their response to the First Consultation Paper.
2 It puts England and Wales on a different footing from other jurisdictions, which also are based on the UNCITRAL Model Law, such as Canada, Hong Kong, and Australia.
3 Aside from the principled objection to deference to the decision of the Tribunal, there are practical issues. Will parties have to argue about how good the arbitrators were? For example, will there be uncomfortable discussions as to whether, for example, ex–high court judges should be given more deference or whether those with commercial experience should be given more deference?
4 Currently, the position is clear and the parties know very clearly what can be dealt with on a s 67 application. However, the Law Commission's recommendation makes matters less certain. There is likely to be case law on what amounts to "interests of justice" in order for new evidence or oral evidence to be given (good for lawyers but not for the end users of arbitration).

As to other recommendations in relation to s 67, the Law Commission considered that there should be consistency of approach to the remedies available across ss 67 to 69. Therefore the draft Bill provides (at clause 10) to include the remedies of (1) declaring the award to be of no effect, in whole or in part, and (2) remitting the award to the tribunal, in whole or in part, for reconsideration with the proviso that the court must not exercise its power to set aside or to declare an award to be of no effect, in whole or in part, unless it is satisfied that it would be inappropriate to remit the matters in question to the tribunal for reconsideration.

The Arbitration Bill, which was closely based on the Law Commission's recommendations, was introduced into Parliament on 21 November 2023 by Lord Bellamy. It had its first and second readings in the House of Lords and was therefore in its early legislative stages prior to the General Election but it was left out of the "wash-up period" (where some bills are passed on an accelerated basis immediately after a General Election has been called) and its fate was therefore left uncertain. However, following the general election in early July 2024 the King's Speech at the State Opening of Parliament re-introduced the Arbitration Bill to Parliament's legislative agenda.

CHAPTER 4

Civil Justice Reforms and the Business and Property Courts of England and Wales

*Masood Ahmed**

I Introduction

The civil justice system is currently experiencing unprecedented levels of procedural reform, which seek to increase access to justice by controlling high, unpredictable litigation costs[1] and reducing the crippling delays in the dispensation of justice. A significant part of the reforms is the government's £1.4 billion investment to digitise the courts and tribunals service to create an entirely digitised justice system.[2] A fundamental component of the digital civil justice system is the integration and enhanced focus on alternative dispute resolution (ADR) procedures to assist in the early settlement of their disputes.[3] To reinforce the digital reform agenda, Parliament has also enacted the Judicial Review and Courts Act 2022 (the 2022 Act), which, among other things, established the Online Procedure Rule Committee (OPRC)[4] which oversees the development of procedural rules for online proceedings across the civil, family, and tribunals jurisdictions. More interestingly, the OPRC's jurisdiction also extends to the pre-action stage (i.e. pre-court stage) of civil disputes as well as existing and future digital pre-action portals. Given these radical developments, it is unsurprising that the current Master of the Rolls, Sir Geoffrey Vos, enthusiastically remarked that "we are now on the brink of a revolution in dispute resolution. We are no longer fixated on court-based systems, but we are in the process of creating a truly holistic Digital Justice System".[5]

---

* **Associate Professor, University of Leicester**.

1 See, for example, the report of Sir Rupert Jackson on "Review of Civil Litigation Costs: Supplemental Report Fixed Recoverable Costs" (July 2017). www.judiciary.uk/wp-content/uploads/2017/07/fixed-recoverable-costs-supplemental-report-online-2-1.pdf, accessed 18 March 2024; see also "Extending fixed recoverable costs: a note on the new rules" (May 2023). https://assets.publishing.service.gov.uk/government/uploads/system/uploads/attachment_data/file/1151873/extending-fixed-recoverable-costs-note-new-rules.pdf, accessed 18 March 2024.

2 His Majesty's Courts and Tribunal Service's (HMCTS) Reform Programme. See also Ministry of Justice, "Policy paper Ministry of Justice Digital Strategy 2025" (April 2022). www.gov.uk/government/publications/ministry-of-justice-digital-strategy-2025/ministry-of-justice-digital-strategy-2025, accessed 18 March 2024.

3 See "Vision for the future of civil and family courts and tribunals" (November 2023). www.gov.uk/government/news/vision-for-the-future-of-civil-and-family-courts-and-tribunals, accessed 18 March 2024.

4 Judicial Review and Courts Act 2022, ss 22–24.

5 The Right Hon Sir Geoffrey Vos, "The Ombudsman Association: keynote address" (21 June 2023). www.judiciary.uk/speech-by-the-master-of-the-rolls-driving-system-change-and-addressing-injustice/, accessed 18 March 2024.

DOI: 10.4324/9781032726243-5

Although the current reforms are primarily focused on lower-value claims, there is no doubt that they will expand to the full range of disputes across the civil justice system, including to high-value and complex domestic and international commercial disputes that are heard in the Business and Property Courts of England and Wales (the B&PC).[6] It is not suggested that the B&PC have lagged in reforming its procedures. Indeed, the B&PC have, in many ways, led the way in implementing procedural innovations. For example, the B&PC pioneered the electronic filing of court documents through its CE filing system, it embraced and encouraged the use of predictive coding in the disclosure process, and it quickly and successfully adopted remote hearings during the COVID-19 pandemic.[7] Furthermore, the Commercial Court (CC) and the Technology and Construction Court (TCC), which form part of the B&PC,[8] have led the way in promoting ADR.[9] For example, before the formal incorporation of ADR within the Civil Procedure Rules (CPR), the TCC pioneered judge-led settlement through the use of early neutral evaluation,[10] and the CC and TCC court guides encourage the use of ADR.[11]

While the B&PC have, thus far, remained immune from the current reforms, two recent major procedural developments will have a significant impact on how B&PC disputes are managed and resolved in the future. The first is the landmark decision of *Churchill v Merthyr Tydfil County Borough Council*,[12] in which the Court of Appeal held that the courts could order disputing parties to engage in ADR or stay the proceedings to enable them to engage in ADR, provided that the order or stay does not undermine the claimant's right to proceed to a judicial hearing. In determining that the courts have the power to compel parties to engage with ADR, the Court of Appeal confirmed that Dyson LJ's controversial comments in *Halsey v Milton Keynes General NHS Trust*[13] – that to compel parties to engage with ADR would undermine their right to a fair trial – were *obiter dicta* and, therefore, not binding on the courts.

6 See Sir Geoffrey Vos, Master of the Rolls and Head of Civil Justice in England and Wales, "Justice in the Digital Age" Speech on the 150th Anniversary of the Technology and Construction Court (2 November 2023). www.judiciary.uk/speech-by-the-master-of-the-rolls-justice-in-the-digital-age/, accessed 18 March 2024 (Vos).

7 N Byrom, "Report and recommendations: The impact of COVID-19 measures on the civil justice system 2020" (Civil Justice Council, Legal Education Foundation, May 2020). www.judiciary.uk/wp-content/uploads/2022/07/CJC-Rapid-Review-Final-Report-f-1.pdf, accessed 18 March 2024.

8 The B&PC consist of the Commercial Court, Business List, Admiralty Court, Circuit Commercial Court, Technology and Construction Court, Financial List, Insolvency List, Companies List, Competition List, Intellectual Property List, Property, Trusts and Probate List, and the Revenue List.

9 See the Commercial Court Guide/TCC Guide and reference to ADR procedures.

10 HM Courts & Tribunals Service, "Technology & Construction Court Guide" (October 2022), s 7.5. www.judiciary.uk/wp-content/uploads/2023/06/The-Technology-and-Construction-Court-Guide.pdf, accessed 18 March 2024.

11 See, for example, The Business and Property Courts of England & Wales, "The Commercial Court Guide (incorporating The Admiralty Court Guide)" (11th Edn 2022) G1.

12 *Churchill v Merthyr Tydfil County Borough Council* [2023] EWCA Civ 1416, [2023] 11 WLUK 492 (*Churchill*).

13 *Halsey v Milton Keynes General NHS Trust* [2004] EWCA Civ 576, [2004] 1 WLR 3002 (*Halsey*).

The second development concerns the recommendations made by the Civil Justice Council in its recent Review of Pre-action Protocols Final Report Part 1 (the PaP Review).[14] The pre-action protocols set a procedural framework that governs litigating parties' pre-court behaviour. They promote party co-operation through the early exchange of information and they encourage the use of ADR procedures. There are currently 17 sector-specific protocols and one general protocol for those disputes that do not fall within the sector-specific protocols. One of the principal recommendations of PaP Review is the introduction of a new General Pre-action Protocol (the General PaP) which has, at its heart, the obligation on the parties to complete the following three sequential procedural steps before issuing court proceedings: (1) the early exchange of relevant information; (2) engagement with an ADR procedure; and (3) if the matter cannot be resolved, the parties must narrow the issues in dispute and complete a stocktake report. Although the specific protocols govern certain types of disputes in the B&PC (e.g. the Construction and Engineering Pre-action Protocol), there is currently no specific protocol for other types of B&PC disputes (e.g. corporate disputes, breach of commercial contracts).

In this chapter, I critically consider the future impact of these two developments on B&PC disputes. I argue that the decision in *Churchill* and the current B&PC procedures provide the judiciary with a unique opportunity to finally develop a consistent jurisprudential body of case law on the issue of compulsory ADR. This will, however, depend on two factors. The first is the need for judges to fully embrace *and exercise* their ADR powers. The second factor is the need for judges to adopt a broader understanding of the full range of ADR procedures – which I call "judicial ADR pluralism" – so that the parties are referred to the most appropriate procedure rather than simply equating ADR to mean mediation. I also consider how *Churchill*, the recommendations of the PaP Review, and the move towards digitisation provide the basis for a new protocol for B&PC disputes.

This chapter is organised into several parts. First, I discuss the rationale underpinning the digital reform agenda and the future vision of the senior judiciary for a fully digital civil justice system. By way of example, I consider the Online Civil Money Claims system (OCMC),[15] which incorporates ADR in the form of opt-out mediation.[16] Second, I focus on the nature and role of the pre-action protocols and the key proposals of the PaP Review. Third, I discuss the issue of compulsory ADR and critically consider the decision in *Churchill*. Finally, I consider the impact of the PaP Review and *Churchill* on the management and resolution of B&PC disputes and the potential for a new protocol.

14 Civil Justice Council, *CJC Review of the Pre-action Protocols Final Report Part 1* (August 2023). www.judiciary.uk/wp-content/uploads/2023/08/CJC-PAP-report-Aug-23-FINAL.pdf, accessed 18 March 2024); Civil Justice Council, *Review of Pre-Action Protocols Civil Justice Council* (November 2021). www.judiciary.uk/wp-content/uploads/2021/11/CJC-PAP-Interim-Report.pdf, accessed 18 March 2024. At the time of writing, the Civil Justice Council published its Final Report Part 1. The Civil Justice Council intends to publish its Final Report Part 2 which considers the sector specific protocols later in 2024.

15 See www.gov.uk/make-court-claim-for-money/make-claim, accessed 18 March 2024.

16 Opt-out means that the parties are automatically referred to mediation, but they can decide to opt out of mediation.

II The Move Towards a Digital Civil Justice System

This part explains the rationale behind the shift towards a digital civil justice system. I consider the approach taken by policymakers and the senior judiciary in embracing technology in digitising pre-action and court procedures, and the importance of data collection. By way of illustration, I discuss the OCMC system as an example of a digital system which incorporates ADR in the form of mediation.

A The Rationale for a Digital Civil Justice System

Digital technologies provide the opportunity to design and create a civil justice system with the individual litigant at its heart. Digital processes help to increase access to justice by making pre-action and court processes and procedures easy to understand and navigate. This means that litigants with limited means can represent themselves more effectively and confidently, thereby avoiding having to incur unpredictable, disproportionate, and potentially substantial legal costs and delays in seeking to vindicate and enforce their legal rights.

Integrating decision trees can help litigants understand their problems better and appropriately formulate their claims or defence. Automated procedures allow litigants to identify and upload key documents to support their cases. Online systems also allow for the greater integration of ADR procedures, which can assist the parties in the early resolution of disputes. Artificial intelligence (AI) can provide litigants with a variety of options in resolving their dispute, and it can signpost litigants, at an early stage, to dispute resolution procedures which may be more suited to the circumstances of their case.

A further valuable feature of a digital system is the ability to collate rich data concerning those for whom the systems are designed. This data can provide valuable insights into the characteristics and demographics of those using the systems, and it can assist in identifying the challenges and difficulties encountered by users, which can help to improve the processes and procedures, such as providing clearer guidance and information to litigants. Digital protocols or portals can assist in transferring information gathered at the pre-action stage to the court process. This can mean that, for example, when parties have exchanged letters explaining their respective positions on the issues in dispute, that information can form the basis of court pleadings, thereby saving the parties the time and cost of drafting a new set of pleadings.

B The Digitalisation of the English Civil Justice System

Digital reforms are underpinned by the policy rationale of increasing access to justice by eliminating the cost and delays of an outdated paper-based court system and replacing it with digital technologies. Indeed, the previous Lord Chancellor, Alex Chalk KC MP, and senior judiciary set out their shared vision for the future of the civil and family courts and the tribunals system, an essential aspect of which is to embrace[17]

17 Lord Chancellor, "Vision for the future of civil and family courts and tribunals" (20 November 2023). www.gov.uk/government/news/vision-for-the-future-of-civil-and-family-courts-and-tribunals, accessed 18 March 2024.

> advances in technology . . . including exploring safe and appropriate use of AI. We want to enable people to resolve their problems earlier and at less cost, for example through mediation or online dispute resolution.

In his extra-judicial speeches, Sir Geoffrey Vos MR has spoken extensively about his future vision of a fully digitised civil justice system which integrates ADR and AI.[18] Until recently, Sir Geoffrey Vos described a future digital civil justice system as consisting of a "funnel" composed of three online tiers with a single entry point. The first tier would be an immediate interface that would provide litigants with information on how to pursue a claim and signpost users to relevant pre-action digital portals or, if applicable, an ombudsman service. The second tier would direct users to engage in a dispute resolution process and for data to be gathered about the dispute. The Official Injury Claim Service (OICS) is an example of a digital pre-action portal.[19] The OICS has been built by the private sector in collaboration with the Ministry of Justice, and it allows litigants with small whiplash claims to resolve their disputes without the need for legal representation. If the matter cannot be resolved through the OICS, then the matter is transferred to the court. Returning to tier two of the funnel, the data collated from the previous tiers will be automatically transferred into the digital court process if the matter cannot be resolved. That vision, however, has recently been modified by the Deputy Head of Civil Justice, Birss LJ.[20] Rather than having a single point of entry, the idea is that the data collated from engagement with the pre-action digital portals will be transferred directly to the courts and tribunals if the dispute cannot be settled. So, if a litigant engages with a pre-action portal like the OICS or engages with an online ADR procedure such as online mediation, and the matter does not settle, then the data from engaging with that process would transfer directly to the courts. As Birss LJ explained:[21]

> [t]he vision is that the provider's system will . . . then be able to refer them on, this next stage may then involve further advice and/or bringing a civil, family or tribunal claim into the courts and tribunals system. The person selects the option to start a court action. The system has the information to do this for them, and they can then immediately see their claim on the court's system – maybe OCMC if it is a small money claim. The data flows to where it is needed when it needs to do so. The data standards will in time mean that all this happens smoothly, without the person having to repeatedly tell their story or repeatedly upload documents.

The OPRC will play a crucial role in this future digital system. It oversees all pre-action protocols and digital pre-action portals, including the OICS. It has the express

18 See Vos, note 6.

19 The OICS was launched on 31 May 2021 following the enactment of the Civil Liability Act 2018. It was developed by the Motor Insurers' Bureau in collaboration with the Ministry of Justice and is governed by the pre-action protocol for personal injury claims below the small claims limit for RTA claims of £5,000. The OICS is often referred to as the "Whiplash Portal".

20 Lord Justice Colin Birss, "Is a focus on data the way to improve access to justice in a multifaceted world?" (30 November 2023) The 24th Competition Law Association Burrell Lecture. www.judiciary.uk/speech-by-lord-justice-colin-birss-is-a-focus-on-data-the-way-to-improve-access-to-justice-in-a-multifaceted-world/#:~:text=To%20focus%20on%20the%20nuts,any%20point%20in%20the%20system, accessed 18 March 2024.

21 Ibid. [49].

authority to make provisions for and to set digital standards about the pre-action space. Thus, by setting digital standards which must be met by all future digital pre-action protocols and pre-action portals, including those created by or in collaboration with the private sector, the OPRC can ensure that appropriate and relevant data is collated from the pre-action space and transferred to the courts.

The removal of the first tier is not only surprising, given the multiple extra-judicial speeches over the past three years explaining the importance of it, but it is also concerning. It is concerning because tier one would provide individual litigants and small businesses vital information, advice and guidance on the nature of their disputes and how best to resolve them. Indeed, in its Proposals for a 21st-century justice system green paper,[22] the Law Society emphasised the significance of tier one as a means of increasing access to justice when it said that[23]

> [t]he development of an online diagnostic tool to support individuals and small businesses to identify and resolve their legal issues must be a cornerstone of reforms to enhance access to justice for low income individuals and small businesses.

Furthermore, although the idea is that the first tier will be replaced with online dispute resolution service providers, it is difficult to see how the vital first point of contact between a litigant and such providers will work: will the dispute resolution service provide the litigant with the essential information as initially contemplated by tier one, or will it simply advise the litigant to engage immediately with its dispute resolution procedure? Also, not all their sector dispute resolution services have online, digital systems and portals – a shift towards digitalisation will require substantial initial and ongoing investment from service providers.

III Digitilisation, ADR and the OCMC System

The OCMC system enables claimants to issue proceedings in respect of money claims of up to £10,000, and defendants may contest those claims online.[24] After pleadings have been filed, the parties are invited to participate in mediation, which is conducted via telephone, to explore whether their dispute can be resolved without continuing to trial. The mediation stage is an opt-out process for cases worth up to £500; that is, disputes are automatically referred to "opt-out mediation" – i.e. if one or both of the parties elect not to have their dispute referred to mediation, then the matter will proceed through OCMC in the usual way.[25] If the dispute is settled through mediation, the parties' agreement is recorded in a settlement agreement. If the mediation does not result in a settlement, then the matter continues through the OCMC and eventually goes to trial, which is conducted online.

22 The Law Society, "Proposals for a 21st-century justice system" (9 October 2023) www.lawsociety.org.uk/contact-or-visit-us/press-office/press-releases/Law%20Society%20publishes%20proposals%20to%20reform%20civil%20justice, accessed 18 March 2024.

23 Ibid.

24 Practice Direction 51R – Online Civil Money Claims Pilot.

25 As described in a presentation delivered David Phillip, Programme Director – Courts Tribunals and Regional Tier, "HMCTS Reform Programme: Online Civil Money Claims and Civil Enforcement" (11 March 2019).

Based on recent HMCTS data, more than 445,000 claims have been issued through OCMC since its introduction in March 2018. They achieved an average user satisfaction rating of 95%, 48.8% of the 7,105 mediation appointments made in 2023 were settled, and, on average, it has taken nine weeks for a directions order to be drawn compared to 34 weeks on paper in 2023. The service was expanded to legal representatives issuing claims against legal representatives up to £25,000 in May 2022. To date, more than 20,000 claims have been issued.[26]

Although HMCTS boast of a 95% user satisfaction with OCMC, the survey questions must be centred around testing and gathering data which provide insights into whether users perceive the procedures and processes, and OCMC as a whole, as procedurally fair, rather than simply asking users whether they found the system easy to use. By doing this, any procedural weaknesses in the system will be identified and remedied, improvements can be made in line with reliable user data that reflects users' concerns and views, and thus, the system can be improved to uphold the principle of procedural fairness. HMCTS has recently evaluated the opt-out mediation stage of OCMC, which provides valuable insights into user experiences and their understanding of the process.[27] Although users have indicated general satisfaction with opting out of mediation, the evaluation reveals that users are unclear on several significant aspects of the process, including the role and nature of the mediator. This valuable data can be used to address the challenges and problems encountered by users and to improve the system accordingly. Ultimately, users will have confidence in the OCMC procedures used to determine their disputes, and they are more likely to accept and comply with outcomes, including compliance with mediation settlement agreements.

IV The Pre-action Protocols and the PaP Review

The protocols embody Lord Woolf's philosophical shift from the "old" adversarial approach to litigation to one that encompasses consensual settlement.[28] The protocols are a procedural framework which formally sits outside the Civil Procedure Rules and, as such, govern the parties' pre-action behaviour as a form of soft law. They promote party co-operation through the early exchange of information, which enables the parties to make informed decisions regarding early consensual settlement. Where settlement cannot be achieved, the parties' engagement with the protocols helps to narrow the issues in dispute, which can, in turn, support more efficient judicial case management. Currently, there are 17 sector-specific pre-action protocols and one general protocol. If a matter does not fall within a specific protocol, the parties must follow the general pre-action protocol. The protocols

26 HM Courts and Tribunals Services, "Fact sheet: Online Civil Money Claims" (27 February 2024). www.gov.uk/government/publications/hmcts-reform-civil-fact-sheets/fact-sheet-online-civil-money-claims, accessed 18 March 2024.

27 HM Courts and Tribunals Services, "HMCTS opt-out mediation evaluation" (21 March 2023). www.gov.uk/government/publications/hmcts-opt-out-mediation-evaluation/hmcts-opt-out-mediation-evaluation-report, accessed 18 March 2024.

28 The Rt Hon Lord Woolf, "Access to Justice Interim Report" (1995); the Rt Hon Lord Woolf, "Access to Justice Final Report" (1996) (Woolf Final Report).

have become increasingly integrated within the CPR and have become, as the Court of Appeal observed in *Jet2 Holidays Ltd v Hughes*,[29] "a highly important part of the litigation architecture".[30]

The Master of the Rolls commissioned an extensive review of the pre-action protocols' current and future role, culminating in the PaP Review. The PaP Review makes several recommendations to reform protocols, including replacing the current general protocol with a new General Pre-action Protocol (the General PaP).[31] At its heart, the General PaP includes three sequential steps the parties must take before issuing court proceedings. The first point is that the General PaP makes clear from the outset that the parties *must* engage with the protocols before issuing proceedings except in urgent cases. The three mandatory sequential steps before proceedings can be issued are:[32]

1 the early exchange of relevant information between the parties – this includes the parties exchanging letters setting out their claims and defences and any key documents;
2 the need for the parties to engage with an ADR procedure – here, the relevant section of the General PaP lists a variety of ADR procedures, explains the benefits of narrowing the issue in the event the matter cannot be settled, and explains that the courts have the power to stay proceedings to allow the parties to engage with ADR;
3 if the matter cannot be settled after taking steps 1 and 2, the parties must review their respective positions, co-operate in narrowing the issue, and complete and file a stocktake report.

The three sequential steps lend themselves well to be incorporated into a future online pre-action protocol. Parties can easily upload their letters, set out their respective positions, and disclose key documents rather than incur the time and cost of managing hard copies.

Advances in online dispute resolution, including online mediation, have become popular, especially during and after the COVID-19 pandemic. The final step will allow the parties to identify, discuss, complete, and file the stocktake online. More importantly, each step will generate valuable data that will provide insights into the nature of the dispute and the parties, identify challenges and areas that require improvement, and provide the basis for informed policy decisions to continue to increase access to justice. Finally, completing the sequential steps will allow the information and data collated to be used as the pleadings for the parties and transferred directly to the digital court process. Later in this chapter, I consider how the General PaP and the *Churchill* decision can form the basis of a new protocol for B&PC disputes. Before that, I turn to the issue of compulsory ADR and the decision in *Churchill*.

29 *Jet2 Holidays Limited v Hughes & Hughes* [2019] EWCA Civ 1858.
30 Ibid. [36].
31 See PaP Review Final Report and Annex 2 Draft General Pre-Action Protocol, note 14.
32 See PaP Review Final Report, note 14.

V Compulsory ADR and *Churchill*

As the OCMC system demonstrates, ADR is a fundamental aspect of the digital and pre-action reforms and a central part of a fully digital civil justice system. The economic and practical virtues of ADR are well known. Disputes that settle before a judicial determination can save the parties the cost, time, and anxiety of the litigation process, and it can provide the parties with the opportunity to resolve their dispute on their terms and to create solutions which the courts may not have the powers to do, such as extracting an apology. The early settlement of disputes also helps preserve the courts' finite resources and furthers the principle of proportionality within the broader civil justice system. ADR forms an integral part of the civil justice architecture. The courts have the power to penalise a party in costs if it has unreasonably refused to consider and engage with ADR during the pre-action stage of the dispute and the court process.[33] However, despite ADR's presence within the civil justice system, the issue of compulsory ADR – whether the courts should compel disputing parties to engage with ADR – has been a controversial and vexed question. In this part, I critically consider the issue of compulsory ADR and the decision in *Churchill*.

A Halsey *and Divergent Judicial Approaches*

The issue of whether the courts have the power to compel litigating parties to engage with ADR and, if they did, whether the courts should exercise that power has been a vexed issue since the controversial comments of Dyson LJ in *Halsey*. In that case, Dyson LJ stated that "to oblige truly unwilling parties to refer their disputes to mediation would be to impose an unacceptable obstruction on their right of access to the court".[34] Despite his stance on compulsory ADR, Dyson LJ explained that the courts could penalise a party in costs for unreasonably refusing to engage with ADR. He also provided a list of non-exhaustive factors that the courts could use to determine unreasonable ADR behaviour.

Dyson LJ's comments on compulsory ADR have contributed to developing inconsistent, divergent, and confusing jurisprudence. On the one hand, the courts have compelled parties to ADR, and where the parties have failed to discharge their ADR obligations, they have not hesitated to penalise parties in costs.[35] On the other hand, the courts have followed Dyson LJ's comments and refused to order parties to engage with ADR or to penalise a party in costs for failing to engage with ADR.[36] In its *Compulsory ADR Report*,[37] the Civil Justice Council concluded that compelling parties to engage with ADR would not, in principle, undermine Article 6 ECHR rights, providing that the parties were not prevented from seeking judicial determination if a settlement

33 See CPR Part 44 – General Rules about Costs.

34 *Halsey*, note 13.

35 See, for example, *Thakkar v Patel* [2017] EWCA Civ 117, [2017] 1 WLUK 447.

36 See, for example, *Gore v Naheed* [2017] EWCA Civ 369, [2017] 5 WLUK 565.

37 *Civil Justice Council, Compulsory ADR Report* (June 2021). www.judiciary.uk/wp-content/uploads/2021/07/Civil-Justice-Council-Compulsory-ADR-report.pdf, accessed 18 March 2024 (Compulsory ADR report).

could not be reached during the ADR process. Two years after the CJC report, the issue came before the courts in *Churchill*, to which I now turn.

B The Decision in Churchill

The claimant commenced proceedings against the local authority for damages to his property caused by Japanese knotweed, which had spread to the claimant's property from neighbouring land owned by the defendant's local authority. In response to the claimant's pre-action letter of claim, the defendant invited the claimant to use its internal Corporate Complaints Procedure (CCP) to resolve the matter. The defendant also clarified that if the claimant decided to issue proceedings without engaging with its CCP, it would apply to the court for a stay and would also seek its costs. The claimant did not, however, engage with the CCP and issued proceedings against the defendant. In response, the defendant applied for a stay of proceedings.

The deputy district judge dismissed the stay application. Although the judge found that the claimant had acted unreasonably by failing to engage with the defendant's CCP and behaved contrary to the general pre-action protocol, he held that Dyson LJ's comments in *Halsey* bound him. Thus, the judge dismissed the defendant's application to stay the proceedings. Given the critical point of principle and practice that the case raised, the judge referred the matter to the Court of Appeal.

The leading judgment of the Court of Appeal was given by Sir Geoffrey Vos MR, to which Lady Chief Justice Carr and Birss LJ agreed. The Court identified the following main issues which required to be resolved:[38]

1. Was the judge right to think *Halsey* bound him to dismiss the defendant's application?
2. If not, can the court lawfully stay proceedings for the parties or order them to engage in a non-court-based dispute resolution process?
3. If so, how should the court decide whether to stay the proceedings for or order the parties to engage in a non-court-based dispute resolution process? and
4. Should the court have allowed the defendant's application for a stay to allow the claimant to engage with the CCP?

On issue 1, the Court held that *Halsey* did not bind the judge because the passage on which the judge relied was not a necessary part of the reasoning that led to the Court of Appeal's decision in that case,[39] i.e. Dyson LJ's passage was *obiter dicta* rather than *ratio decidendi*. The Court explained that the Court in *Halsey* was concerned with whether

38 *Churchill*, note 12, [6].

39 *R (on the application of Youngsam) v The Parole Board* [2019] EWCA Civ 229, [2020] QB 387, in which Leggatt LJ explained the meaning of the Latin terms *ratio decidendi* and *obiter dicta*: "It therefore seems to me that, when the ratio decidendi is described as a ruling or reason which is treated as 'necessary' for the decision, this cannot mean logically or causally necessary. Rather, such statements must, I think, be understood more broadly as indicating that *the ratio is (or is regarded by the judge as being) part of the best or preferred justification for the conclusion reached:* it is necessary in the sense that the justification for that conclusion would be, if not altogether lacking, then at any rate weaker if a different rule were adopted" [emphasis added].

a costs' sanction should be imposed against the successful parties because they had refused to mediate. In *Halsey*, the Court held that there should be no sanction for costs as it had not been established that the parties' refusal was unreasonable. The Court also identified several factors as relevant in deciding whether a refusal to mediate was unreasonable.[40] In that context, Dyson LJ had commented on ADR compulsion, which was not necessary in reaching the court's conclusions on the costs' questions decided in the appeals. The factors the Court identified in *Halsey* as relevant to the issue of unreasonable refusal to engage with ADR were relevant to whether or not the Court had the power to require the parties to mediate.

The Court of Appeal in *Churchill* identified four elements of Dyson LJ's judgment in *Halsey*, indicating that his comments were not to be regarded as part of the best or preferred justification for the conclusion he reached. First, Dyson LJ's statement of the issue clarified that the decision was about sanctions for costs and not whether to order parties to participate in mediation. Secondly, Dyson LJ's comments are in a section of the judgment entitled "general encouragement of the use of ADR". Thirdly, the Court in *Halsey* expressly stated that it had heard arguments on whether the court had the power to order parties to submit their dispute to mediation against their will. That had only been raised for the first time in oral argument. Fourthly, Dyson LJ was guided on the general approach in dealing with the costs issues raised by the appeals and the factors that should be considered in deciding whether a refusal to agree to ADR was unreasonable. The question of whether the court had the power to mandate ADR was no part of the best or preferred justification for these conclusions.[41]

On issue 2, the Court considered domestic cases, the European Court of Human Rights (ECtHR), and pre-Brexit cases from the Court of Justice of the European Union (CJEU), as well as relevant legislation and the Civil Procedure Rules. On the CPR, the Court referred to several rules. First, CPR 1.4(1) provides that the court must "further the overriding objective by actively managing cases". CPR 1.4(2)(e) explains that active case management includes "encouraging the parties to use an alternative dispute resolution procedure if the court considers that appropriate and facilitating the use of such procedure". Secondly, CPR 3.1 relates to the court's general powers of management. It says expressly at CPR 3.1(4) that, when giving directions, the court "will take into account whether or not a party has complied with [the PD] and any relevant pre-action protocol". CPR 3.1(5) provides that the court may order a party to pay money into court if it has "without good reason, failed to comply with a rule, practice direction or a relevant pre-action protocol". Thirdly, CPR 26.5(1) allows a party, when filing a completed directions questionnaire, to "make a written request for the proceedings to be stayed while the parties try to settle the case by alternative dispute resolution or other means". CPR 26.5(3) also allows the court to stay the proceedings, even without the parties requesting it, "[i]f the court otherwise considers that such a stay would be appropriate".

40 The factors include the nature of the dispute, the merits of the case, whether other settlement methods have been attempted, whether the costs of mediation would be disproportionately high, whether any delay in setting up and attending ADR would have been prejudicial, and whether the ADR process has a reasonable prospect of success.

41 *Churchill*, note 12, [19]–[21].

The Court also referred to several ECtHR cases,[42] including *Deweer v Belgium*, which Dyson LJ relied upon in *Halsey*. *Deweer* was concerned about a Belgian butcher who had allegedly committed an offence of selling meat at an illegal profit. The public prosecutor ordered the butcher to close his shop until either his prosecution was completed or he paid a fine of 10,000 Belgian francs. He paid the fine under protest but brought successful proceedings before the ECtHR for breach of Article 6(1). The ECtHR held that the fine had been paid, and the butcher's right to a hearing had been waived under the threat to close the shop and destroy the business. The ECtHR said that "[t]he waiver, which has undeniable advantages for the individual concerned as well as for the administration of justice, does not in principle offend against the [ECHR]".[43] The ECtHR continued as follows:[44]

> Nevertheless, in a democratic society too great an importance attaches to the "right to a court" . . . for its benefit to be forfeited solely by reason of the fact that an individual is a party to a settlement reached in the course of a procedure ancillary to court proceedings. In an area concerning the public order (ordre public) of the member States of the Council of Europe, any measure or decision alleged to be in breach of Article 6 calls for particularly careful review.

The ECtHR made clear that the pressure brought to bear on Mr Deweer by the threat to close his shop if he did not pay the fine was a constraint that was incompatible with Article 6.

In the case of *Alassini v Telecom Italia SpA*,[45] the CJEU considered whether Italian law, which mandated compulsory engagement with ADR, infringed Article 6 rights. The CJEU decided that it did not and concluded that

> it is settled case law that fundamental rights do not constitute unfettered prerogatives and may be restricted, provided that the restrictions, in fact, correspond to objectives of general interest pursued by the measure in question and that they do not involve, about the objectives pursued, a disproportionate and intolerable interference which infringes upon the very substance of the rights guaranteed.[46]

The decision in *Alassini* was subsequently applied in *Menini v Banco Popolare Società Cooperativa*[47] in the context of Directive 2013/11/EU of 21 May 2013 on alternative dispute resolution for consumer disputes.[48]

The Court of Appeal then turned its attention to domestic case law, particularly the leading modern authority on the constitutional right of access to the court as an essential element of the rule of law: *R (UNISON) v Lord Chancellor*.[49] In *UNISON*, the UK Supreme Court held that the right of access to the courts could only be curtailed

42 Other cases include *Tolstoy Miloslavsky v United Kingdom* (1995) 20 EHRR 442, [1995] 7 WLUK 198; *Z and others v United Kingdom* (2002) 34 EHRR 3, [2001] 5 WLUK 297; and *Momcilovic v Croatia* (2019) 69 EHRR 14, [2015] 3 WLUK 795.

43 *Churchill*, note 12, [49].

44 Ibid.

45 Joined Cases C-317/08, C-301/08, C-319/08 and C-320/08 *Alassini v Telecom Italia SpA* [2010] 3 CMLR 17.

46 Ibid. [63].

47 Case C-75/16 *Menini v Banco Popolare Società Cooperativa* [2018] CMLR 15.

48 Ibid. [61].

49 *R (on the application of UNISON) v Lord Chancellor* [2017] UKSC 51, [2020] AC 869.

by express primary legislation. Therefore, the statutory instrument increasing fees to bring claims to the Employment Tribunal was unlawful because it prevented access to justice. In that case, the statutory instrument increasing fees for the commencement of Employment Tribunal cases (the fees order) was considered unlawful since it prevented access to justice. However, the Court in *Churchill* noted that *UNISON* was concerned with an impediment that prevented access to a judicial determination and not with the circumstances in which it might be considered proportionate to delay such access for a legitimate objective, such as achieving resolution of the dispute by other means.

The Court explained that the essential question was whether *UNISON* meant that a court may not be stayed or delayed to allow such steps to occur without primary legislation allowing it. In his Lordship's judgment, the answer to that question was no for the following five reasons: (1) *UNISON* was not concerned with either staying existing proceedings for other dispute resolution processes to take place or with mandating the parties to participate in them. It was not even worried about the situation once proceedings had been issued. (2) *UNISON* did not say anything to oppose the proposition that the court has a long-established right to control its own process. That right is entrenched in the Civil Procedure Act 1997, which established the CPR to govern the practices and procedures of the court and provided that rule-making should make the civil justice system accessible, fair, and efficient. The settling of cases as quickly as can reasonably be achieved and at a proportionate cost to the parties supported those aims. (3) None of the authorities referred to in *UNISON* suggested that the court cannot make orders that delay or prevent the resolution of existing proceedings in aid of making the court system accessible, fair, and efficient. (4) Whilst the CPR itself is not primary legislation, nothing in *UNISON* suggests that one of the fundamental premises of the overriding objective and even the CPR itself, namely the promotion of out of court dispute resolution by various means, could be unlawful without primary legislation authorising it expressly. The overriding objective requires the court to manage cases actively and to encourage and facilitate ADR, and expressly contemplates stays for such processes to be undertaken. (5) Several authorities that were not cited to the Supreme Court in *UNISON* support the proposition that the court can, and indeed should, in an appropriate situation, stay cases whilst out of court attempts to resolve the disputes take place.[50]

Having completed its review of the CPR and relevant authorities, the Court of Appeal concluded that the courts do have the power to lawfully stay proceedings for or order the parties to engage with ADR because (1) *UNISON* was not authority for the proposition that a statutory basis was required for the court to be able to mandate ADR. It was clear from that judgment that the court had the power to control its own processes and could, for legitimate reasons, place constraints on the right of access. (2) The court had the power to take many steps that postponed parties' access to a trial.

50 See, for example, *Guinle v Kirreh* [1999] 8 WLUK 24, [2000] CP Rep 62; *R (on the application of Cowl) v Plymouth City Council* [2001] EWCA Civ 1935, [2002] 1 WLR 803 [14]; *Shirayama Shokusan Co Ltd v Danovo Ltd (No 2)* [2004] 1 WLR 2985 [12]–[20] (Blackburne J); *Uren v Corporate Leisure (UK) Ltd* [2011] EWCA Civ 66, [2011] 2 WLUK 107 [73] (Smith LJ); *Mann v Mann* [2014] EWHC 537 (Fam), [2014] 1 WLR 2807 [16]–[17] and [36] (Mostyn J); *Bradley v Heslin* [2014] EWHC 3267 (Ch), [2014] 10 WLUK 287 [24]; and *Lomax v Lomax* [2019] EWCA Civ 1467, [2019] 1 WLR 6527.

It could, for instance, adjourn proceedings. (3) The decision in *Deweer v Belgium* did not, contrary to the conclusion in *Halsey*, conclude that mandatory ADR breached Article 6 of the ECHR. *Deweer* concerned coercion into arbitration and the fact that that violated the right to a fair trial. (4) It was clear from the ECtHR and CJEU case law that court-mandated ADR was compatible with the Article 6 right to a fair trial. (5) The Civil Justice Council's Compulsory ADR Report[51] supported the general view that mandatory ADR was compatible with Article 6 and therefore endorsed the general conclusions of the Court of Appeal in *Churchill*.

On issue 3, the Court refused to provide a list of factors which would assist the courts in determining when to exercise its powers to compel parties to engage with ADR; it would be a matter for the courts to determine in the circumstances of each case.[52] His Lordship went on to state that the court should only stay proceedings for, or order, the parties to engage in a non–court-based dispute resolution process provided that the order made "does not impair the very essence of the claimant's right to proceed to a judicial hearing, and is proportionate to achieving the legitimate aim of settling the dispute fairly, quickly and at reasonable cost".[53]

As for the factors that a court should consider, Sir Geoffrey Vos MR explained that the overriding objective identified by the appellant, the Bar Council, and the *Halsey* factors were all likely to be relevant. His Lordship observed that the *Halsey* factors mirrored those identified by the Bar Council.[54]

Finally, on issue 4, the Court allowed the appeal on this point but declined to order a stay of the proceedings. It held that if the judge had not concluded that *Halsey* bound him to refuse a stay, he would have granted one to allow the claimant to engage with the CCP. However, the Court found little point in granting a stay of the claim now, as the court could not properly grant a mandatory injunction requiring the claimant to allow the defendant to treat the knotweed, which had neither been sought nor argued.

The decision is a significant development in civil procedure and dispute resolution. By finding that Dyson LJ's comments on Article 6 point were *obiter* and therefore did not bind the courts, *Churchill* has finally confirmed that the courts can compel disputing parties to engage with ADR in appropriate cases. Thus, as a matter of law, judges are no longer bound by Dyson LJ's comments in *Halsey*. The decision provides a detailed exposition of the necessary case law at all levels and reinforces its

51 Compulsory ADR Report, note 37.

52 Ibid. [60].

53 *Churchill*, note 12, [65].

54 The Bar Council submitted that the following factors were relevant to the exercise of the court's discretion: (1) the form of ADR being considered; (2) whether the parties were legally advised or represented; (3) whether ADR was likely to be effective or appropriate without such advice or representation; (4) whether it was made clear to the parties that, if they did not settle, they were free to pursue their claim or defence; (5) the urgency of the case and the reason-ableness of the delay caused by ADR; (6) whether that delay would vitiate the claim or give rise to or exacerbate any limitation issue; (7) the costs of ADR, both in absolute terms, and relative to the parties' resources and the value of the claim; (8) whether there was any realistic prospect of the claim being resolved through ADR; (9) whether there was a significant imbalance in the parties' levels of resource, bargaining power, or sophistication; (10) the reasons given by a party for not wishing to mediate: for example, if there had already been a recent unsuccessful attempt at ADR; and (11) the reasonableness and proportionality of the sanction, if a party declined ADR in the face of an order of the Court.

conclusions by identifying and explaining the procedural law underpinning the courts' powers to compel parties to ADR. The Court makes the obvious but powerful point that the courts retain the power to control their own procedures.

This judicial clarification has long been awaited. I have consistently argued that Dyson LJ's comments were *obiter* and have demonstrated, through a detailed analysis of the ADR jurisprudence, how judicial misunderstanding of those comments has resulted in divergence and inconsistencies in judicial approaches and, consequently, has led to confusing and contradictory messages for litigating parties and their lawyers on their ADR obligations.[55] Indeed, ten years after *Halsey*, Lord Dyson, speaking extra-judicially, agreed that his comments were *obiter* when he said, "[Masood] Ahmed of Leicester University . . . in 2012 suggested that what Halsey had to say about compulsory mediation was obiter (which in my view it was)".[56]

It was always clear that the courts had the power to compel parties to engage with ADR – it is an integral part of the overriding objective and the court's case management powers, and it is reinforced by the courts' powers to penalise parties in costs for unreasonably refusing ADR. However, this latter point of costs sanctions has created what I have previously referred to as "implied compulsory mediation" – the situation in which, before *Churchill*, the courts would formally reject the idea of compelling parties to engage with ADR. Still, they would later penalise those parties in costs, which, I have previously argued, is a form of implied compulsion to engage with ADR.

The decision also reinforces the current civil justice reform programme, which seeks to integrate further and enhance ADR's role and function within the pre-action space and during the court process. Indeed, in *Churchill*, Sir Geoffrey Vos MR explained that the conclusion of the Court "is supported by the Civil Justice Council's June 2021 Report on Compulsory ADR, which expressed the view that 'any form of ADR which is not disproportionality onerous and does not foreclose the parties' effective access to the court will be compatible with the parties' Article 6 rights". The Report stated that "we think the balance of the argument favours the view that it is compatible with Article 6 for a court or a set of procedural rules to require ADR". As discussed earlier, OCMC incorporates opt-out mediation, and the Ministry of Justice has recently confirmed its intentions to expand the use of opt-out mediation to higher-value claims.

The decision also provides fertile ground to enhance the role of the protocols and ADR within the digital environment. It also reinforces the role and powers of the OPRC in governing the pre-action space and setting data standards for digital portals from service providers. It also potentially strengthens the three sequential steps in the proposed General PaP. Parties and their lawyer will not be clear that the courts can

55 See, for example, M. Ahmed, "Implied compulsory mediation" (2012) Civil Justice Quarterly 51; M. Ahmed, Mediation: the need for a united, clear and consistent judicial voice' (2018) Civil Justice Quarterly 13; M. Ahmed & D. Quek Anderson, "Expanding the scope of dispute resolution and access to justice" (2019) Civil Justice Quarterly 1; M. Ahmed, "A more principled approach to compulsory ADR" (2020) Journal of Personal Injury Law 277.

56 Lord Dyson MR, "Halsey 10 Years On – The Decision Revisited" in Lord Dyson, *Justice: Continuity and Change* (Bloomsbury 2018) 383.

and, in appropriate cases, will exercise their powers and stay proceedings issued in breach of any applicable protocol.

There are, however, concerns regarding the Court of Appeal's guidance on the factors the courts should consider when deciding whether to exercise their discretion in ordering parties to ADR or staying proceedings in favour of ADR. It will be recalled that the Court of Appeal declined to lay down fixed principles as to what will be relevant in determining this issue. Instead, the Court of Appeal stated that the factors identified by the Bar Council and those set out in *Halsey* would be relevant. Although I agree with the Court of Appeal's approach in not setting a fixed principle, not least because it has the undesirable effect of creating a rigid list of factors and can restrict the courts' discretion, I believe the Court of Appeal missed a unique opportunity to revisit and dismiss the *Halsey* merits factor which has led to the development of contradictory and confusing ADR jurisprudence.

Finally, the courts must embrace and exercise their powers in making ADR orders or staying proceedings in appropriate cases. Not every case will be suited for ADR, which is why the Court of Appeal made clear that it will be for the courts to determine the issue on a case-by-case basis. If, however, a particular case is suited for ADR, as many will be, then the court should not hesitate to make an ADR order, and when making such an order, the courts should make an order to refer parties to the most appropriate ADR procedure rather than simply opting for mediation. Mediation is the most popular ADR procedure among the judiciary and policymakers. The strong judicial promotion of mediation has elevated it to the pre-eminent ADR procedure in resolving civil disputes. However, this has the danger of creating two dominant dispute resolution streams: litigation and mediation. Furthermore, this preference for one particular type of procedure over other forms of ADR restricts the courts' ability to effectively further the overriding objective of encouraging and facilitating *appropriate* ADR procedures. What is required is judicial ADR pluralism – the promotion of a range of ADR procedures – so that parties have a choice of the most suitable procedure for their dispute.

VI Impact on the B&PC Disputes

In this final part, I consider the impact *Churchill* and the PaP Review will have on B&PC disputes and propose the essential elements of a new pre-action protocol for the B&PC.

A ADR Powers and Judicial ADR Pluralism

The B&PC are well suited and prepared to adapt to the decision in *Churchill* and the PaP Review proposals. The CC and TCC have a long history of incorporating ADR within its procedures. The CC has led the way in developing ADR orders, and the TCC has pioneered various ADR procedures, including judicial early neutral evaluation and judicial mediation, which are prominently featured within the CC and TCC court guides. The language used in the guides encourages the parties to consider and engage with ADR. For example, the parties are "given the opportunity to ask the court if they feel NDR may benefit them". The apparent impact of *Churchill* will mean that the courts can and should make ADR orders in appropriate cases, regardless of the parties' wishes. Given the long history of ADR within the CC and TCC, the B&PC is uniquely positioned to lead the way in developing a consistent body of case law on the issue of compulsory ADR. This opportunity will rest upon the judges in B&PC fully embracing and exercising their ADR powers and distancing themselves from the authorities, which followed *Halsey*'s reasoning on the issue of compulsory ADR. The judges in the King's Bench Division have demonstrated a willingness to not only endorse their ADR powers but have also exercised their powers. Take, for example, *Hadley v Przybylo*, which concerned a dispute regarding the parties' costs budgets. Master McCloud did not hesitate to order the parties to engage in ADR, using appropriately qualified costs professionals, before the court conducted the costs' budgeting exercise. In another decision, Master McCloud endorsed using judicial early neutral evaluation. He set out a generic version of an early neutral evaluation order that could be adapted to suit other case proceedings in the King's Bench Division. That guidance has now been incorporated within the King's Bench Guide.

The reference in the CC and TCC guides to a range of ADR procedures also potentially provides fertile ground for promoting judicial ADR pluralism. Although some of the language emphasises mediation, the range of ADR procedures covered in both guides is to be welcomed. Those procedures include the range of ADR procedures expressly set out in the General PaP and, therefore, allow the courts to consider and recommend the most appropriate ADR procedure for the case's particular circumstances.

B The General PaP and the B&PC

The final point is the potential for a pre-action protocol for the B&PC that would apply to disputes that do not fall within the scope of specific protocols such as the Construction and Engineering Protocol. In this section, I focus on the three sequential steps of the General PaP to explain why I think it provides a strong procedural basis for disputes in the B&PC.

Before considering the General PaP, let me first deal with the potential argument against having a protocol for the B&PC or having a less prescriptive protocol that "softens" the stocktake requirement. It may be argued that, given the high value and complex nature of the disputes heard in the B&PC, there is no need for a protocol, or a simple protocol should suffice which does not require the parties to complete a stocktake report. The principal rationale for this argument would be that a protocol or a highly prescriptive protocol will lead to the front-loading of costs and the possibility of satellite litigation. Indeed, there is some weight in that argument. The B&PC is a world-leading centre for commercial dispute resolution and a highly respected judiciary. It has a stellar reputation for the work that it does. It attracts disputes from around the world, and it is a leader in procedural innovations. However, that does not detract from the need to ensure that the courts' resources are managed carefully and that the principle of proportionality is upheld. This means that the parties, regardless of whether they are individuals with a small claim or an international litigant with a multimillion-pound claim, must assist the court in furthering the overriding objective, which should apply equally to all.

The proposed General PaP provides a robust procedural framework for the development of a new B&PC protocol. The essence of such a protocol would be the three sequential steps and the need for the protocol to be digitised. The complex and high-value nature of the disputes heard in the B&PC generates vast volumes of documents that can be more efficiently and effectively dealt with through the online environment by, for example, using predictive coding in the disclosure process. In essence, predictive coding is the review of documents undertaken by computer software, which analyses the documents and then "scores" them for relevance to the issues in the case. The process aims to identify the documents relevant to the case while reducing the time and cost of the review by reducing the number of irrelevant documents. Predictive coding was embraced in *Pyrrho Investments Limited v MWB Property Limited*,[57] in which the court recognised and praised the ability of predictive coding to save substantial costs in the disclosure process. The second ADR step would also lend itself well to B&PC disputes, where clients are represented by sophisticated law firms accustomed to using and facilitating online ADR procedures. As discussed earlier, the B&PC successfully adapted to remote and online hearings during the COVID-19 pandemic which demonstrates that a culture and practice exists among the B&PC judges and practitioners working with digital processes and procedures. Finally, the stocktake procedure should remain, albeit in a slightly less prescriptive form. Therefore, the third step, which requires the parties to narrow the issues and complete a stocktake report, should also apply to the B&PC disputes. This will not only help the parties to better understand the issues in dispute, but it will also assist in the possible settlement of the case at a later stage and, more significantly, it will assist in the more efficient management of judicial resources.

The B&PC are well placed to embrace and adapt to the current and future civil justice reforms. The digitalisation of civil procedure and increasing emphasis on the role of ADR will allow the B&PC to modernise its procedures and thereby reinforce its international reputation as a leading centre for commercial dispute resolution. To fully realise these benefits, however, the B&PC judges must begin to develop a more principled approach to the issue of compulsory ADR, and there must be a bespoke pre-action protocol for B&PC disputes which promotes constructive pre-action conduct and reinforces efficient judicial case management.

57 [2016] EWHC 256 (Ch), [2016] 2 WLUK 413.

CHAPTER 5

Resolving Airline Passenger Disputes by Alternative Dispute Resolution Methods

An Appraisal of the UK System

*George Leloudas**

I Introduction

Passenger disputes with airlines for their death, bodily injury, delay and the loss, damage, destruction and delay of their baggage have historically been the remit of courts. This was not the result of airlines imposing onerous terms on their customers to limit the litigation forums. Instead, the international legal framework governing such claims established a uniform code to be applied by the courts of State parties. This code, designed to be uniform and exclusive of resort to domestic laws, sets the conditions and venues for passengers to establish the airlines' liability.

This framework was established in 1933 when the 1929 Warsaw Convention (WC29) came into force.[1] It was conceived to protect "the fledgling and still fragile aviation industry".[2] While the WC29 was amended several times,[3] the four litigation forum

* **Professor of Law, Member of the Institute of International Shipping and Trade Law.**

1 Warsaw Convention for the Unification of Certain Rules Relating to International Carriage by Air (adopted 12 October 1929, entered into force 13 February 1933) 137 LNTS 11.

2 *Morris v KLM* [2002] 2 AC 628 [12] per Lord Steyn.

3 The Warsaw Convention 1929 was amended by the Hague Protocol to Amend the Convention for the Unification of Certain Rules Relating to International Carriage by Air (adopted 28 September 1955, entered into force 1 August 1963), 478 UNTS 371, the Guadalajara Convention Supplementary to the Warsaw Convention for the Unification of Certain Rules Relating to International Carriage by Air Performed by a Person Other than the Contracting Carrier (adopted 18 September 1961, entered into force 1 May 1964) 500 UNTS 32 and the Montreal Additional Protocols 1975 which consist of the Montreal Additional Protocol No 1 to Amend the Convention for the Unification of Certain Rules Relating to International Carriage by Air, Signed at Warsaw on 12 October 1929, as Amended by the Protocol done at The Hague on 28 September 1955 (adopted 25 September 1975, entered into force 15 February, 1996) ICAO DOC 9145, the Montreal Additional Protocol No 2 to Amend the Convention for the Unification of Certain Rules Relating to International Carriage by Air, Signed at Warsaw on 12 October 1929, as Amended by the Protocol done at The Hague on 28 September 1955 (adopted 25 September 1975, entered into force 15 February 1996), ICAO Doc. 9146 and the Montreal Protocol No 4 to Amend the Convention for the Unification of Certain Rules Relating to International Carriage by Air signed at Warsaw on 12 October 1929 as Amended by the Protocol done at The Hague on 28 September 1955 (adopted 25 September 1975, entered into force 14 June 1998), ICAO Doc 9148. The Guatemala City Protocol to Amend the Convention for the Unification of Certain Rules Relating to International Carriage by Air signed at Warsaw on 12 October 1929 as Amended by the Protocol done at The Hague on 28 September 1955 (adopted 8 March 1971) ICAO Doc 8392 and the Montreal Additional Protocol No 3 to Amend the Convention for the Unification of Certain Rules Relating to International Carriage by Air signed at Warsaw on 12 October 1929 as Amended by the Protocols done at The Hague on 28 September 1955 and at Guatemala City on 8 March 1971 (adopted 25 September 1975, entered into force 15 February 1996), ICAO Doc 9147 never came into force.

DOI: 10.4324/9781032726243-6

provisions (for which see later in Section II) remained intact until 2003 when the Montreal Convention 1999 (MC99)[4] came into force to replace the WC29 and its amendments and ensure "protection of the interests of consumers in international carriage by air and the need for equitable compensation based on the principle of restitution".[5] Despite this shift of focus from protecting the industry to protecting consumers-passengers, MC99 did not change the four litigation forum provisions of WC29 but added a fifth jurisdiction only available for passengers' injury and death claims.[6]

This international legal system is designed to provide a level playing field between airlines and their passengers; airlines that fly internationally are well aware of the jurisdictions they need to defend claims from their passengers, and passengers are protected from terms and conditions imposed by airlines that attempt to restrict their litigation options.

This almost 100-year-old system, for the reasons discussed in Section III, does not make provision for the resolution of passenger disputes by alternative means, be that arbitration, mediation, adjudication, etc., and has its exclusive focus on resolving them through courts. However, this one-sided focus is lagging domestic initiatives to streamline consumer-protection disputes to alternative forums so that the judicial systems are not burdened with thousands of relatively low-value claims, and their resolution does not usually raise complex evidentiary and legal issues.

While these initiatives did not have aviation in mind at first, they have become an integral part of airline passenger disputes due to the popularity of domestic consumer protection regulations, which are more flexible in terms of the means of resolving disputes within their scope of application and they produce a more significant number of claims. The comparison becomes more evident with judicial activism enabling some of these regulations to contest the exclusive nature of the international legal framework (see Section V) and raise questions about the potential reform of the international legal framework to accommodate them.

This chapter does not aim to analyse the debate on the co-existence of domestic consumer protection legislation and the MC99. Still, it will examine the role that alternative means of resolving airline passenger disputes (ADR) have played so far, what role they should play in the future, and whether they can be integrated into the MC99.

II Court Jurisdiction in Montreal Convention 1999

The MC99 provides the exclusive framework for resolving passenger disputes with airlines involving bodily injury, death, and delay,[7] as well as disputes involving the loss, damage, destruction, and delay (LDDD) of checked-in baggage and carry-ons

4 Montreal Convention for the Unification of Certain Rules for International Carriage by Air (adopted 28 May 1999, entered into force 4 November 2003) 2242 UNTS 309.

5 Ibid., Preamble.

6 Ibid., art 33.

7 See arts 17.1 and 19.

arising from international air carriage.[8] It also covers disputes for cargo LDDD from international air carriage.[9] The jurisdictions where a passenger or cargo interest is permitted to bring a claim against the airline are also identified as part of this exclusive framework; which one to choose is the option of the claimant:[10]

1 domicile of the airline;
2 principal place of business of the airline;
3 place of business of the airline through which the contract of carriage has been made;
4 place of destination of the carriage in question,

provided that these countries are parties to the MC99.

Providing a detailed analysis of each jurisdiction is outside the scope of this chapter,[11] but a few points must be raised to inform our discussion. Of these four forums, the first two (domicile and principal place of business of the airline) usually direct claimants to the country where the airline is based, namely where it is incorporated.[12] This results from commercial airlines adhering to strict ownership and control requirements, which require them to have their place of incorporation in the same jurisdiction as their main place of business. These jurisdictions are not linked to the passenger's itinerary but to the airline's business and give the airline certainty that the claims will be filed before this country's courts.

The other two jurisdictions (numbers 2 and 3) relate to the claimant's itinerary, either the place where the ticket is purchased or the country of destination for their trip. The requirement that the ticket be bought via an airline's "place of business" links the claim to the airline's operational network, with US courts accepting that the premises of an authorised agent of a carrier can be considered an establishment of the airline for this Article.[13] Similarly, the place of destination as a forum links the itinerary to the claim, as it is expected that both the passenger and the airline have links to this country. One thing to note here is that under the Convention, the place of destination in return itineraries (e.g. LHR-ATH-LHR) is the place of origin (namely the UK), which increases the chances that the claimant and the airline have strong links to the jurisdiction in question.[14]

The Warsaw Convention 1929 (and its amendments) did not provide for the right to bring a claim in the country where the claimant was living; this was resisted because the claimant's residence jurisdiction might not be linked to the itinerary or the airline's network of operations. Still, the main reason for resisting its inclusion was the concern that the litigation floodgates would open as passengers could bring claims where they

8 See arts 17.2 and 19.
9 See arts 18 and 19.
10 See art 33.
11 See Timothy M. Ravich, Grégory Laville de la Plaigne and Romain Verté, "Article 33 Jurisdiction" in George Leloudas, Paul S. Dempsey, Laurent Chassot (eds), *The Montreal Convention. A Commentary* (Elgar 2024) (*Montreal Convention Commentary*) and George Leloudas et al., *Shawcross and Beaumont on Air Law* (LexisNexis, Issue 187, 2024) Vol 1, Division VII [416] ff (*Shawcross and Beaumont*).
12 *Montreal Convention Commentary*, n 11, [33.14].
13 Ibid., [33.42]–[33.45].
14 See art 1.

reside irrespective of their actual itinerary, especially in the United States, which is considered the most expensive jurisdiction, even if the airline has no operational connection to the jurisdiction of their residence.[15]

However, this resistance gave way (after a long fight) in MC99,[16] where a fifth jurisdiction was added permitting claimants to bring claims for death or bodily injury (but not for passenger delay, baggage, and cargo LDDD claims) where they have their principal and permanent residency at the time of the accident, provided that the country is a party to the Convention and the airline has a direct (by operating its aircraft) or indirect (e.g. via code-sharing or leasing agreements with other airlines) relation to this jurisdiction. The fifth jurisdiction was a compromise to enable passengers to bring a claim where they live while protecting airlines' interests by only permitting claims where the defendant has a commercial presence. This dual requirement might explain why the inclusion of the fifth jurisdiction has not opened the litigation floodgates as some delegates have predicted during the drafting of the MC99.

Overall, this arrangement does not prevent forum shopping after multi-casualty accidents, yet it works well in most other situations, providing certainty and stability in applying the Convention. To this effect, the principle of exclusivity of Article 29 MC99 has played a significant role, as the claimant must file the claim in one of the said forums, which have "exclusive" jurisdiction over the dispute. This provision has been chiefly used by airlines to "restrain" passengers from bringing claims in non-Convention jurisdictions and re-direct them to the regime of the Convention. At the same time, Article 26 MC99 prevents airlines from restricting the jurisdictions available to the claimant under the Convention via their terms and conditions and Article 27 permits airlines to add jurisdictions to the prescribed ones via their contract conditions.

III ADR in Montreal Convention 1999

The drafters of the MC99 disagreed on whether to permit arbitration to settle disputes arising from the carriage of passengers and baggage. This discussion followed the drafting of Article 34 MC99; Article 34 permits arbitration clauses for cargo claims to be included in contracts of carriage by air, giving an additional way of resolving cargo disputes. The delegate of Sweden to the Montreal Convention Conference provided a brief explanation of why the drafters did not permit arbitration clauses to cover passenger disputes:[17]

> Arbitration may, in Europe, be extremely expensive; its cost could reach the amount mentioned in the draft Convention for the first tier of liability. The Delegate of Sweden therefore did not wish to see an arrangement whereby passengers, upon purchasing their tickets, agreed on arbitration.

15 *Shawcross and Beaumont*, n 11, [441.1].

16 Ibid.

17 ICAO, "International Conference on Air Law – Volume I – Minutes" (10–28 May 1999), Doc 9775-DC/2, p 188 (Montreal Convention 1999 Minutes Vol 1).

Several delegates from European countries agreed with this view, prominent among them the French delegate:[18]

> Having recourse to such a system could only occur when it involved a balanced situation with two parties of virtually equal strength. That was why in the *travaux preparatoires* the issue of arbitration in respect of cargo had been included, since it was difficult to envisage an individual involved in arbitration with an airline.

Overall, the delegates were concerned that airlines could use arbitration to exercise undue influence on claimants, predominantly by increasing costs to force claimants to settle or abandon their claims. While several arbitration rules deal with such concerns by having a set of provisions for controlling arbitral expenses, the truth remains that this was a valid concern at the time of drafting the Convention. ADR methods, such as adjudication, which provide cheaper and more balanced ways to resolve disputes than arbitration, were not on the drafters' radar and were not even considered. As such, the delegates retained the court-focused system with its inherent weaknesses in terms of delays and forum shopping because they thought it provided better protection from manipulation for the passenger. However, they did not discuss in detail the impact of the safeguards built in Article 34, such as the right of the claimant/cargo interest to choose the place of arbitration among the forums of Article 33 and the requirement for arbitrators to apply the provisions of the MC99 to the dispute.

The MC99 does not preclude referring passenger disputes to arbitration or other alternative dispute resolution methods after they have arisen.[19] Essentially, it permits ad-hoc non-litigation procedures to resolve passenger disputes. Several (especially arbitration and mediation) are regularly used to resolve passenger claims under the Conventions, especially in multi-fatal aircraft accidents where global settlements are typical. Yet, these would usually be accompanied by a court action to save the limitation period of two years of the MC99.[20] This is necessary because initiating alternative dispute resolution proceedings does not stop the limitation period of the MC99.

In that respect, the MC99 does not preclude using alternative dispute resolution methods for passenger claims provided they are not agreed upon before the accident, for example, as part of the airline's terms and conditions, but are opted for in its aftermath. The logic here is that the claimants will take legal advice in the aftermath of an accident and will make an informed decision on their potential choices for resolving a dispute. The MC99 does not regulate this alternative option, as it does with cargo arbitration, but leaves it to domestic arbitration laws and the general provision of the Convention; for example, it is plausible that the claimant files a claim in one of the five forums of the MC99 to protect the limitation period but arbitrate the dispute in a different jurisdiction. In principle, this option is not available to cargo arbitrations as Article 34 requires that the arbitration "shall, at the option of the claimant, take place within one of the jurisdictions referred to in Article 33".

18 Ibid.

19 Ibid. and Michael Chatzipanagiotis, "Article 34 Arbitration" in George Leloudas, Paul S. Dempsey, Laurent Chassot (eds), *The Montreal Convention. A Commentary* (Elgar 2024).

20 See art 35.

IV Aviation Consumerism and Passenger Complaints

The drafters of the MC99 were not keen on ADR methods for passenger claims, demonstrating a conservative and (somewhat outdated) view. One reason for such an approach was that at the time of drafting the MC99, the full effect of consumerism in international civil aviation was not apparent. While the Conventions had produced a fair share of case law over the years, this was nothing compared to consumer protection legislation's influx of cases from the mid-noughties to today. The reasons behind the consumerisation of air travel can be briefly described as follows:[21]

> The expansion of low-cost/charter carriers and the regular failures of full-cost air carriers to deliver the "innovative products, [and] personalised services" promised to their passengers have contributed significantly to this trend: "Airlines are now less service-oriented and more impersonal. As a consequence, passengers are less likely to relate personally to air crew and more likely to see them as representatives of an airline that has emphasised cost rather than service, and consequently someone that they can vent their anger on". . . .
>
> This inclination is further supported by a legislature-driven desire to create a consumer-friendly environment in which grievances are dealt with through claims and complaints. The resulting rule-bound culture has fostered the establishment of consumer-advocacy groups, which use advertising, demonstrations, and lobbying to promote their agendas and communicate their hostility to corporate organisations that do not uphold their part of the bargain. Consumer activism – combined with the introduction of conditional fee arrangements (CFA), after-the-event insurance (AEI), legal-expenses insurance (LEI), and claims-management companies – has arguably increased public awareness of consumer rights, demystified the complexities of claims handling, and lifted litigation costs from the shoulders of the consumer/claimant [quotations omitted].

This decline in airline confidence was amplified by the MC99's rigid litigation system and a pro-carrier interpretation of its terms despite the change in public attitudes towards airlines[22] but was driven mainly by a general dissatisfaction with the air travel experience. This trend was most recently expressed in the 2023 Aviation Consumer Survey published by the Civil Aviation Authority (CAA):[23]

> The proportion of recent flyers who were satisfied with their most recent flight has fallen from 80% in 2022 to 79% this year. This is a small change and is not in itself a cause for concern. However, a decline of this kind has occurred every year since 2019, and consequently the cumulative, longer-term trend is more noteworthy. In March 2016, 9 in 10 consumers (90%) were satisfied with their most recent journey, a figure considerably higher than the one recorded in 2023 (79%). Satisfaction saw a decline during the pandemic, much like flight frequency. However, unlike flight frequency, satisfaction has continued to fall post-pandemic, rather than returning to previous levels.

These feelings seem to be fuelled by the increasing number of disruptions faced by air travellers. In 2023, only 42% of air passengers faced no travel problems (the

21 George Leloudas, *Risk and Liability in Air Law* (Informa Law 2009) [3.44]–[3.45] (*Leloudas Risk*).
22 Ibid., ch 5.
23 CAA, "CAP 2622: Wave Twelve: UK Aviation Consumer Survey: Full Survey Report" (January 2024) p 9, www.caa.co.uk/our-work/publications/documents/content/cap2622/, last accessed 17 May 2024.

corresponding shares were 38% in 2022, 45% in 2021, 65% in 2020, and 56% in 2019).[24] Flight delays seem to be one of the most prevalent forms of air travel disruption, with 22% of passengers experiencing a flight delay in 2023.[25]

To deal with such disruptions, domestic consumer protection legislation emerged that was initially designed to supplement (rather than take over) the Conventions. The most prominent legislation to do so was the (European) Regulation 261/2004 on denied boarding compensation and compensation and assistance to passengers in the event of cancellation or long delay of flights (Regulation 261),[26] with many to follow. The Preamble highlighted the need for a stronger consumer-protection focus by "raising the standards of protection set by that Regulation both to strengthen the rights of passengers and to ensure that air carriers operate under harmonised conditions in a liberalised market". In this context, the Regulation identified three situations, namely denied boarding, cancellations, and delays, that inconvenience passengers regularly and aimed to address their impact.

Similarly, Regulation 1107 / 2006 concerning the rights of disabled persons and persons with reduced mobility when travelling by air was enacted to protect disabled passengers from unjustified denied boardings from airlines:

> Disabled persons and persons with reduced mobility should therefore be accepted for carriage and not refused transport on the grounds of their disability or lack of mobility, except for reasons which are justified on the grounds of safety and prescribed by law.[27]

These Regulations were designed to accompany the Conventions, not interfere with their application sphere or breach the principle of exclusivity. Disputes concerning denied boarding and flight cancellations are not part of the Conventions' regimes, so, in principle, there is no direct conflict with them. This relation explains why Regulation 261 provides the affected passengers the right to compensation based on the distance of their affected flights;[28] this compensation is supplemented by assistance and care measures, such as reimbursement of the ticket cost, return or re-routing flights, and provision of refreshments, meals, hotel accommodation, transport between the airport and place of accommodation, etc.[29] However, claiming damages for delayed flights is part of Article 19 of the Conventions, and to avoid any conflict with them, the text of

---

24 Ibid., p 40.

25 Ibid., p 41.

26 Regulation (EC) No 261/2004 of the European Parliament and of the Council of 11 February 2004 establishing common rules on compensation and assistance to passengers in the event of denied boarding and of cancellation or long delay of flights, and repealing Regulation (EEC) No 295/91 OJ L 46, 17.2.2004, pp 1–8. The Regulation has been assimilated into the British legal systems following Brexit and in 2023 was amended by the Aviation (Consumers) (Amendment) Regulations 2023, SI 1370/2023. The amendment does not change the philosophy of the Regulation but codifies some of the significant decisions of the Court of Justice of the European Union. As such, our analysis here is valid for both the EU and the British version of the Regulation.

27 Preamble of Regulation (EC) No 1107/2006 of the European Parliament and of the Council of 5 July 2006 concerning the rights of disabled persons and persons with reduced mobility when travelling by air OJ L 204, 26.7.2006, pp 1–9. The Regulation is now part of assimilated law in the UK.

28 See art 7 which provides that passengers will receive compensation amounting to (i) £220 for all flights of 1500 kilometres or less; (ii) £350 for all flights between 1500 and 3500 kilometres; (iii) £520 for all flights not falling under (i) or (ii).

29 See arts 8–10.

the Regulation did not give delayed passengers the right to compensation but instead provided a set of assistance and care measures.[30]

When the Court of Justice of the European Union (CJEU) was asked to decide on whether such measures conflict with the MC99, it justified their co-existence with the Convention's exclusive regime on the basis that they cover damage that is "almost identical for every passenger, redress for which may take the form of standardized and immediate assistance or care for everybody concerned",[31] while the MC99 covers "individual damage, inherent in the reason for travelling, redress for which requires a case-by-case assessment of the damage caused and can consequently only be the subject of compensation granted subsequently on an individual basis".[32]

Despite the criticism against this artificial distinction,[33] the logic of this interpretation is straightforward. To respect the exclusivity of the Convention under Article 29, only those areas of (international) carriage outside its scope can be regulated domestically. This is why the Regulation gives the right of compensation to denied boarding and cancellation claims (which do not fall into the scope of the Conventions) and does not provide for the right to compensation in cases of delay (which is regulated in Article 19 MC99), which was left to the MC99 regime to determine.

V Judicial Activism

This sensitive balance between the two regimes was permanently disturbed by the case of *Sturgeon v Condor Flugdienst GmbH* (*Sturgeon*),[34] which made the need for ADR in aviation passenger disputes necessary. The CJEU, in the *Sturgeon* case, held that flight delays over three hours must be treated as cancellations and attract the compensation regime of Article 7 of Regulation 261 (see Section IV). However, the text of Article 7 on purpose does not give such right to passengers who experience delays (for the reasons explained in Section IV). As such, the CJEU rewrote the Regulation to read that passengers who arrive at their destination with more than a three-hour delay can claim compensation under it. This compensation does not require proof of actual damages or a causative link but is based on the distance of the flight.[35]

This activist decision surprised the European judicial system, with several domestic courts refusing to apply it "because the European Court supposedly overstepped its competence in extending the rights under the Regulation beyond its wording".[36] But the CJEU, in the joined cases of *Nelson v Deutsche Lufthansa GmbH* and *R (on*

30 See arts 8 and 9.

31 Case C-344/04 *R (on application of International Air Transport Association) v Department for Transport* [43] [2006] ECR I-403, [2006] 2 CMLR 20.

32 Ibid.

33 For a strong criticism of the relationship between Regulation 261 and the MC99, see Laurent Chassot and Paul S Dempsey, "Article 29 Exclusivity" in *Montreal Convention Commentary*, n. 11.

34 Joined cases C-402/04 and C-432/07 *Christopher Sturgeon v Condor Flugdienst GmbH* and *Stefan Böck and Cornelia Lepuschitz v Air France SA* [2009] ECR I-10923.

35 Namely (i) £220 for all flights of 1500 kilometres or less; (ii) £350 for all flights between 1500 and 3500 kilometres; and (iii) £520 for all flights not falling under (i) or (ii).

36 *Shawcross and Beaumont*, note 11, Division VIIA [51].

the application of TUI Travel) v Civil Aviation Authority,[37] confirmed its decision in *Sturgeon* and justified it by making a further artificial distinction between "loss of time" and "delay" to accommodate the two regimes:[38]

> a loss of time cannot be categorised as "damage occasioned by delay" within the meaning of Article 19 of the Montreal Convention, and, for that reason, it falls outside the scope of Article 29 of that convention. . . . First of all, a loss of time is not damage arising as a result of a delay, but is an inconvenience, like other inconveniences inherent in cases of denied boarding, flight cancellation and long delay. . . . Next, a loss of time is suffered identically by all passengers whose flights are delayed and, consequently, it is possible to redress that loss by means of a standardised measure. . . . Lastly, there is not necessarily a causal link between, on the one hand, the actual delay and, on the other, the loss of time considered relevant for the purpose of giving rise to a right to compensation under Regulation No 261/2004 or calculating the amount of that compensation.

Since then, domestic European courts have accepted this distinction between delay and loss of time and the right to compensation for delayed arrivals of more than three hours at the destination.[39] Most recently, the Canadian Federal Court of Appeals approved the equivalent provision of the Canadian regulations, following the CJEU logic.[40] In the UK, this logic has been approved in *Dawson v Thomson Airways Ltd* and *Gahan v Emirates*, which have accepted the reasoning of the CJEU and have not been overturned following Brexit. Furthermore, the Aviation (Consumers) (Amendment) Regulations 2023 (see note 26) have made such decisions part of the assimilated Regulation 261 as they unequivocally provide in Article 3(7) and (8) that the obligation to pay compensation for such delays "does not constitute a liability for damage occasioned by delay for Article 19 of the Montreal Convention".

The other related issue that needs to be addressed here is jurisdiction under Regulation 261. While the MC99 has four forums for passenger delay claims (the fifth is reserved for personal injury or death claims) and baggage claims (see Section II), the Regulation does not contain any provisions regarding jurisdiction. In that respect, it is more flexible than the Convention and permits ADR mechanisms agreed upon before the flight to resolve such disputes.

The relevant case law has established that complaints under the Regulation can be brought at the place of departure and the place of destination of the flight in question.[41] For example, a Regulation 261 claim can be brought in either country if a flight from London to Milan is delayed or cancelled. This arrangement has been extended to connecting flights that are part of a single itinerary. For example, the passenger can bring a claim to the UK or Greece on an itinerary from London to Athens via Milan and Paris. In addition, case law has established that a claim under Regulation 261 can be brought to the country of the carrier's domicile and the country where the airline has a branch office involved in the carriage contract. While the last

37 Joined Cases C-581/10 and C-629/10, *Nelson v Deutsche Lufthansa GmbH* and *R (on the application of TUI Travel) v Civil Aviation Authority* [2013] All ER (Comm) 385.

38 Ibid., [49]–[53].

39 See *Shawcross and Beaumont*, note 11, Division VIIA [53].

40 *IATA v Canadian Transport Agency and Attorney General of Canada* [2022] FCA 211.

41 For a detailed analysis of the relevant case law, see *Shawcross and Beaumont*, note 11, Division VIIA [38]–[44].

two forums resemble the MC99's, the place of departure is unavailable as a forum in MC99 delay claims, and the place of destination is defined differently in the MC99 (see also Section II).

So, in the first itinerary mentioned (one way from London to Milan), delay claims under MC99 cannot be brought to the UK (as it is the itinerary's departure place). At the same time, if this itinerary was on a return basis, i.e. London-Milan-London, the MC99 delay claims cannot be filed in Italy as it is not the destination for the Convention's purposes; the same will happen in the second itinerary on a return basis, i.e. London-Milan-Paris-Athens and back to London; an MC99 delay claim cannot be brought in Greece as it is not the country of departure. Still, in all these scenarios, a Regulation 261 claim can be filed in Italy or Greece as they are the destination countries for the Regulation purposes. In that respect, the MC99 and the Regulation provide two jurisdictional systems regarding delay that do not always point in the same direction. Unsurprisingly, in Case C-213/18 *Guaitoli v easyJet Airline Co Ltd*,[42] the CJEU held that the two jurisdiction regimes are to be determined independently, although this might lead to having the claims heard before different forums.

VI The Effect of Judicial Activism on Passenger Complaints

The impact of this judicial rewriting of Regulation 261 is evident in the most recent (2023) statistics released by the two aviation ADR providers operating in the UK, namely Aviation ADR and CEDR.[43] The work of these two aviation ADR providers is supplemented by the CAA's Passenger Advice and Complaints Team (PACT), which deals with complaints against airlines that are not members of any of the two ADR providers.[44] These three providers cover the following types of disputes between airlines and their passengers:

- complaints for denied boarding or cancellation of flight under Regulation 261;
- complaints for delay of flights under Regulation 261 and the MC99;
- complaints for the LDDD of checked-in baggage and carry-ons under the MC99;
- complaints by passengers with reduced mobility under Regulation 1107;
- any disputes arising where the consumer alleges that the business is not trading fairly – PACT has no authority to deal with such disputes.

The number of complaints filed before the two aviation ADR providers is astonishing.[45] In 2019, approximately 32,500 complaints were logged before the two ADR bodies; in

42 ECLI:EU:C:2019:927.

43 See Aviation ADR www.aviationadr.org.uk/ and CEDR www.cedr.com/consumer/aviation/make-a-complaint/, last accessed 17 May 2024.

44 See CAA, "How the CAA can help. If you are not satisfied with the response from your airline or airport". www.caa.co.uk/passengers/resolving-travel-problems/how-the-caa-can-help/how-the-caa-can-help/, last accessed 17 March 2024.

45 The statistics derive from the 2023 annual reports that the two providers compiled to comply with Reg 11 (and Schedule 5) of The Alternative Dispute Resolution for Consumer Disputes (Competent Authorities

2020, a total of 39,554 complaints; in 2021, more than 26,000 complaints were logged; in 2022, approximately 23,000 complaints were logged; and in 2023, approximately 55,700 complaints were logged – a significant increase over the previous years that might be attributed to "some unforeseen circumstances seen this year such as environmental issues like the fires in Europe or the air traffic control problems experienced recently",[46] as well as "disruption of flights due to ground handling issues experienced by airports around the UK".[47] To understand the magnitude of those figures, one must consider that they don't include the complaints filed before the CAA PACT and those that ended up in the judicial system.

In 2023, the vast majority of complaints submitted before the two aviation ADR providers (47,184 out of 55,700) were under Regulation 261, with the remaining claims split among Regulation 1107 (77 complaints), claims for the LDDD of checked-in and carry-on bags (1942 complaints), and several other smaller categories, such as medical issues, in-flight facilities and services, etc. Of the 47,184 complaints under Regulation 261, the vast majority of them were for compensation, namely 15,865 complaints because the flight in question was cancelled, 18,907 complaints for compensation because the flights were delayed (the *Sturgeon* compensation right), and 1256 complaints for compensation because the passengers were denied boarding. The second-largest group of complaints was the payment of expenses due to the cancellation, delay, and denied boarding of the flights, namely 2,053 complaints. The third-largest group was claims for the LDDD of checked-in and carry-on baggage, namely 1,942. Similar divisions have been experienced in the past years; for example, in 2022, Regulation 261 complaints amounted to 20,957 out of 26,000 complaints, with compensation complaints amounting to 16,148 out of 20,957.

In addition, the 2023 Aviation Consumer Survey indicated that 41% of the passengers who formally complained wanted financial compensation (an increase of 7% from 2022), 40% complained as a way of expressing their disappointment (an increase of 8% from 2022), 38% wanted the airline/airport to make changes so that the issue was less likely to happen in the future, and 36% wanted an apology from the airline/airport.[48]

It is evident from the foregoing that Regulation 261 complaints account for the lion's share of passenger-related claims in the UK. The most popular are complaints for compensation because the flights were delayed (the *Sturgeon* right). These figures also demonstrate that Regulation 261 delay claims have taken over the delay claims of MC99, as there were no reported delay court cases under the MC99 in the UK in 2022 and 2023 and no ADR claims for passenger delay under the MC99 in 2023.

We believe that the main reason for the popularity of Regulation 261 is its relative ease of use (which we see more about in Section V). Its legal framework gives the impression of a more straightforward regime in that terms such as delay have been defined in a mechanical manner that leaves little to interpretation; the same applies

and Information) Regulations 2015 (as amended). The reports can be found in the following links: www.aviationadr.org.uk/ and www.cedr.com/consumer/aviation/reports/, last accessed 17 March 2024.

46 2023 Aviation Consumer Survey, n 23, p 40.

47 Aviation ADR 2023 report, n 45, [3].

48 2023 Aviation Consumer Survey, n 23, p 52.

to the compensation provided under the Regulation where there is no requirement to prove the actual damage that the passenger suffered as a result of the delay (cancellation or denied boarding) but is linked to the distance of the disrupted flight.

On the contrary, the delay regime under the MC99 is complicated in that delays are identified on a case-by-case basis by reference to "the length of the flight, weather conditions or events like congestion at airports or ATC problems".[49] In addition, to be awarded damages for delay under MC99, the claimants must prove that they suffered damage from the delay and its quantum. This task is not always easy, as several countries do not compensate for emotional damages, such as a loss of enjoyment or loss of income caused by delay.[50] One also has to consider that Regulation 261 claims can be brought at the place of departure or arrival of the flight, either of which would usually be the country of the passenger's residence – with the MC99 not providing for the residence of the claimant (which is reserved for bodily injury and death claims) as a potential forum.

Last but not least, we believe that the availability of a relatively straightforward dispute resolution system that does not have many formalities and does not require the instruction of lawyers has undoubtedly contributed to the amplification of the number of complaints filed under Regulation 261 before the two aviation ADR providers. We now turn our attention to that system to explain its operation.

VII ADR in Air Passenger Disputes

The use of Regulation 261 triggered a myriad of claims as passengers were given a relatively easy legal tool to receive compensation as well as a series of care and assistance measures; the number of claims we discussed in Section VI makes the use of out-of-court settlement systems not only advisable for the benefit of consumers but essential to prevent the clogging of the judicial system, especially of county courts. Still, it creates doubts about the efficiency of Regulation 261 – producing 47,184 complaints per year in the UK alone (without considering the CAA PACT complaints and those ending up in court), despite the dissatisfaction with airlines, also questions the role and purpose of the Regulation (this is a discussion outside the scope of this chapter and relates to its reform). Such complaints fit nicely into the reasoning for using ADR schemes: they mainly consist of low-value claims (£520 is the maximum amount a passenger can get under Regulation 261 – see Section IV) that are not evidence-heavy and can be quickly resolved by an independent intermediary rather than via the more expensive and lengthier judicial process.

Aviation is a particular case in the context of consumer ADR, as the use of ADR by airlines is not mandatory, making it the only regulated sector without compulsory schemes. Most British airlines are part of two voluntary schemes, namely CEDR Aviation and ADR Aviation, while several non-British airlines are also part of the

49 Wolf Müller-Rostin and Jae Woon (June) Lee, "Article 19 Delay" in *Montreal Convention Commentary*, n. 11, [19.11].

50 Ibid., [19.24]–[19.33] and *Shawcross and Beaumont*, note 11, Division VII [1023].

same schemes.[51] Overall, 32 airlines are registered with an ADR scheme that arguably covers 80% of those departing the UK by air.[52] Still, most non-British airlines that fly to/from the UK are not members, and complaints against them must be filed before the CAA PACT.

The basic philosophy of the Aviation ADR Schemes is that a passenger's complaint that falls into one of the categories in Section VI and is against an airline that subscribes to either of the two schemes will be determined by an independent adjudicator appointed by either scheme. The decision of the adjudicator becomes binding only when the passenger accepts it. Our analysis herein follows the 2022 Rules of the Aviation ADR Scheme as it was by far the more popular one, with 46,996 complaints filed before it in 2023 (in contrast, the CEDR Scheme received 8,706 complaints).[53]

Airline passengers can refer complaints to the ADR Scheme if they have followed the subscribed airline's complaints procedure and (1) have not received a response from the airline (a so-called deadlock letter) within eight weeks as to whether the airline accepts the complaint or (2) the airline rejects the complaint.[54] The geographical scope of application of the scheme covers direct flights with their origin and destination in the UK or directly connecting flights with their origin, destination, or connection taking place in the UK.[55] This is quite broad as it covers flights that depart from, connect via, or terminate in the UK (whether they are part of a more extensive itinerary with connecting flights or not).

The schemes will not entertain complaints from the same passenger about an incident affecting the same flight that has been the subject of an existing or previous valid application to the scheme or a complaint that has been the subject of court proceedings or other ADR procedures unless they have been abandoned, stayed or suspended.[56] Also, the schemes will not entertain complaints of more than £25,000 in value and complaints that have not been filed within "12 months from the date upon which the Airline gave their final response on the Complaint (or, where no response is given, it has been more than 12 months since the Passenger's last attempt to contact the Airline)".[57] Once a passenger files a complaint, airlines must submit their defences to the ADR Scheme within 28 days of being notified of the complaint.[58] No party can add evidence once the adjudicator determines that the complaint file has been completed.[59]

The decision-making process has been simplified to facilitate the resolution of complaints and keep costs under control. Once the complaint is filed with the ADR

51 For a list, see www.aviationadr.org.uk/ and www.cedr.com/consumer/aviation/companies-covered/, last accessed 17 May 2024.

52 See CAA, "Alternative dispute resolution. Information on CAA-approved ADR" www.caa.co.uk/passengers/resolving-travel-problems/how-the-caa-can-help/alternative-dispute-resolution/, last accessed 17 May 2024.

53 The Rules can be located in www.aviationadr.org.uk/, last accessed 17 May 2024.

54 Rule 1.1.2.

55 Rule 1.1.3.

56 Rule 1.2.4.

57 Rules 1.2.5 and 1.2.6.

58 Rule 3.2.

59 Rule 3.3.

Scheme, the adjudicator assesses whether it falls within the scheme's scope; if not, the passenger is notified within three weeks.[60] If the complaint is accepted, it will be passed to the airline, which has 28 days to confirm whether it wishes to defend or settle the complaint.[61] A third alternative is for the airline to notify the adjudicator (within 14 days) that "it considers that the complaint raises a genuinely complex and novel issue" and a particular procedure must be followed.[62]

If a settlement is reached at this stage, the airline has 28 days to implement it, for example, by compensating the passenger.[63] But suppose the airline decides to defend the complaint. In that case, the passenger has seven calendar days to comment on the airline's defence, provided the defence raises new evidence not offered in the original passenger's response.[64] Once the passenger comments to the airline's defence, the file is completed, and no further evidence is accepted, apart from exceptional circumstances authorised by the scheme's Chief Adjudicator.[65]

From that moment onwards, the complaint will be determined in writing within 90 calendar days unless it involves a highly complex issue, in which case the 90-day deadline will be extended and the parties informed.[66] Deciding on the complaint does not usually require a hearing unless the parties agree otherwise, which is rare. The language used in the decision (and any oral proceedings) is the language used by the carriage contract.[67] The passenger can withdraw from the complaints process at any stage and bring a claim to court. The airline does not have the right to withdraw from the process unilaterally unless the complaint involves a complex issue.[68]

One potential issue that might delay the decision is that the complaints involve a legal issue that has not been determined in the past and is currently the subject of court proceedings either in the UK or in European courts (see, for example, the aftermath of *Sturgeon* in Section V): in that case, the passenger is given the option of either proceeding with its complaint before the adjudicator or putting it on hold until the judicial decision is rendered; if the passenger agrees to put it on hold, the ADR Scheme must inform the CAA.[69]

Overall, the ADR system seems to be working as intended from the perspective of offering a low-cost and quick way of resolving complaints. In 2023, the two schemes reported that the average time to resolve complaints was between 32 and 77 days,[70] which can only be described as lightning speed. They also reported that they refused to deal with a minority of complaints (6,708 complaints out of the 55,700 received ones), with the vast majority of them (92.93% and 71%, respectively) because they were out of the schemes' scope.[71]

60 Rules 4.2 and 4.3.
61 Rule 4.4.
62 Ibid. For the special procedure, refer to appendix 4 of the Rules.
63 Rule 4.5.
64 Rule 4.6.
65 Rule 4.7.
66 Rule 4.8.
67 Rule 9.11.
68 Rule 6.
69 Rule 5.
70 See the respective 2023 Annual Reports, n 47.
71 Ibid.

While the number of annual complaints seems to correlate to the gravity of disruptions experienced during the year, there is an expectation that the figures shall (rather than will) increase as the 2023 CAA Customer Survey indicated that only a small proportion of consumers express dissatisfaction with how their travel issue is handled by making a complaint. In 2023, 56% of the passengers took no action whatsoever, 12% filed a claim for expenses incurred and/or compensation, 15% made a formal or informal complaint, 16% decided to avoid flying with the disrupted airline/airport in the future, and 17% warned friends and family about flying with the disrupted airline/airport in the future.[72]

At the same time, the current level of complaints might be fuelled by low satisfaction with the airlines' complaints handling process. As the Survey indicated, only 43% trust airlines to handle complaints effectively.[73] Similarly, only 50% of the passengers who complained to the airline or the airport were satisfied with the complaint process overall – the level of satisfaction has dropped by 2% since 2022 and 13% since 2019, the pre-COVID years.[74] At the same time, the level of satisfaction with the claims handling process was much lower than that with other elements of the travel experience, such as booking, with an 87% satisfaction rate, travelling to and from the airport in the UK with 81%, onboard and on-flight experience with 76%, airport experience with 76%, and value for money with 67%.[75]

The statistics in this section indicate that the number of claims that end up in the two ADR systems is unlikely to reduce significantly. Our final section will propose some ideas on how to improve the system.

VIII Some Thoughts on the Way Forward

The level of trust in the ADR Schemes, evidenced by the vast number of complaints filed before them, indicated that the use of ADR for at least the non-MC99 disputes must become mandatory for airlines operating to/from the UK to avoid not only spillover into the judicial system but also the unnecessary use of CAA resources in resolving disputes via PACT. The British Government indicated in 2023 that it aimed to make aviation ADR Schemes mandatory,[76] but it is unlikely that this will happen before the 2024 elections. It is important to note that the MC99 disputes (baggage LDDD and MC99 delay claims) cannot be the subject of a mandatory regime for the reasons we mentioned in Section III. That will create a dual system that might confuse passengers, yet we believe that the relatively low number of MC99 claims that end up in ADR will not distort the benefits of having a mandatory system for non-MC99 disputes.

72 2023 Aviation Consumer Survey, n 23, p 44.
73 Ibid., p 49.
74 Ibid., p 74.
75 Ibid., p 15.
76 Department for Transport, "Consultation outcome. Response to the aviation consumer policy reform Consultation" (June 2023). www.gov.uk/government/consultations/reforming-aviation-consumer-policy-protecting-air-passenger-rights/outcome/response-to-the-aviation-consumer-policy-reform-consultation, last accessed 17 May 2024.

At the same time, we believe that a rapprochement of the jurisdiction provisions of the two regimes needs to be achieved. While we will not delve into the debate of amending the MC99 to incorporate the essence of consumer protection regulations, we believe that creating such a regime is the best way forward, provided it enables passenger ADR and unifies the forums for judicial and out-of-court actions against airlines. Long are the days of the Montreal Diplomatic Conference with the mistrust of European delegates for ADR; its extended use has shown that, in certain instances, it provides a better service to the consumer than court litigation. Such a unified regime will provide certainty of the applicable law to passengers and airlines, reduce costs, limit the number of parallel claims, and enable cheaper and quicker resolution of disputes.

However, the aviation ADR schemes are not required to publish the adjudicators' decisions. This has the effect that thousands of cases interpreting the content of consumer protection regulations and the baggage provisions of the MC99 are not published, which leaves a gap in knowing how the legal instruments are interpreted in the UK. The provision that novel and complex cases will be referred to the CAA is insufficient to close this gap, as there is no discernible manner to publicise such cases. Also, they constitute a small part of the case law produced by the adjudicators.

We believe it is misplaced to argue that the adjudicators provide for the mechanical application of legal instruments, and their decisions have little precedential value. The existing case law demonstrates that issues of evidence submitted by the airlines (e.g. weather reports, crew statements) remain open to interpretation and shape the final decision of the adjudicators. As such, we believe it is necessary for at least a sample of cases to be published (after anonymising personal data) as it will enable the development of the case law on consumer protection regulation and will assist courts in the interpretation of those cases that end up in the judicial system. Furthermore, the publication of such cases will also inform the debate about the future of consumer protection regulations, especially Regulation 261.

It is also important to note that the ADR adjudicators decide baggage claims and delay claims under the MC99, cases that the law's application is not as mechanical and raises issues of interpretation of an international convention: with only a handful of MC99 baggage cases and no delay cases published the last few years in the UK, it is necessary to have access to issues of interpretation that have the potential to shape the understanding of the MC99 globally. Reducing the number of judicial decisions is a success for the proponents of the ADR system, as these cases (or a significant proportion of them) have been withdrawn from the judicial system. Yet, without publishing their outcomes, a considerable interpretation gap is created concerning the MC99 that has wider than the UK repercussions.

PART 2

JURISDICTION-RELATED ISSUES, OTHER REMEDIES, AND THE POSITION OF THIRD PARTIES

CHAPTER 6

Anti-suit Injunctions in International Litigation

Two Important Niche Issues

*Andrew Tettenborn**

I Introduction

Just as a successful general does his best to give battle on ground carefully selected by him, a good international commercial lawyer will always try to ensure by judicious use of arbitration provisions or exclusive jurisdiction clauses (EJCs for short) that if they have to fight it will be exclusively in a tribunal of their own choosing. Such clauses, however, are only as effective in so far as a party can ensure they are observed, and enforcing them is often easier said than done.

The traditional English[1] anti-suit injunction, or ASI, is not only a vital weapon in this connection: it has also become a vastly more effective one since Brexit freed London law firms and English courts from the previous rule[2] that any right to interfere with foreign legal proceedings stopped abruptly at the boundaries of the EU.[3] This chapter builds on this development, and takes the opportunity to look at two fairly specialised but nevertheless important aspects of the use of ASIs in a commercial context. These are, first, their application to foreign preliminary and interlocutory proceedings; and secondly, how far such orders are available to control derivative claims brought by those not directly party to an agreement containing the relevant arbitration clause or EJC.

---

* **Member of the Institute of International Shipping and Trade Law.**

1 Traditionally English, but more accurately Commonwealth and common-law: see S. Gee, *Gee on Commercial Injunctions* (7th Edn, Sweet & Maxwell, 2021), ch 14, s 3. The United States accepts them: *Grupo Mexicano de Desarrollo SA v Alliance Bond Fund Inc*, 527 US 308, 318–319 (1999). Civil law jurisdictions are less receptive to such claims, though some allow them.

2 Laid down by the ECJ in its decisions in *Turner v Grovit (C-159/02)* [2004] ECR I-3565 and *West Tankers Inc v Allianz SpA (C-185/07)* [2009] ECR I-00663 on the basis that this interfered with the full faith and credit on which the Brussels scheme was based. This rule was reinforced post-Brexit by the same court in *The Alexandros T (C-590/21)* [2023] EUECJ C-590/21, saying that awards of damages for suing in EU courts in breach of contract were just as objectionable as ASIs.

3 This is because of the lapse of the Brussels I Recast Regulation (Regulation (EU) No 1215/2012) in the UK following Brexit, and the subsequent refusal of the EU to allow the UK to join the alternative scheme regulated by the 2007 Lugano Convention. (The prospect of EU and UK membership of the 2019 Hague Judgments Convention makes no difference here, since this deals with enforcement rather than jurisdiction matters.) For examples of English courts exercising this new freedom, see *Ebury Partners Belgium SA/NV v Technical Touch BV* [2022] EWHC 2927 (Comm), [2023] 1 Lloyd's Rep 575 and *QBE Europe SA/NV v Generali España de Seguros y Reaseguros* [2022] EWHC 2062 (Comm), [2023] Lloyd's Rep IR 192.

DOI: 10.4324/9781032726243-8

II ASIs: Preliminary and Interlocutory Proceedings

A contract containing an arbitration clause or an English EJC[4] implicitly forbids substantive court proceedings abroad: that is the reason why such clauses exist in the first place, and also explains why ASIs are very readily available against defendants who seek openly to flout them.[5] But this leaves a different question unanswered. How far, if at all, do such clauses bar a party from seeking *interlocutory* remedies against litigants in foreign courts, such as search orders, interlocutory injunctions, freezing injunctions, arrest of ships, or *saisie-conservatoire* requests in civil law jurisdictions? The issue here is slightly different. Even a litigant concerned with keeping a substantive claim in a given jurisdiction may well be happy with the idea that they, or even their opponents, may engage in satellite litigation to safeguard their interests anywhere where relevant assets can be found.

What, then, is the position? The answer to this question is of course ultimately a matter of interpretation of the relevant arbitration agreement or EJC. There is nothing to stop parties spelling out in detail what is and is not allowed,[6] or even agreeing that no proceedings of any kind whatever can be brought abroad.[7] Nevertheless, absent specific provision the presumption is that an ordinary arbitration or EJC clause is intended to distinguish between substantive and interlocutory proceedings, with the former barred and the latter allowed.[8] The question is where that line should be drawn, and when particular proceedings cross it so as to justify an ASI. In this connection different types of interlocutory proceedings need some separate discussion.

A Freezing Injunctions

Seeking relief in the nature of a freezing injunction *prima facie* does not fall foul of an arbitration or EJC clause so as to give rise to the possibility of an ASI.[9] However, the

4 From now on, "EJC" will be used specifically to refer to an EJC referring to the English courts. Even though a person suing in Ruritania in the face of an ECJ giving exclusivity to the courts of Utopia is just as much in breach of contract as someone doing so in defiance of a provision stipulating an English forum, the English courts will steer clear of such disputes even if they otherwise have jurisdiction over the defendant: *Airbus Industrie G.I.E. v Patel* [1999] 1 AC 119.

5 See later, and also S. Gee, *Gee on Commercial Injunctions* (7th ed, Sweet & Maxwell, 2021), ch 14, s 11. Where the EJC is covered by the 2005 Hague Convention on Choice of Court Agreements there is no explicit requirement to issue an ASI (see art 7, making it clear that this is governed by the law of the court seized), but it may well be that this factor would incline a court even more in favour of granting relief.

6 As they rather sensibly did in *Ultisol Transport Contractors Ltd v Bouygues Offshore SA* [1996] 2 Lloyd's Rep 140 (exclusive English jurisdiction clause, but express permission "to bring proceedings in rem to obtain conservative seizure or other similar remedy . . . in any state or jurisdiction where such vessel or property may be found").

7 As seemingly happened in *Mantovani v Carapelli* [1978] 2 Lloyd's Rep 63: see the interpretation of that case in *Re Q's Estate* [1999] 1 Lloyd's Rep 931, 934–936.

8 For statements of the principle, see e.g. Jonathan Hirst QC in *The Kallang (No.2)* [2008] EWHC 2761 (Comm), [2009] 1 Lloyd's Rep 124 [78] ff; *SRS Middle East FZE v Chemie Tech DMCC* [2020] EWHC 2904 (Comm) [35]–[36], [39]–[40] (Andrew Baker J), and *Aquavita International SA v Indagro SA* [2022] EWHC 892 (Comm) [18]–[21] (Foxton J). In *Petromin SA v Secnav Marine Ltd* [1995] 1 Lloyd's Rep 603, 613, Colman J seemingly suggested that the fact that the foreign proceedings were limited to obtaining security went merely to the discretion whether to issue an ASI: but this seems heterodox, if only because the same distinction seems equally to apply to claims for damages, where there is no element of discretion.

9 See *Re Q's Estate* [1999] 1 Lloyd's Rep 931, *SRS Middle East FZE v Chemie Tech DMCC* [2020] EWHC 2904 (Comm), [2021] 1 Lloyd's Rep 371 [37] (Andrew Baker J).

prima facie qualification is important, and at least two limits of this principle need to be borne in mind. For one thing, freezing injunctions can morph into more substantial claims, and as soon as a respondent goes beyond pure freezing relief and pursues anything in the nature of substantive proceedings, matters are different.[10] And it also remains highly arguable that a suit for freezing relief that was excessive, unnecessary, or disproportionate would itself be seen as vexatious and oppressive and thus liable to be enjoined on that basis.[11]

B Foreign Security Proceedings

An English freezing injunction merely exists to make assets available for execution; it does not give the claimant any kind of security over them.[12] Many jurisdictions, however, go further and allow a claimant to freeze assets in order to secure their claim. Does this make a difference? In *Ispat Industries Ltd v Western Bulk Pte Ltd*,[13] Teare J held that on principle it did not. In that case owners in dispute over a charterparty with a London arbitration clause had obtained Rule B attachments[14] in New York against the charterers' assets. His Lordship upheld the arbitrators' refusal to award damages to the charterers on the basis that this amounted to a breach of the arbitration agreement: *a fortiori*, he would of necessity have refused an ASI. Similarly, in *SRS Middle East FZE v Chemie Tech DMCC*,[15] Andrew Baker J accepted that under a Middle Eastern construction contract with a London arbitration clause, it was acceptable for the constructor to seek provisional attachment in the Sharjah courts, a remedy that again gave a measure of preference over its clients' property there.

On the other hand, as with freezing orders, in order to take advantage of this dispensation the proceedings must be genuinely ancillary. As soon as they stray over into claiming any kind of decision on the merits, then the ordinary rule applies and an ASI runs as of course. (This, on the facts, was held to follow in the *SRS Middle East* case itself, where the proceedings actually threatened to go a good deal further, and an injunction was issued to keep them in proper bounds.)

C Ship Arrest

It has been established for over 40 years that arbitration clauses or EJCs *prima facie* do not bar ship arrest, provided that the substantive issue is arbitrated or litigated in

---

10 Compare the ship arrest case of *Sam Purpose AS v Transnav Purpose Navigation Ltd* [2017] EWHC 719 (Comm), [2017] 2 Lloyd's Rep 50.

11 A point left open by Andrew Baker J in *SRS Middle East FZE v Chemie Tech DMCC* [2020] EWHC 2904 (Comm), [2021] 1 Lloyd's Rep 371 [38]. It is suggested that relief should be available here: there is no good reason for such litigation and conversely every justification for suppressing it. Compare the decision in the ship arrest case of *The Joker* [2019] EWHC 3541 (Comm), [2021] 2 CLC 1, discussed later.

12 See *The Angel Bell* [1981] QB 65 and *Flightline Ltd v Edwards* [2003] EWCA Civ 63, [2003] 1 WLR 1200 [47] (Jonathan Parker LJ); also *Company 1 v Company 2* [2017] EWHC 2319 (QB), [2018] 1 Lloyd's Rep 115.

13 [2011] EWHC 93 (Comm), [2011] Arb LR 3.

14 See the Federal Rules of Civil Procedure, Title XIII, Rule B. Such attachments not only freeze assets but also give a preference over them.

15 [2020] EWHC 2904 (Comm), [2021] 1 Lloyd's Rep 371; see esp [35]–[36], [39]–[40]. See too *Aquavita International SA v Indagro SA* [2022] EWHC 892 (Comm) [21] (Foxton J).

the chosen court and not the place of arrest. The point was first made in *The Rena K*[16] (technically a case of stay of proceedings, but nothing turns on this). In that case, cargo interests arrested a vessel in England over a cargo claim subject to London arbitration. On the owners' complaint the Court of Appeal ordered the arrest lifted, but only on condition of provision by the owners of equivalent security, the reasoning being precisely that the original arrest had been unobjectionable. Six years later the same result was reached in the converse context of an ASI concerning an arrest abroad. In *The Lisboa*[17] a vessel was arrested in Italy over a cargo claim arising out of a contract with an English EJC. The Court of Appeal refused to order the lifting of the arrest, Lord Denning MR saying simply that the reference in the EJC to "any and all legal proceedings" did not include "proceedings to enforce a judgment or award or to obtain security";[18] and since then this has been accepted as representing the law.[19]

However, while it is clear that arrest is not as such impermissible, the line between the acceptable and the unacceptable can be fairly nuanced.

First, the protection given to the right of arrest is narrow. Arrest for any purpose further than a simple obtaining of security is not permitted.[20] In *Kallang Shipping SA v AXA Assurances Sénégal*[21] the facts were superficially analogous to *The Lisboa*, in that cargo had arrested a vessel abroad – here in Dakar – in the face of a London arbitration clause. But in *Kallang*, unlike *The Lisboa*, cargo had additionally demanded as the price of release not only security but an irrevocable submission to Senegalese jurisdiction. Distinguishing the earlier cases, Gloster J unsurprisingly said that this arrest had been made for an improper purpose. She upheld an ASI preventing cargo from demanding such a submission, making the point that such a demand amounted to a clear attempt to circumvent the arbitration clause, and therefore both it and the arrest in support of it were a breach of contract.[22] More recently, the same reasoning was applied in *The Sam Purpose*[23] to an arrest abroad coupled with an application for default judgment, with an order being made to compel the respondent to discontinue the latter application.[24]

Secondly, arrests are not necessarily justifiable even if they are made simply for security. If it is clear that adequate security for a claim will be forthcoming as of course even without an arrest, for example from a shipowner's P&I Club, then it seems

16 [1979] 1 QB 377.

17 [1980] 2 Lloyd's Rep 546.

18 [1980] 2 Lloyd's Rep 546, 548.

19 See e.g. *Kallang Shipping SA v AXA Assurances Sénégal* [2006] EWHC 2825 (Comm), [2007] 1 Lloyd's Rep 160 [36] (Gloster J), *The Sam Purpose* [2017] EWHC 719 (Comm), [2017] 2 Lloyd's Rep 50 [9]; and *Ispat Industries Ltd v Western Bulk Pte Ltd* [2011] EWHC 93 (Comm), [2011] Arb LR 3 [46] (Teare J).

20 It seems, moreover, that the arrest is wrongful, and hence capable of spawning a claim for damages, even if the same arrest for the legitimate purpose of obtaining security would have been permissible: see *The Sam Purpose* [2017] EWHC 719 (Comm), [2017] 2 Lloyd's Rep 50.

21 [2006] EWHC 2825 (Comm), [2007] 1 Lloyd's Rep 160. See too *LLC Eurochem North-West-2 v Tecnimont SpA* [2023] EWCA Civ 688 [72].

22 Furthermore, because it was a breach of contract, the Commercial Court in later proceedings also held cargo liable in damages: see *Kallang Shipping SA v AXA Assurances Sénégal (No 2)* [2008] EWHC 2761 (Comm), [2009] 1 Lloyd's Rep 124.

23 [2017] EWHC 719 (Comm), [2017] 2 Lloyd's Rep 50.

24 *The Sam Purpose* [2017] EWHC 719 (Comm), [2017] 2 Lloyd's Rep 50.

that the justification for allowing parallel proceedings falls away and the arrest itself will be regarded as wrongful and will be restrained, together with any subsequent proceedings, by ASI.[25]

Thirdly, it goes without saying that any right to seek security can be ousted by agreement. If, for example, an English jurisdiction agreement specifically provides for the affording of reasonable security by the defendant and the latter tenders such security, this implicitly excludes any right that might otherwise exist in the claimant to arrest in order to give themselves further assurance.[26]

D Interim Injunctions

If seeking the freezing of funds or the provision of security is permissible despite an EJC or arbitration clause, logically one might have thought that seeking provisional or interim relief abroad with a view to preserving the status quo fell to be treated in much the same way. Indeed, exactly such a principle was hinted at by Blair J in *U & M Mining Zambia Ltd v Konkola Copper Mines Plc*.[27] So if, for example, there was a dispute as to the termination of a contract for the operation of some facility abroad, the owner would probably not be in breach of an arbitration or jurisdiction clause by seeking a local interim injunction telling the operator to vacate the site immediately.[28]

However, matters are again nuanced here. As with ship arrest, there is a fine line between interlocutory proceedings genuinely ancillary to court or arbitral proceedings before an agreed tribunal, which are *prima facie* permitted, and those apt to duplicate or interfere with such proceedings, which are not. Take the facts of *Orient Express Lines (Singapore) Pte Ltd v Peninsular Shipping Services Ltd*.[29] An agency agreement involving an importer of vessels into Bangladesh contained a London arbitration clause. Following an alleged breach by the principal in terminating the arrangement and using the services of another import agent, the agent obtained an interlocutory injunction in Bangladesh restraining its replacement. In later ASI proceedings in England, the issue arose of whether the interlocutory proceedings in Bangladesh had infringed the arbitration agreement. Burton J had no doubt that they had, and could have been restrained. They had, he said, gone "way beyond supporting the arbitration or preserving the status quo pending the arbitration".[30]

More recently, Foxton J reached a similar conclusion in *Aquavita International SA v Indagro SA*.[31] Brazilian buyers chartered a ship to carry fertiliser from China

25 So held in *The Joker* [2019] EWHC 3541 (Comm), [2021] 2 CLC 1 and *A v B* [2020] EWHC 3657 (Comm), [2021] 2 CLC 47.

26 *M/V Pacific Pearl Co Ltd v Osios David Shipping Inc* [2022] EWCA Civ 798, [2023] 1 All ER (Comm) 213. This case concerned an ex post facto jurisdiction agreement (the ASG2 London form for collisions at sea sponsored by the Admiralty Solicitors Group in the City), but nothing turns on this.

27 [2013] EWHC 260, [2013] 2 Lloyd's Rep 218 [63]. See too Foxton J in *Aquavita International SA v Indagro SA* [2022] EWHC 892 (Comm) [25] (referring to applications abroad aimed at "holding the ring").

28 This was the result in the *Konkola* case, the country concerned being Zambia. The point did not have to be decided in that case, however, because the matter was pre-empted by the arbitration agreement itself. Because the agreement allowed such proceedings, the ASI was therefore discharged.

29 [2013] EWHC 3855 (Comm).

30 [2013] EWHC 3855 (Comm) [34].

31 [2022] EWHC 892 (Comm).

to southern Brazil; the charter provided for London arbitration. In the event, the buyers allegedly failed to pay the sellers, who still had the bills of lading and told the shipowners not to deliver except against them. The buyers, faced with arbitration proceedings between them and the shipowners about who was entitled to delivery of the fertiliser, sought an order from the Brazilian courts for a physical handover to them. In ASI proceedings brought in England by the shipowners, the buyers argued that order they had sought was explicitly interlocutory, was intended to preserve the status quo, and said nothing about who actually had the right to the cargo. Foxton J, however, was unconvinced. The fact that proceedings were in name interlocutory was not conclusive. To escape the effects of jurisdiction and similar clauses they had, he thought, also to have two other features. First, they should not have the effect of giving one party the benefit of an essential *fait accompli*; and secondly, they should be such that their result was of little or no relevance to the eventual outcome of the main proceedings.[32] Neither of the latter factors was, he held, present in this case. It followed that an ASI should issue.

In essence, it is suggested, the important point to be drawn from that case is this: if the interlocutory proceedings will not pre-empt the issue, and there is good reason to bring them in the foreign jurisdiction, they will probably be seen as permissible, but otherwise they will be problematical.

III ASIs and Derivative Claims

We now pass from interlocutory proceedings to another awkward topic: derivative claims. Where A sues B abroad in breach of a contractual obligation owed directly to B under an arbitration clause or EJC, an ASI goes almost automatically unless there is a very strong reason not to grant it.[33] This is for the very good reason that a blatant breach of contract, for which damages are almost invariably an inadequate remedy, should normally be nipped in the bud.[34] Indeed, in contrast to cases involving a plea of *forum non conveniens*, courts will not be particularly concerned with the relative advantages or otherwise of allowing the foreign suit or with preserving the appearance of comity (comity demanding here that agreements be respected).[35]

32 [2022] EWHC 892 (Comm) [21] onwards.

33 See *The Angelic Grace* [1995] 1 Lloyd's Rep 87, and *Donohue v Armco Inc* [2001] UKHL 64, [2002] CLC 440, esp [24]–[25] (Lord Bingham), also S. Gee, *Gee on Commercial Injunctions* (7th ed, Sweet & Maxwell, 2021), ch 14, s 11. This rule is now applied almost as of course: e.g. *Specialised Vessel Services Ltd v Mop Marine Nigeria Ltd* [2021] EWHC 333 (Comm), [2021] 2 CLC 72 and *Maersk AS v Mercuria Energy Trading SA* [2021] EWHC 2856 (Comm).

34 The point about inadequacy of damages has been made repeatedly. See e.g. *Continental Bank NA v Aeakos Compania Naviera SA* [1994] 1 WLR 588, 598 (Steyn LJ), *OT Africa Line Ltd v Magic Sportswear Corp* [2005] EWCA 710, [2005] 2 Lloyd's Rep 170 [33]–[34] (Longmore LJ), *Clearlake Shipping Pte Ltd v Xiang Da Marine Pte Ltd* [2019] EWHC 2284 (Comm), [2020] 1 All ER (Comm) 61 [18] (Andrew Burrows QC).

35 *Times Trading Corp v National Bank of Fujairah* [2020] EWHC 1078 (Comm), [2020] 2 Lloyd's Rep 317; *AIG Europe SA (formerly AIG Europe Ltd) v John Wood Group Plc* [2021] EWHC 2567 (Comm) [8] (Jacobs J). Nor will courts be very impressed with arguments that the jurisdiction of the foreign court under its own law is mandatory: see *The Yusuf Cepnioglu* [2016] EWCA Civ 386, [2016] 1 Lloyd's Rep 641 [34]–[37], [57]–[58], and also T. Raphael, *The Anti-Suit Injunction* (2nd ed, OUP, 2019), paras 8.31–8.44.

But what about the case where suit is brought not by A but by C, where C is someone exercising A's rights or someone otherwise closely connected in interest with A? Logically there is a problem here: if C is not party to any contract between A and B, there will almost certainly be no direct obligation binding them not to sue. Nevertheless, for some time it has been clear that this does not necessarily leave B without a remedy. The courts retain a parallel jurisdiction in equity to issue ASIs to restrain suits whose bringing is "vexatious or oppressive" even if not a breach of contract, and this has been held to cover many such situations.[36] This section deals with when they will do so, and on what terms.

A Transferees and Assignees

The first category is assignees and transferees. Imagine C is an assignee of A's rights under a contract containing an EJC or arbitration provision. If C tries to sue in England without abiding by the provisions as to jurisdiction, the action will normally be stayed.[37] But what if C sues abroad? An English court cannot stay a foreign action; and even if the benefits of a contractual obligation can be transferred the burdens cannot, from which it follows that there is normally no direct breach of contract in issue.[38] Nevertheless the general rule is clear. C will be regarded as acting vexatiously bringing a suit abroad that would have amounted to a breach of contract if brought by A,[39] and for that reason C is susceptible to an anti-suit injunction: witness a series of cases where relief has been given against insurer-assignees[40] and miscellaneous other transferees.[41] Moreover, despite the lack of any direct breach of contract, the principles applied here are similar to those applicable where there has been such a breach. An order will go as of course in the absence of good reason, with little regard to the advantages or disadvantages of allowing C to litigate in the foreign jurisdiction.[42]

36 See generally *Kallang Shipping SA v Axa Assurances Senegal* [2006] EWHC 2825 (Comm), [2007] 1 Lloyd's Rep 160 [19]–[20] (Gloster J) and *Impala Warehousing & Logistics (Shanghai) Co Ltd v Wanxiang Resources (Singapore) Pte Ltd* [2015] EWHC 811 (Comm), [2015] 2 All ER (Comm) 234 [60] (Blair J).

37 As of right if there is an arbitration agreement within the New York Convention: Arbitration Act 1996, s 9, combined with s 82(2) (see *The Leage* [1984] 2 Lloyd's Rep. 259, 262, decided under previous legislation but still in point). It is suggested that the same would apply to an exclusive jurisdiction agreement covered by the 2005 Hague Convention (Civil Jurisdiction and Judgments Act 1982, s 3D). The grant is otherwise discretionary (see *The El Amria* [1982] 2 Lloyd's Rep 28), though in practice the discretion is likely to be nearly always exercised in favour of a stay.

38 If the burdens can, exceptionally, be transferred, then clearly this problem does not arise. An example is s 3 of the Carriage of Goods by Sea Act 1992, providing for the passing to an indorsee of the burden of a bill of lading. See e.g. *ZHD v SQO* [2021] EWHC 1262 (Comm), [2021] 2 CLC 91 (ASI against transferee of bill of lading preventing cargo claim in Vietnam where bill required arbitration in London), and also *Times Trading Corp v National Bank of Fujairah* [2020] EWHC 1078 (Comm), [2020] 2 Lloyd's Rep 317.

39 See in particular *The Jay Bola* [1997] 2 Lloyd's Rep 279, 286 (Hobhouse LJ), 291 (Scott V-C).

40 Apart from *The Jay Bola*, see *The Jordan Nicolov* [1990] 2 Lloyd's Rep 11 (insurer-assignee of cargo claim), and compare *The Leage* [1984] 2 Lloyd's Rep 259 (a stay of proceedings case concerning an assignee of charter hire).

41 For example, transferees of a warehouse receipt: *Impala Warehousing & Logistics (Shanghai) Co Ltd v Wanxiang Resources (Singapore) Pte Ltd* [2015] EWHC 811 (Comm), [2015] 2 All ER (Comm) 234.

42 See *Impala Warehousing & Logistics (Shanghai) Co Ltd v Wanxiang Resources (Singapore) Pte Ltd* [2015] EWHC 811 (Comm), [2015] 2 All ER (Comm) 234 [115] (Blair J).

B Subrogation Claimants

Many ASI cases in practice concern subrogated underwriters bringing claims abroad which would have been barred to their insureds under EJCs or arbitration clauses. Where the claim is brought in the insured's name, as it is in common law jurisdictions, the insured can clearly be enjoined,[43] as can the insurer[44] because the latter, by conniving at and indeed assisting the insured's own breach, is seen as acting wrongfully by infringing the equitable rights of the person sued.[45] Moreover, as with assignees, the "as of course" approach applicable in cases of ordinary breach of contract will obtain in such cases.[46]

Moreover, it seems that this continues to be the case where, as in many civil law jurisdictions, there is a possibility of a direct action by the underwriter himself, not involving a technical takeover of the rights of the assured. A straightforward example was *The Jay Bola*.[47] A voyage charter contained a London arbitration clause; damage to steel carried under it was in due course made good by cargo underwriters. The Court of Appeal restrained the latter from then claiming against the disponent owner in Brazil under a Brazilian statute allowing a subrogated insurer to sue in its own name. And in 2019 it was confirmed that the same result would, but for the then applicable EU law, have been reached in the case of an insurer suing a wrongdoer in Italy directly in tort.[48]

IV Claims Against Underwriters: The Effect of Foreign Insurance Direct Action Statutes

In common law systems, if a person is insured against liability the victim has strictly speaking no direct claim against the insurer. They merely have a right, if the insured becomes insolvent, to invoke the Third Parties (Rights against Insurers) Act 2010 or similar legislation to claim a statutory transfer of the insured's right to indemnity. It follows that if the victim sues on the basis of this statutorily transferred right, they are

43 Though even here it may be appropriate to join the insurers: *OT Africa Line v Magic Sportswear Corp* [2005] EWCA Civ 710, [2005] 2 Lloyd's Rep 170 [14].

44 E.g. *West Tankers Inc v RAS Riunione Adriatica di Sicurta SpA* [2005] EWHC 454 (Comm), [2005] 1 CLC 347; *Whitesea Shipping & Trading Corp v El Paso Rio Clara Ltda* [2009] EWHC 2552 (Comm), [2010] 1 Lloyd's Rep 648; *Daiichi Chuo Kisen Kaisha v Chubb Seguros Brasil SA* [2020] EWHC 1223 (Comm), [2020] 2 Lloyd's Rep 137.

45 *West Tankers Inc v RAS Riunione Adriatica di Sicurta SpA* [2005] EWHC 454 (Comm), [2005] 1 CLC 347 [70]–[71] (Colman J), see too *Aline Tramp SA v Jordan International Insurance Co* [2016] EWHC 1317 (Comm), [2017] 1 Lloyd's Rep 467, and *Airbus SAS v Generali Italia SpA* [2019] EWCA Civ 805; [2019] 1 CLC 903 [86], [93]–[96] (Males LJ). The equitable rights are important here, since damages in equity are in principle available for breach of them even if there is no question of an ASI: see *The Frio Dolphin* [2021] EWHC 554 (Comm), [2021] 1 CLC 552.

46 See *The Yusuf Cepnioglu* [2016] EWCA Civ 386, [2016] 1 Lloyd's Rep 641 [32]–[35]; also *Clearlake Shipping Pte Ltd v Xiang da Marine Pte Ltd* [2019] EWHC 1536 (Comm) [37] (Bryan J). Previously there had been controversy: *The Jay Bola* [1997] 2 Lloyd's Rep 279 supported the position in *The Yusuf Cepnioglu*, while *The Hari Bhum* [2004] EWCA Civ 1598, [2005] 1 Lloyd's Rep 67 suggested the opposite.

47 [1997] 2 Lloyd's Rep 279. See too *Charterers Mutual Assurance Association Ltd v British & Foreign, etc.* [1998] Int L Pr 838 [45]–[46]. In *The Hari Bhum* [2004] EWCA Civ 1598, [2005] 1 Lloyd's Rep 67 the same was assumed.

48 See *Airbus SAS v Generali Italia SpA* [2019] EWCA Civ 805.

susceptible to an ASI on the same basis as an assignee, as described in the previous paragraph. This is highly important as regards EJCs and arbitration clauses contained in P&I Club rules and liability insurance policies governed by English law, since it means that suits brought in common law jurisdictions can generally be enjoined.

In many civil law jurisdictions, however, the system for claims against insurers is different. The victim in effect is given a direct right against a liability insurer. This in turn raises the question: what happens if the victim sues in a civil law jurisdiction to enforce such a direct right despite an EJC or arbitration provision in the underlying insurance contract between the assured and the underwriter?

The point came up for decision in *The Yusuf Cepnioglu.*[49] A cargo being carried for Turkish cargo owners suffered damage, and cargo underwriters paid out. The underwriters then invoked a Turkish direct action statute to sue the carriers' P&I club in Turkey. Relying on a London arbitration clause in the P&I entry, the club sought an ASI. The Court of Appeal, upholding Teare J, granted it. Even though technically neither cargo nor its insurers had been party to the contract contained in the club rules and equally were not assignees of any rights arising under it, they were still in essence attempting to invoke its provisions against the club. It followed that they were susceptible to an ASI, and indeed subject to the same strong presumption in favour of the grant of such an order as would have applied in the case of such a party or its assignee.

Despite the relief for insurance interests this case brings, however, there is a twist: it may not cover all foreign direct action statutes. Whether it does depends on how the claim works under the foreign legal system. There may apparently be cases where the foreign law direct claim against the insurer, properly analysed according to the foreign law concerned, is seen as not an exercise in enforcing the insurance contract but as an independent claim, "in substance a claim to enforce an independent right of recovery",[50] in which case an ASI will not be available.[51] Such cases are, it has been said, typified by situations where the defences that would have been available to the insurer against the assured are substantially curtailed if the claimant is the victim.[52] No such case has yet arisen, but it seems merely a question of time before the point is taken by an insurance claimant.

While the point is now settled up to Court of Appeal level and can now only be disturbed by the Supreme Court, it is still, with respect, a little difficult to see why this should be so. For one thing, wherever the existence of a claim is conditioned on

49 [2016] EWCA Civ 386, [2016] 1 Lloyd's Rep 641, commented on in A Dickinson, "The Right to Rome? The Law Applicable to Direct Claims against Insurers, and Anti-suit Injunctions" (2016) 132 LQR 536. (See too the earlier decision in *Charterers' Mutual Assurance Association v British & Foreign Marine Insurance Co Ltd* [1997] I L Proc 838.) This was followed in *UK P&I Club NV v República Bolivariana de Venezuela* [2022] EWHC 1655 (Comm), [2022] 1 WLR 4856, where an ASI would have issued but for Venezuela's state immunity, and in *QBE Europe SA/NV v Generali España de Seguros y Reaseguros* [2022] EWHC 2062 (Comm).

50 The words of Teare J at first instance in *The Yusuf Cepnioglu* [2015] EWHC 258 (Comm) [6].

51 *The Yusuf Cepnioglu* [2016] EWCA Civ 386, [2016] 1 Lloyd's Rep 641 [16] (Longmore LJ). See too the earlier decision of Moore-Bick J in *The Hari Bhum* [2003] EWHC 3158 (Comm), [2004] 1 Lloyd's Rep 206 [16]–[19], and also *The Prestige (No 2)* [2013] EWHC 3188 (Comm), [2014] 1 Lloyd's Rep 309.

52 See again Teare J at first instance in *The Yusuf Cepnioglu* [2015] EWHC 258 (Comm) [37]–[38].

the existence of an insurance contract, then it is a little hard to see why it is not in substance a claim to enforce the latter whatever its incidents under the governing law.[53] For another, one of the main cases relied on in *The Yusuf Cepnioglu*, *The Prestige (No 2)*,[54] concerned a rather different issue: namely, whether a direct action statute claimant was bound by an arbitration award made under a term contained in a P&I Club entry. But in the ASI situation the issue is different: namely, whether the claimant is acting vexatiously or oppressively in such a way as inequitably to defeat the right of the insured to insist that any claims against it be arbitrated. And in that situation, it is submitted that the answer to this question cannot turn on whether the claim under a foreign legal system can be classified as "in substance a claim to enforce an independent right of recovery".

V Other Connected Claimants and ASIs

In the case of assignees and those in a closely analogous situation, such as direct claimants against insurers, it is not difficult to see why they should be bound by EJCs and arbitration clauses in the relevant contracts. In substance, if not in form, they are trying to obtain payment on the footing of those contracts (or complain that a contractual duty of which they had the benefit has been broken, which comes to the same thing). But if you wish to invoke someone else's rights arising under a contract, there is every reason why you should have to take the rough with the smooth; there is therefore abundant justification for orders aimed at ensuring that you abide by any provisions in the relevant agreements requiring you to arbitrate, or to litigate exclusively in an English court.

What, however, of others who are neither party to a contract containing an EJC nor classifiable as assignees, but are nevertheless connected in interest with a party to it? Imagine, for example, that an agent of a contracting party, having paid money on its behalf to a counterparty, now seeks to get it back as money paid by mistake; or that a guarantor sues a creditor seeking a declaration of the non-liability of the principal debtor. Can such people be injuncted in the same way, or should they be able to argue that they can ignore the agreement because a contract binding X cannot bind Y merely because Y happens to have some close connection with X?

Until recently it was assumed they could, and that they were beyond the reach of an ASI. In *Star Reefers Pool Inc v JFC Group Co Ltd*[55] in 2012, the obligations of a number of one-ship charterers were guaranteed by their Russian parent JFC. The charters, but not the guarantee documents, provided for London arbitration. The owners made claims against the charterers and an arbitration commenced; JFC countered by suing in Moscow for a negative declaration that the charterers, and hence it, were not liable. The owners sought an anti-suit injunction against JFC. Teare J granted it, but the Court of Appeal disagreed. However much the Moscow suit might have been designed

53 As seemingly assumed by Aikens J in *Youell v Kara Mara Shipping Co Ltd* [2000] 2 Lloyd's Rep 102.

54 [2013] EWHC 3188 (Comm), [2013] 2 CLC 562 (upheld [2015] EWCA Civ 333, [2015] 1 CLC 596).

55 [2012] EWCA Civ 14, [2012] 1 CLC 294. Cf *IBM United Kingdom Ltd v LzLabs GmbH* [2022] EWHC 2094 (TCC).

to put a spoke in the wheel of the arbitration, JFC's invocation of its own courts under a contract with no EJC of its own could not be seen as unconscionable or vexatious.

However, times may be changing, and the reach of ASIs may be extending. *Star Reefers* predated a number of later cases[56] determining the boundaries of what should be regarded as oppressive or abusive;[57] and at least some more recent authority suggests that those boundaries may now have expanded.

Qingdao Huiquan Shipping Co v Shanghai Dong He Xin Industry Group Co Ltd,[58] for example, concerned the position of the agent of a party to an EJC. Faced with a claim by carriers to a lien over cargo for charter hire and a refusal to deliver without payment, cargo receivers agreed to pay $640,000 for release under a contract containing an English law and London jurisdiction clause. The money was paid by the receivers' agents in Qingdao in China, and the cargo was duly released. Later, however, the agents then sued in Qingdao to recover the payment, alleging a subsequent side-letter agreed between them and the owners allowing them to do so. Despite the agents' (entirely correct) observation that they were party neither to the settlement agreement nor to the EJC in it, Bryan J injuncted the suit, holding that they were still in substance seeking to rely on the terms of the settlement agreement and therefore had to take it warts and all.[59] *Star Reefers* was not cited: yet it is difficult to see much distinction between the cases. In both, the foreign proceedings were under an allegedly separate agreement in some way ancillary to the agreement with the arbitration clause or EJA clause;[60] in neither was the injuncted person party to, or a person taking over rights under, the latter agreement.

Another case raising the same kind of issue was *Aon UK Ltd v Lamia Corp SRL*.[61] Following an air disaster in Colombia which killed several passengers, it transpired that the airline had no effective insurance cover. The passengers' relatives brought suit in Florida against the brokers who had arranged the cover for the airline, alleging that the latter had been negligent. The brokers pointed out that they had acted under a contract that contained a London arbitration clause,[62] and on that basis sought an ASI to stop the Florida proceedings. The deputy judge granted relief. The main ground of his decision was fairly orthodox: because the passengers were essentially suing as third party beneficiaries of the broking contract, they had to take it warts and all, in

56 Notably *The Yusuf Cepnioglu* [2016] EWCA Civ 386, [2016] 1 Lloyd's Rep. 641 and *Dell Emerging Markets (EMEA) Ltd v IB Maroc.com SA* [2017] EWHC 2397 (Comm), [2017] 2 CLC 417.

57 The same can also be said of two cases following it, *Navig8 Pte Ltd v Al-Riyadh Co for Vegetable Oil Industry* [2013] EWHC 328 (Comm), [2013] 2 Lloyd's Rep 104 (no injunction for alleged carrier under bill of lading governed by English law against holder seeking to sue in a court in Jordan which would ignore aspects of that law) and *Golden Endurance Shipping SA v RMA Watanya SA* [2014] EWHC 3917 (Comm), [2015] 1 Lloyd's Rep. 266 (bill of lading holder not bound by terms of charter).

58 [2018] EWHC 3009 (Comm), commented on, on slightly different grounds, in M. Phua, "Injunctive Enforcement of Arbitration Agreements against Non-Parties: Two Complications" [2019] LMCLQ 518.

59 [2018] EWHC 3009 (Comm) [36]. Cf the expressions used in *The Yusuf Cepnioglu* [2016] EWCA Civ 386, [2016] 1 Lloyd's Rep 641 [14]–[16], [45]–[46] and *Fair Wind Navigation v ACE Seguradora* [2017] EWHC 3352 (Comm) [5]–[8], [6].

60 Admittedly Bryan J was decidedly sceptical about the existence of the alleged agreement: see [2018] EWHC 3009 (Comm) [38]. But he accepted that he did not have to decide that issue at this point.

61 [2022] EWHC 3323 (Comm).

62 This slightly oversimplifies matters, since many of the facts remained to be proved, but it adequately describes the legal background.

the same way that an assignee had to. But he went on to suggest that even if the action was a direct tort action alleging that the passengers had been foreseeable victims of the brokers' incompetence, the result would probably have been the same: the essence of the tort claim was a breach of duty arising because of negligent performance of the broking contract, and in such a case the passengers could not be allowed to bring it without respecting the terms of that contract, including the arbitration clause.[63]

We shall have to see how all this works out in practice in the future. The equities, however, seem to be in favour of the grant of an ASI in cases like this; so also arguments of litigational efficiency. If one had to bet on such matters, the better position is probably that in future the scope of what counts as oppressive or vexatious will be expanded rather than curtailed. To this extent at least, we may not yet have seen the end of the bull run of the ASI.

63 See [2022] EWHC 3323 (Comm) [128]–[132].

CHAPTER 7

Jurisdiction and Enforcement of Judgments in the EU – the UK Judicial Space Post-Brexit

Francesco Munari[*]

I Introductory Remarks

When two legal systems separate from each other, very many complex consequences can arise.

In the case of Brexit, the consequence was not simply the one that early Brexiteers simplistically and enthusiastically had advocated, i.e. the recovery of the UK sovereign power to shape its rules without EU constraints. Much more than that, Brexit wiped out countless legal relationships based on the existence of rules forged within the EU (1) having direct effect and (2) presuming membership of the UK in the Union.

These legal relationships were grounded on a unique rationale, a sort of "grundnorm" governing the whole being together of EU States, namely the principle of mutual trust.[1]

The collapse of this general principle of EU law in the legal realm concerning UK and the EU has deprived the remaining Member States (and specifically the UK as the "counterpart" of any legal relationship with them) of the possibility to continue to rely on such rules. And more importantly, it has prevented the adoption of any other unilateral or bilateral rules aiming at restoring the status and the quality of the legal relationships as existing when the UK was an EU member.

The foregoing is particularly true for the *corpus juris* concerning private international law, which, in the EU perspective, all Member States shared through the legal instruments adopted under Article 81 of the TFEU (Judicial Cooperation in Civil Matters);[2] Brexit left the UK largely bereft of the EU *acquis* on this matter, which

---

* **Full professor of EU law, University of Genoa. Partner, Deloitte Legal (Italy), Head of practice of International and EU law.**

1 For further reference on the principle of mutual trust, see E. Regan, "The role of the principles of mutual trust and mutual recognition in EU law" [2018] *Il Diritto dell'Unione europea* 231; C. Rizcallah, *The Principle of Mutual Trust in European Union Law* (Larcier 2022); Matti Pellonpää, "Reflections on the Principle of Mutual Trust in EU Law and Judicial Dialogue in Europe", in K. Karjalainen et al. (eds), *International Actors and the Formation of Laws* (Springer 2022) 29; E. Storskrubb, "Mutual Trust in Civil Justice Cooperation in the EU", in A. Bakardjieva Engelbrekt et al. (eds), *Trust in the European Union in Challenging Times* (Palgrave 2019), 159; M. Hazelhorst, "Mutual Trust Under Pressure: Civil Justice Cooperation in the EU and the Rule of Law" [2018] *Netherlands International Law Review* 103.

2 On the evolution of EU judicial co-operation in civil matters, see: J. Basedow, *EU Private Law: Anatomy of a Growing Legal Order* (Intersentia 2021) 43 ff.; E. Rodriguez Pineau, "Article 81", in H. Blanke, S. Mangiameli (eds), *Treaty on the Functioning of the European Union – A Commentary* (Springer 2021) 1529; M. Wilderspin, "Article 81 TFEU" in M. Kellerbauer et al. (eds) *The EU Treaties and the Charter of Fundamental Rights: A Commentary* (OUP 2019) 853; M. Ancel & H. Gaudemet-Tallon, *Compétence*

DOI: 10.4324/9781032726243-9

actually represented (and still represents for EU members) the most important source of private international law of European States. Besides, without EU membership, the UK could not simply "recast" such rules as part of its domestic legislation, for they implied to be bound by the principle of mutual trust, and thus to share the advantages of participating to the so-called European judicial space.

This chapter will therefore aim to summarise the situation concerning the status of the judicial co-operation between the UK and the EU Member States as now existing subsequently to the withdrawal of the former from the Union.[3] After a short analysis of the sources of private international law that, at present, characterise the legal scene for European states, outlined in Section II, Section III will provide an assessment of those instruments that – after Brexit – have become unavailable in the bilateral relationship between the UK and EU States, in particular as regards allocation of jurisdiction and recognition of judgments in (international) civil and commercial matters. Sections IV and V then investigate the practicability of filling the lacunae generated by Brexit with the 1968 Brussels Convention, or the 2007 Lugano Convention, i.e. existing treaties on these topics either previously applied within the EC, or presently governing judicial co-operation in civil and commercial matters between the EU States and other European countries. Sections VI and VII will then

---

et exécution des jugements en Europe (LGDJ 2018); T. Hartley, *Civil Jurisdiction and Judgments in Europe* (OUP 2017); P. Stone & Y. Farah (eds), *Research Handbook on EU Private International Law* (Cheltenham 2017); G. van Calster, *European Private International Law* (Hart 2016); S. Leible (ed.) *General Principles of European Private Law* (Kluwer 2016); P. Beaumont & M. Danov, "The EU Civil Justice Framework and Private Law: Integration through (Private International) Law" [2015] *Maastricht Journal of European & Comparative Law* 706; Permanent Bureau of the HCCH, *A commitment to private international law: essays in honour of Hans Van Loon* (Intersentia 2013); K. Lenaerts, "The contribution of the European Court of Justice to the area of freedom, security and justice" (2010) 59 ICLQ 255; J. Heymann, *Le droit international privé à l'épreuve du fédéralisme européen* (Paris: Economica 2010); P. Stone, *EU Private International Law. Harmonisation of Laws* (Edward Elgar 2006); P. Partsch, *Le droit international privé européen* (Larcier, 2003).

3 For further insights on the topic concerning Brexit and private international law see P. Beaumont, "Some Reflections on the Way Ahead for UK Private International Law after Brexit" [2021] *Journal of Private International Law* 1; Reid Mortensen, "Brexit and Private International Law in the Commonwealth" [2021] *Journal of Private International Law* 18; Policy Department for Citizens' Rights and Constitutional Affairs, Directorate-General for Internal Policies, *Ensuring Efficient Cooperation with the UK in civil law matters. Situation after Brexit and Options for Future Cooperation* (PE 743.340 – March 2023); A. Briggs, *Civil Jurisdiction and Judgments* (Routledge 2021) 44; L. Merrett & A. Sommerfeld, "Incentives for Choice of Law and Forum in Commercial Contracts: Predicting the Impact of Brexit" (2020) 28 *European Review of Private Law* 627; L. Gilles, "Appropriate Adjustments Post Brexit: Residual Jurisdiction and Forum Non Conveniens in UK Courts" [2020] JBL 161; M. Poesen, "Civil and commercial private international law in times of Brexit: Managing the impact, and fostering prospects for a future EU-UK cooperation" in R. Sacco (ed.), *Brexit: A Way Forward* (Vernon Press, 2019) 254; E. Crawford & J. Carruthers, "Brexit: The Impact on Judicial Cooperation in Civil Matters Having Cross-border Implications – A British Perspective", [2018] *European Papers* 183; M. Pilich, "Brexit and EU Private International Law: May the UK Stay in?" [2017] *Maastricht Journal of European and Comparative Law* 382; J. Fitchen, "The Private International Law Consequences of Brexit" [2017] *Nederlands Internationaal Privaatrecht* 411; B. Hess, "Back to the Past: BREXIT und das europäischeinternationale Privat- und Verfahrensrecht" [2016] *Praxis des Internationalen Privat- und Verfahrensrechts* 409; P. Jeney, "The European Union's Area of Freedom, Security and Justice without the United Kingdom – Legal and Practical Consequences of Brexit" [2016] *ELTE Law Journal* 117; G. Croisant, "Fog in Channel – Continent Cut Off. Les consequences juridiques du Brexit pour le droit international privé et l'arbitrage international" [2017] *Journal des tribunaux* 24; E. Lein, "Unchartered Territory? A Few Thoughts on Private International Law Post Brexit" (2016) *XVII Yearbook of Private International Law* 33.

consider other multilateral and "non-preferential" treaties potentially fit to replace the former *acquis*, and in particular the Hague Conventions covering our subject matter, i.e. the available instruments to allow for relevant reciprocal collaboration among the EU members and the United Kingdom. More precisely, they will refer to the 2005 Hague Convention on choice-of-court agreements and the 2019 Hague Convention on the recognition and enforcement of foreign judgments in civil and commercial matters shall be briefly commented. Finally, Section VIII will conclude in favour of adhesion by the UK to the latter.

II The Cut-Off Caused by the UK Withdrawal From the European Union as Regards the Formerly Existing Sources of Private International Law Governing European Judicial Co-operation

It is common ground among legal scholars that sources of private international law pertaining to each legal system have either an international (i.e. supranational) origin or a domestic one. In fact, however, domestic rules of private international law have become less and less relevant over time, in connection with the growing importance and diffusion of international and supranational instruments. This is particularly true within the EU, where – as already mentioned – a far-reaching and detailed regime on this topic has been in force for decades, initially as international conventions and later on as EU regulations. As far as this chapter is concerned, reference is particularly made to the so-called Brussels I *bis* Regulation (i.e. Regulation no 1215/2012),[4] which is the backbone piece of (recast) EU legislation on jurisdiction and recognition of civil and commercial judgments within the EU.

Before Brexit, there was an alignment between the UK and other EU States, in so far as their private international law encompassed EU sources, international conventions (dealt with later), and domestic rules.

The Withdrawal Agreement[5] provided that there would be a continued application of these instruments during the Transition Period;[6] however, no provisions on judicial co-operation on civil and commercial matters were envisaged after 1 January 2021, either in the EU-UK Trade and Cooperation Agreement[7] or in any of the other treaties aimed at regulating the EU-UK legal relationship after Brexit.[8]

4 [2012] OJ L 351/1. A consolidated version of the Brussels I *bis* Regulation is available at https://eur-lex.europa.eu/legal-content/EN/TXT/?uri=CELEX%3A02012R1215-20150226.

5 Agreement on the Withdrawal of the United Kingdom of Great Britain and Northern Ireland from the European Union and the European Atomic Energy Community [2020] OJ L 29/7.

6 See Title VI of the Withdrawal Agreement.

7 Trade and Cooperation Agreement between the European Union and the European Atomic Energy Community, of the one part, and the United Kingdom of Great Britain and Northern Ireland, of the other part [2021] OJ L 149/10.

8 Reference is made to the Agreement between the European Union and the United Kingdom of Great Britain and Northern Ireland concerning security procedures for exchanging and protecting classified information [2021] OJ L149/2540 ("EU-UK Security Agreement"), or to the Agreement between the Government of the United Kingdom of Great Britain and Northern Ireland and the European Atomic Energy Community for Cooperation on the Safe and Peaceful Uses of Nuclear Energy [2021] OJ L150/1 ("Euratom-UK Cooperation Agreement").

The UK has thus lost the legislative tools that previously allowed both a coordination of its jurisdiction with that of other EU Member States, and a recognition of judgments rendered by UK courts in all such States.[9] Clearly, this phenomenon cuts both ways, but its effects are not equal, because the remaining 27 EU States still enjoy the benefit of belonging to the European judicial space in their relationships, with the only exception of the UK, whereas the latter has lost such a benefit with 27 jurisdictions. Furthermore, legal instruments of this sort cannot be unilaterally conceived, since they need exactly an agreement, i.e. a treaty.

III No Revival of 1968 Brussels Convention as Amended

Absent any specifically agreed "new" bilateral instrument between the UK and the EU to foster judicial co-operation in civil and commercial matters, we now consider the state of play as regards the relevant international conventions.

The first instrument to be investigated is the ancestor of Brussels I *bis*, namely the 1968 Brussels Convention on jurisdiction and the enforcement of judgments in civil and commercial matters,[10] as amended. Since the UK had been party to this Convention, some authors argued that it could revive as a substitutive tool for permitting the UK to remain somehow within the European judicial space.[11] Such an argument has little merit, however,[12] and in any case has been set aside by an official declaration of the UK Government to the European Council dated January 29, 2021, stating that, as of January 1, 2021, the 1968 Brussels Convention had ceased to apply.[13] The reason for this declaration is a little unclear, for the application of the (old) 1968 Brussels Convention would have been rather an advantage for the UK, lacking any other available legal instruments.

This aside, however, the UK declaration reflects reality. The Convention was conceived, negotiated and always applied in parallel with EC law; and it was set aside when the EU decided to enhance the level of intra-EU judicial co-operation and adopted the Brussels I (and later I *bis*) Regulations. The Brussels Convention never existed, nor was meant to operate, outside the framework of the European Communities. This conclusion seems confirmed by the fact that, even though Denmark as a Member State opted out of the adoption by the EU of measures on co-operation

9 See A. Dickinson, "Realignment of the Planets – Brexit and European Private International Law" [2021] *IPRax* 213, 216; V. Lazić & C. Okoli, "Private international law and cooperation in civil and commercial matters after Brexit – legislative gaps and future developments", in A. Łazowski & A. Cygan (eds.), *Research Handbook on Legal Aspects of Brexit* (Edward Elgar 2022), 221.

10 [1972] OJ L299/32. The consolidated version of the Convention is published in [1998] OJ C 27.

11 *Inter alia*, A. Dickinson, "Back to the Future: the UK's EU Exit and the Conflict of Laws" (2016) 12 Journal of Private International Law 195; J. Ungerer, "Consequences of Brexit for European Private International Law" (2019) 4 European Papers 395.

12 V. Lazić & C. Okoli (supra note 6) at 224 consider this argument "surprising".

13 The declaration (which is a letter from the UK mission to the European Union, unpublished but easily available on the internet) reads as follows: "The Government of the United Kingdom hereby notifies the Secretary-General of the Council of the European Union that it considers that the Brussels Convention 1968 and the 1971 Protocol, including subsequent amendments and accessions, ceased to apply to the United Kingdom and Gibraltar from 1 January 2021, as a consequence of the United Kingdom ceasing to be a Member State of the European Union and of the end of the Transition Period".

in civil and commercial matters,[14] the Brussels I and I *bis* Regulations, and not the 1968 Brussels Convention, formed the basis of the specific bilateral agreements between the EC and Denmark.[15] Moreover, when the Member States decided to extend the Brussels Convention regime to other States with whom they shared "parallel" fundamental freedoms, a "parallel" convention was signed, i.e. the 2007 Lugano Convention,[16] which is in force among the EU States and the members of EFTA, that is, the European Economic Area, plus Switzerland.

The next question is therefore whether the Lugano Convention could be extended to the UK after Brexit.

IV The (Understandable) Refusal by the EU to Allow the UK Access to the 2007 Lugano Convention

A treaty arrangement which might have been available to keep the UK judicial system aligned with those of the EU (and EEA) States was the 2007 Lugano Convention.[17]

Indeed, as a former EU State, the UK was already party to the Convention, and, while moving over to the "opposite side" of the EU among the Convention's contracting parties, it could have taken advantage of the rules on jurisdiction allocation and recognition of judgments contained in such a Convention. And in fact, the UK had filed a request to become a party to it.[18]

Not surprisingly, the non-EU contracting parties, i.e. Norway, Iceland and Switzerland, were in favour of this solution, because it would maintain unaltered their relationship with the UK jurisdiction concerning the matters covered by the Lugano Convention.

In May 2021, however, a reasoned opposition came from the European Commission, which took the view that "the European Union should not give its consent to the accession of the United Kingdom to the 2007 Lugano Convention".[19]

The reason for this position is clear, and mirrors the rationale governing substantial and civil procedural rules of co-operation among European States. To quote further from the Commission's Communication:

> [f]or the European Union, the Lugano Convention is a flanking measure of the internal market and relates to the EU-EFTA/EEA context. . . . The United Kingdom is a third country without a special link to the internal market. Therefore, there is no reason for the European Union to depart from its general approach in relation to the United Kingdom.

---

14 See Protocol (No 22) on the Position of Denmark, [2012] C 326/212 ff.

15 [2005] OJ L 299/62; [2009] OJ L 149/80.

16 Convention on jurisdiction and the recognition and enforcement of judgments in civil and commercial matters [2007] OJ L339/3.

17 On this topic (and also for a more general assessment) see also Trevor Hartley, "Post-Brexit. The New Shape of English Private International Law", in Jonathan Harris and Campbell McLachlan (eds.), *Essays in International Litigation for Lord Collins* (OUP 2022), 226, 231

18 See inter alia A. Łazowski and A. Cygan (supra note 7), 225.

19 See the "Communication from the Commission to the European Parliament and the Council. Assessment on the application of the United Kingdom of Great Britain and Northern Ireland to accede to the 2007 Lugano Convention" COM (2021) 222 final.

Cuius commoda, eius incommoda, says the Latin adage. And in fact, the package of treaties governing the present relationship between the UK and the EU, in particular the TCA mentioned earlier,[20] are far from establishing a sort of internal market, and substantially differ from the rules applied within the EEA. In this vein, there seems to be coherence in excluding the UK from those jurisdictions enjoying a special relationship as far as judicial co-operation is concerned.

As a consequence, the Commission recommended to set the future relationships with the UK in the field of civil judicial co-operation within the "general regime" provided for by the Hague Conventions, which shall be analysed later.

V The Situation of International Conventions on Private International Law Ratified by or Through the EU With Third Party States

Among the private international law sources with a supranational origin one needs now to consider also conventions entered into by States within typical fora in which they decide – on a general basis – to co-operate for the unification or harmonisation of private international law.

This is specifically the case with conventions concluded within the framework of the Hague Conference on Private International Law, some of which are quite important for civil and commercial matters, such as the 2005 Convention on choice of court agreements, the 2019 Convention on the Recognition and Enforcement of Foreign Judgments in Civil or Commercial Matters, the 1965 Convention on Service, the 1970 Convention on Evidence, the 1970 Convention on Divorce, the 1980 Convention on Child Abduction, and the 1996 Convention on Protection of Children.[21]

As far as the European (EC/EU) States are concerned, the goal of fostering judicial co-operation at an international level has been constantly pursued. This goal was strengthened especially following the Treaty of Amsterdam, when the EU Member States entrusted the European institutions, in particular the Commission, with the power to negotiate private international law treaties, including those stipulated within the Hague Conference. The competence to conclude such treaties would be exclusive to the EU, in accordance with the principle of pre-emption, as regards international agreements potentially impacting on existing common rules adopted at EU level.[22] Therefore, it was not only a matter of taking the opportunity to speak one single voice within the Hague Conference; rather, it was, to some extent, an obligation stemming from the EU treaties themselves.

---

20 See note 4.

21 All these instruments can be found at www.hcch.net/en/instruments/conventions. While this paper limits its treatment to two of these conventions, for a more general analysis see H. van Loon, "Le *Brexit* et les conventions de La Haye" [2019] *Revue critique de droit international privé*, 353. Also relevant for the commercial environment between the EU and the UK is the post-Brexit regime on service, on which see recently D. Nitschmann, *Der Zustellungsverkehr mit dem Vereiningten Königreich: eine Studie unter besonderer Berücksichtigung der Rechtsentwicklungen seit dem Brexit* (Mohr Siebeck 2023). On the future of HCCH activities, see M. Lehmann, "Incremental international law-making: The Hague Jurisdiction Project in context" (2023) 19 Journal of Private International Law 41.

22 *Inter alia*, see CJEU Opinion 1/2013 of 14 October, 2014, ECLI:EU:C:2014:2303; CJEU Judgement of 5 November 2002, *Commission v Kingdom of Belgium (Open skies)*, ECLI:EU:C:2002:628.

In any case, over the decades very many international conventions had been concluded by the EC/EU on behalf of its Member States, including some related to private international law. Besides, the impact of private international law on internal market rules or on EC/EU fundamental freedoms has been never questioned, this being confirmed by the already quoted 1968 Brussels Convention, as well as by the other conventions entered into at a later stage by the EC Members, that have now been transposed into EC/EU regulations.[23]

Brexit therefore had a significant impact on the need by the UK to reset its position as an "independent contracting party" under international treaties formerly concluded via the EC/EU. This is true in all those cases in which the treaties had been concluded by the EU only, i.e. treaties to which the Member States were not party in their own right. But it is also true for those treaties that, although ratified in addition by Member States, can be considered as having been incorporated in the EU *acquis*, because in this case the UK cannot necessarily claim an automatic disentanglement of these treaties from the EU legal system.

Having been a member of the EU for almost 50 years, it comes as no surprise that the UK faced the risk of a substantial legal vacuum also as far as many legal relationships covered by private international law conventions were concerned. Such risk was addressed in the Withdrawal Agreement, whose Article 129(4) established that

> during the transition period, the United Kingdom may negotiate, sign and ratify international agreements entered into in its own capacity in the areas of exclusive competence of the Union, provided those agreements do not enter into force or apply during the transition period, unless so authorised by the Union.

This provision allowed therefore the UK to adhere or accede to some conventions during the transition period, thus avoiding the "cliff-edge" otherwise inevitable after 1 January 2021.[24]

With that said, as far as the private international law conventions are concerned, the aim to "take back control" through Brexit proved to be in fact a hurdle rather than an opportunity for the UK.

VI The Hague Convention on Choice of Court Agreements

It would be clearly beyond the scope of this chapter to consider all private international law conventions formerly applied to the UK as an EU Member State. Our aim will be therefore to shed some light on two such instruments only. One is the Choice of Court Convention concluded in Hague on 30 June 2005, which the EU ratified in 2015 and UK has adhered to using Article 129(4) of the Withdrawal Agreement.[25]

23 Reference is made e.g. to the 1980 Rome Convention on the law applicable to contractual obligations, now replaced by Regulation 593/2008 [2008] OJ L 177/6, as amended.

24 See also R. Wessel, "Consequences of Brexit for International Agreements Concluded by the EU and Its Member States" (2018) 55 *Common Market Law Rev.*, 101, 106.

25 On this topic see also A. Casey, "Holding out Hope for the Hague Judgments Project Thirty Years Later: The Future of Express English Jurisdiction Clauses in Light of the London-Lugano Lacuna (Brexit, Brussels, and Beyond)" (2023) 3 Plassey Law Review 10; M. Ahmed & P. Beaumont, "Exclusive choice of

As far as private international law matters are concerned, choice of court agreements are among the most important clauses of international commercial contracts, and as such have served as the backbone of the co-operation in private international law issues among European States since the 1968 Brussels Convention and through to the Brussels I *bis* Regulation.

The 2005 Hague Convention also deals with this topic, and protects choice of court clauses agreed between the parties to international contracts.

More precisely, both legal instruments give validity to exclusive choice of court agreements, and establish the obligation of a not chosen court to suspend or dismiss proceedings to which such agreements apply.[26]

Yet, while in principle both the 2005 Hague Convention and Brussels I *bis* Regulation share the same scope and purposes, the respective provisions are not identical.[27] In particular, one of the most important differences concerns the different level of effectiveness of choice of court agreements respectively provided for by the Convention and the Regulation. The Brussels I *bis* Regulation actually improved such effectiveness, in particular with a revision of the rule on *lis pendens* in order to ban altogether the so-called (Italian-type) torpedo actions.[28] However, such an enhanced protection of the choice of court clauses is not provided for by the 2005 Hague Convention, which is still modelled on the regime set forth by Brussels I Regulation, i.e. Regulation 44/2001. Hence a risk of abusive use of the *lis pendens* rules to delay the outcome of the dispute was still material under such previously applicable regime and the same is probably going to occur for disputes falling within the scope of the 2005 Hague Convention. In this vein, one might expect a revival of torpedo actions in respect to cases when a court of a non-EU Member State is a prorogated court, including a court in the UK.

Moreover, some grey areas exist that deserve particular attention. For one thing, the 2005 Hague Convention has a scope of application which is more limited than that of the Brussels I *bis* Regulation.[29] For instance, the Convention does not apply to choice of court clauses contained in contracts of "carriage of passengers and goods". Moreover, issues of application of the Convention may also arise in cases where the choice of court agreement is "asymmetric", as in the case of consumer contracts, or contracts involving employer and employee. In these situations, the Convention does not apply,[30] whereas, again, the Brussels I *bis* Regulation provides a full-fledged series of rules to determine the court having jurisdiction in all civil and commercial matters. It is thus a much easier and complete tool for identifying the competent court also within international contracts than the Hague Convention.

---

court agreements: some issues on the Hague Convention on choice of court agreements and its relationship with the Brussels I recast especially anti-suit injunctions, concurrent proceedings and the implications of BREXIT" (2017) 13 Journal of Private International Law 386.

26 See, respectively, Articles 5 and 6 of the Convention and Articles 25 ff. of the Regulation. Cf. A. Kistler, "Effect of exclusive choice-of-court agreements in favour of third states within the Brussels I Regulation Recast" [2018] Journal of Private International Law 66.

27 On the topic, see also Matthias Weller, "Choice of Court Agreements under Brussels Ia and under the Hague Convention: Coherences and Clashes" (2017) 13 Journal of Private International Law 91.

28 See art 31 of the Regulation.

29 See art 2 of the Convention.

30 See art 2.1 of the Convention.

Finally, uncertainties still remain as regards the relevant date from which the 2005 Hague Convention applies in contracts containing choice of court clauses and involving EU-UK relationships. According to the Convention, the UK became a party to the Convention on the date when it became binding on EU Member States (i.e. 1 October 2015).[31] By contrast, in its Notice to the reference to Article 16 of the Convention, the European Commission expressed the view that the Convention "will apply between the EU and the United Kingdom to exclusive choice of court agreements concluded after the Convention enters into force in the United Kingdom as party in its own right to the Convention", which is 1 January 2021 (i.e. the end of the Transition Period).

This different view has implications for litigation involving UK and EU States' courts. If the court seized is a UK one, it will consider that the Convention applies to agreements on choice of court entered into after 1 October 2015; but if the court seized is in the EU, it will apply the Convention only to clauses entered into after 1 January 2021, hence giving full priority to the Brussels I *bis* Regulation before that date.[32]

Again, these "substantial" differences stem from the different nature of the normative instruments at stake. The 2005 Hague Convention (like all other treaties on international judicial co-operation in private international law matters) merely intends to ease business relationships, and is not at all rooted on common values and principles, such as those binding the EU States. Therefore, such differences do not come as a surprise when considering the "new normal" of EU-UK relationships in these matters; yet, these issues will have to be carefully considered in relevant civil and business relationships involving EU and UK courts.

VII The Hague Convention on the Recognition and Enforcement of Foreign Judgments in Civil or Commercial Matters

From the end of the Transition Period, and hence the sunset of Brussels I *bis* Regulation as the main tool for co-operation in judicial matters between the EU States and the UK, the closest available substitute is provided by the Hague Convention of 2 July 2019 on the Recognition and Enforcement of Foreign Judgments in Civil or Commercial Matters.[33]

On 29 August 2022 the EU acceded to this Convention, on behalf of its Member States, and the Convention entered into force on 1 September 2023 for all EU States except Denmark,[34] clearly without prejudice to the fact that, within the EU judicial space, the Brussels I *bis* Regulation continues to apply.[35] At the time this chapter was

31 See the status table at www.hcch.net/en/instruments/conventions/status-table/?cid=98.

32 V. Lazić, C. Okoli (supra note 6) at 230; A. Dickinson (supra note 6). Some EU judges have upheld this view already: e.g. Rechtbank Amsterdam, 28–02–2022, C/13/713166/KG ZA 22–81, ECLI:NL:RBAMS:2022:1453.

33 For a commentary see M. Weller, J. Ribeiro-Bidaoui, M Brinkmann & N. Dethloff (eds.), *The HCCH 2019 Judgments Convention: cornerstones, prospects, outlook* (Hart 2023); P. Nielsen, "The Hague 2019 Judgments Convention – from failure to success?" (2020) 16 Journal of Private International Law 205.

34 See www.hcch.net/en/instruments/conventions/status-table/?cid=137.

35 This carve-out option is expressly allowed by art 26(4) of the Convention.

written, the only non-EU State which had ratified the Convention was Ukraine;[36] thus, at that time this instrument provides an international tool for judicial co-operation concerning relationships between each of the 26 EU contracting parties and Ukraine. The United Kingdom had not ratified the Convention yet.

The general provisions of the Convention are indicated in its Article 4, under which, in particular, "[a] judgment given by a court of a Contracting State (State of origin) shall be recognised and enforced in another Contracting State (requested State) in accordance with the provisions of this Chapter".

The court seized for recognition cannot review the merits of the judgment rendered in the State of origin, and can refuse recognition "only on the grounds specified" in the Convention:[37] for instance, if the judgment is not enforceable in such State, or if it is subject to review in the State of origin, provided that – as far as these two latter cases are concerned – the refusal or recognition does not prevent a subsequent application for recognition or enforcement of the judgment.

Like the 2005 Hague Convention, and for the same reasons highlighted in the preceding section, one should underline that the 2019 Hague Convention is only a substitute, and falls short of replicating the scope and deepness of the judicial co-operation established among the EU States by the Brussels I *bis* Regulation. Nevertheless, it seems the only instrument plausibly available to the UK to establish a mutually agreed regime in this matter. In addition, the European Commission expressly pushed for this solution when it denied the UK access to the Lugano Convention, and at the same time "invited" the UK to consider joining the 2019 Hague Convention.[38]

It is widely known that one of the most striking differences between the Hague Convention and a normative instrument such as the Brussels I *bis* Regulation is the lack in the Convention of rules concerning jurisdiction allocation among the contracting parties, or establishing homogeneous criteria for determining jurisdiction in each contracting State. That said, however, one should consider that the Convention assumes that any judgment rendered in a contracting State is eligible for recognition when one or more of the criteria established by its Article 5 are met. Each contracting party is therefore left with the choice to unilaterally determine the basis of its domestic jurisdiction, provided that judgments rendered in any such contracting party can be recognised under the Convention only if the domestic court could adjudicate the case under any of the conventional criteria.

In this vein, it may well be that the 2019 Hague Convention cannot work as a "double instrument", meaning one relating both to allocation of jurisdiction and to recognition of judgments, as with the EU Brussels I *bis* Regulation (and its ancestors). Yet it does provide convergence in establishing the criteria for jurisdiction among the contracting parties, unless they are prepared to allow domestic judgments that will not be recognised in other States. It has, therefore, at least an indirect impact on domestic rules on civil jurisdiction.

36 Some States have signed it, without ratifying it.
37 These grounds are in particular established by arts 5 to 7 of the Convention.
38 See note 9.

In essence, if one leaves aside the totally different scale of co-operation offered within the EU/EEA judicial space (which, once again, is justified by other "substantial" shared values going well beyond private international law), it seems reasonable to believe that the Convention appears to be a very innovative and unprecedented tool for international judicial co-operation in civil and commercial matters. Moreover, combined with the Choice of Court Convention, it probably represents the best available option to avoid a total reset of the "good old days" in which the UK jurisdiction in these matters was totally integrated with those of the other EU members.

VIII Concluding Remarks: What Remains and What Can Be Expected for Future Judicial Co-operation Between EU States and the UK in Civil and Commercial Matters

From 1 January 2021, UK jurisdiction is totally independent from those of the EU Member States, and – with the notable exception of the matters covered by the Choice of Court Convention (and within its limits as briefly set out earlier) – no co-ordination exists either concerning allocation of jurisdiction, or judgments recognition.

Compared to commercial arbitration, for which the New York Convention regime has not changed for decades (and was never affected by the EC/EU legal system), there is no doubt that a big change has occurred with Brexit.

Needless to say, each of the concerned States has resumed its "sovereign power" to adopt whatever measure it deems fit in order to oppose exorbitant jurisdiction implemented by courts abroad or to deny recognition of foreign judgments. To take the easiest examples, UK courts now have a larger scope to apply the *forum non conveniens* doctrine,[39] and have fully resumed their power to issue anti-suit injunctions – which had entirely disappeared after *Turner v Grovit*[40] – in a case where a party validly claims that UK courts have jurisdiction on a given matter and that a court of an EU Member State has been wrongly seized.[41]

Yet such injunctions, as well as any similar orders, do not exactly satisfy the need of co-operation in judicial matters. Nor do they help the facilitation of international (business) relations, whose support should obviously continue in the EU-UK present and future relationships.

One cannot exclude the possibility that, gradually, the strong connections forged during almost 50 years of UK membership in the EC/EU will fade away, with the UK enhancing its relationships outside the European continent and, at the same time, the EU members doing the same with third countries.

However, it cannot be denied that, throughout all these decades, UK-EU judicial co-operation has been mutually beneficial, and that this is especially true for the legal services offered in the UK, that have been able to operate as a "catalyst" for many

39 See F. Farrington, "A return to the doctrine of *forum non conveniens* after Brexit and the implications for corporate accountability" (2022) 18 Journal of Private International Law 399.

40 ECLI:EU:C:2004:228; [2004] ILPr 25. Also relevant is *Allianz SpA v West Tankers Inc (Case C-185/07)* ECLI: EU:C:2009:69; [2009] ILPr 20.

41 See A. Mammadzada, "The Rebirth of the European "Anti-Suit Injunction" Post-Brexit", in B. Soyer (ed.), *Damages, Recoveries and Remedies in Shipping Law* (Routledge 2023).

international judicial disputes involving EU parties, including those not necessarily related with the UK legal system.

As a matter of fact, the legal service industry in the UK is the second largest in the world, coming immediately after the United States. It has been constantly growing over the past 20 years and in 2021 has generated a turnover of roughly $45 billion, compared to roughly $30 billion for France, $27 billion for Germany, and $18 billion for Italy. More than that, the pull factor exercised by the UK legal services for non-UK stakeholders is demonstrated by the fact that the value of legal services exports from the UK is seven times higher than its imports.[42]

At the same time, and not surprisingly, EU Member States have implemented (or announced) the establishment of international chambers, in which pleadings can take place in English, and briefs and exhibits can be submitted in English. Purposes of these developments is to increase the judicial attractiveness of their legal system and compete with other fora, namely the British ones, as far as cross-border commercial disputes are concerned. The Paris commercial court is the most notable example, having established its international chambers in 2018 already, but other followers exist.[43]

In this "market" of (international business) legal services, it is clearly fundamental to be able to rely on judgments that may circulate relatively easily in many countries, especially those having the stronger links with the parties concerned.

The foregoing makes a clear case for the UK – and especially for the related legal services' stakeholders – to adhere to any international instrument capable of fostering international judicial co-operation, starting from the 2019 Hague Convention, which is, and will probably remain, the only reasonably available solution for the coming years. And in fact, on 27 June 2024 the UK ratified the 2019 Hague Convention, which will enter into force between the UK and all other contracting States (meanwhile also Uruguay has adhered) as at 1 June 2025.

Alas, within the EU-UK judicial relationships, gone are the times of the mutual trust principle inspiring *also* the creation and implementation of a system of rules allowing allocation of jurisdiction and recognition of judgments. But in the more prosaic Brexit fallout, the advantages for the UK of remaining (well) connected with the EU Member States appear to be even stronger, and the UK certainly made a good choice in catching the opportunity to maintain solid co-operation with the EU member States within the Hague Convention treaties.

---

42 See www.statista.com/topics/8517/legal-services-industry-in-the-uk/#topicOverview. For a first empirical assessment, see also M. Danov, "Cross-border litigation: Evaluating the Brexit impact – a socio-legal model for data analysis" (2020) 27 Maastricht Journal of European and Comparative Law 199.

43 E.g. for Germany see B. Hess & T. Börner, "Chambers for International Commercial Disputes in Germany: The State of Affairs" [2019] Erasmus Law Review 33.

CHAPTER 8

Sailing Round Judgments From EU Member States After Brexit. Time Charters and the "Shipping Company's" Right of "Pass-Through" Under the Amended Emissions Trading Directive 2023

*Simon Baughen**

I Introduction

On 1 January 2024 shipping became subject to the Emissions Trading Scheme (ETS) of the EU pursuant to the amended Emissions Trading Scheme Directive 2023/957. Ships trading to, from, and within the EU will have to surrender allowances in respect of CO_2 emissions on these voyages by 30 September of the year following the year in which the emissions occurred. The obligation of surrendering allowances is being phased in over the years 2024 and 2025, and for voyages starting or ending outside the EU there will be a 50% discount on the amount of allowances to be surrendered. The first allowances for calendar year 2024 will need to be surrendered by 30 September 2025, and the party responsible will be the "shipping company" which could be the registered owner, or the bareboat charterer or the ship manager. The surrender of allowances may also affect time charterers as the 2023 ETS Directive provides for a "pass-through" under which Member States are to provide the "shipping company" with a statutory right of reimbursement for the cost of all surrendered allowances from the party contractually responsible for the operation of the vessel, and for the provision of its fuel – the bareboat charter or the time charterer. Given that under most time charters the owner will be the party responsible for acquiring and surrendering allowances, the "pass-through" opens up the prospect of a new "torpedo" in the near future. This chapter will examine the impact of the revised ETS Directive 2023 on parties connected with vessels trading to, from, and within the EU and on possible responses available to time charterers in the English High Court if faced with "pass-through" claims against them by the "shipping company" which are directly opposed to the contractual position under the time charter as regards responsibility for acquiring and surrendering allowances.

II The Revised EU Emissions Trading Directive 2023 and the Right to Pass Through

On 16 May 2023, the Official Journal published Directive 2023/959, amending the ETS Directive, and Regulation 2023/957, and the Monitoring, the Reporting

*** Professor of Shipping Law, Member of the Institute of International Shipping and Trade Law, Swansea University.**

DOI: 10.4324/9781032726243-10

and Verification (MRV) Regulation 2015/757. Shipping entered the ETS from 1 January 2024 as regards CO_2 emissions and as from 1 January 2026 the ETS will also apply to emissions from two other greenhouse gases (GHGs): methane (CH_4) and nitrous oxide (N_2O). The reporting obligations under the MRV Regulation were extended from CO_2 to these other two greenhouses gases as from 1 January 2024. By 30 September each year, emissions allowances in respect of a ship's CO_2 emissions for voyages into, out of, and within the EU during the previous calendar year will have to be surrendered. Entry into the ETS is phased in over the first two calendar years with surrender of allowances being 1,000 for 2024, 70% for 2025, and 100% for 2026. For voyages starting from or ending outside the EU only 50% of those allowances will need to be surrendered, although this may rise when the Commission completes its review of the Directive in the light of IMO developments in 2028. The first surrender of allowances, in respect of 2024 must take place by 30 September 2025.

The obligation to surrender allowances, which will entail acquiring the necessary allowances for that year in the first place, will fall on the "shipping company". The "Shipping company" is defined as

> the shipowner or any other organisation or person such as the manager or the bareboat charterer, which has assumed the responsibility for the operation of the ship from the shipowner and has agreed to take over all the duties and responsibilities imposed by the International Management Code for the Safe Operation of Ships and for Pollution Prevention.[1]

In many cases this will point to the vessel's ship manager that is already undertaking the CO_2 emissions reporting obligations for the vessels under the Monitoring, Reporting and Verification Regulation 2015, as well as under the IMO's parallel mandatory Data Collection Scheme. However, the Commission on 22 November 2023 introduced an Implementing Regulation whereby the "shipping company" for the purposes of the ETS will be the shipowner unless there is a clear written delegation to either the demise charterer or the ship's manager, satisfying the criteria specified in the Implementing Regulation.[2] On 31 January 2024 the EU Commission published their list showing which shipping companies are to be associated with the different administering authorities of the Member States under the EU ETS. The list will be updated every two years. All shipping companies now have 40 days from the publication of the list to open a maritime operator holding account (MOHA) used to deliver and trade emission allowances within 40 days, and shipping companies that are not on the list must open an account within 65 working days of the first port of call falling within the scope of the EU ETS Directive. The "shipping company" must nominate at least two "authorised representatives" when opening the account.

A "shipping company" that fails to surrender allowances becomes liable to an excess emissions penalty of 100 euros per tonne of CO_2 and is still liable for surrender of the required allowances. Failure for two consecutive years makes a ship subject to penalty of expulsion or detention (in the port of the flag state if that is a Member State of the EU). If the "shipping company" is a ship manager, that penalty will apply to

1 Art 3(w).
2 Implementing Regulation (EU) 2023/2599 of 22 November 2023.

all vessels under their management.[3] The responsibility for ensuring surrender by the shipping company by 30 September each year of allowances in respect of emissions in the previous calendar year falls on the administering authority. This will be:

> the Member State where that is the flag State of the vessel or;
> if the flag state not a Member State, the most frequently visited EU port state within previous 4 years, or;
> if there have been no EU visits within that time the Member State where a ship of the shipping company has started or ended its first voyage.[4]

Article 3gc of the 2023 ETS Directive requires Member States to

> take the necessary measures to ensure that *when the ultimate responsibility for the purchase of the fuel and/or the operation of the ship is assumed by a different entity than the shipping company pursuant to a contractual arrangement*, the shipping company is entitled to reimbursement from that entity for the costs arising from the surrender of allowances. [emphasis added]

The justification for the entitlement is set out in Recital 32.

> The emissions from a ship depend, inter alia, on the vessel energy efficiency measures taken by the shipowner, and on the fuel, the cargo carried and the route and the speed of the ship, which can be under the control of a different entity from the shipowner. The responsibilities for purchasing fuel or taking operational decisions that affect the greenhouse gas emissions of the ship can be assumed by an entity other than the shipping company under a contractual arrangement. At the time the contract is negotiated, the latter aspects, in particular, would not be known and thus the ultimate emissions from the ship covered by Directive 2003/87/EC would be uncertain.
>
> However, unless the carbon costs were passed on to the entity operating the ship, the incentives to implement operational measures for fuel efficiency would be limited. In line with the "polluter pays" principle and to encourage the adoption of efficiency measures and the uptake of cleaner fuels, the shipping company should therefore be entitled, under national law, to claim reimbursement for the costs arising from the surrender of allowances from the entity that is directly responsible for the decisions affecting the greenhouse gas emissions of the ship.[5]

Article 3(g) (c) will therefore result in each Member State enacting a statutory right for the "shipping company" to be reimbursed from the different entity – the time charterer – in respect of the cost of allowances surrendered in connection with voyage into, out of, and within the EU within the period of the time charter. This may come as an unwelcome surprise to time charterers, as they will assume that the shipowner under most standard forms of charter will have no right to claim reimbursement for the costs of surrendered ETS allowances. It will amount to a financial incentive to time

3 Art 11(a).
4 Art 3gf.
5 The justification for the pass-through is stated as being the application of the "polluter pays" principle. One may wonder why the time charterer is singled out under the "polluter pays" principle, in that voyages in and out of the EU will involve commercial operations involving a chain of participants, including the shipowner, the shipper, the ultimate receivers of cargoes carried on such voyages, all of whom are involved in the pollution to which this principle applies.

charterers to contribute to reduction of GHG emissions from the chartered vessels, through ordering slow-steaming or re-routing. This will have consequences on their own contracts with sub-charterers and under bills of lading under which they are the carrier. Both the right to order slow-steaming and re-routing and the possibility of recovery of any emissions allowances for which they have to reimburse the "shipping company" will have to be achieved by contractual provisions in bills of lading and sub-charters. There is no statutory right of pass-through for the time charterer.

An example of these coming ETS costs was given by Safety4Sea in late September 2022,[6] who posited the example of a voyage from Brazil to Rotterdam, using the carbon credit price at that date of US$85 per metric tonne of carbon emitted. The example has been updated in line with the phase-in period in the amended Directive, and with the carbon credit price of €63.4 per metric tonne as of 2 February 2024,[7] and takes a Capesize dry bulk voyage carrying iron ore from Ponta da Madeira in Brazil to Rotterdam (4,100 nm) for 2024, the first year in which shipping will be subject to the ETS. Assuming a Capesize speed of 14 knots, this would take around 12 days: at 62 tonnes per day, this corresponds to 744 tonnes of fuel consumed, emitting 2,300 tonnes of CO_2. As the voyage starts outside Europe, only half the emissions qualify for allowances – 1,150 tonnes. Forty per cent of this will need to be covered for 2024, 460 tonnes. Therefore, at a carbon credit price on 2 February 2024 of €63.4 mt of carbon emitted, the total cost for the carbon allowance would be €29,164, plus a small addition for consumption in port. This compares with a fuel cost for the voyage of around €520,000 (equivalent to 8%). But two years later, in 2026, the cost for the carbon allowance would rise to 100% for half the emissions, almost € 72,910 – equivalent to 20% of the total fuel bill for the voyage. Under a time charter with trading limits within the EU, there may be several such voyages in a calendar year, generating allowances of €1,000,000 and more, and it will be worthwhile for the "shipping company" to claim the annual cost of these allowances from the time charterer under the statutory "pass-through" which Member States must provide under the revised Directive.

III Responsibility of EUA Allowances Under Time Charters

The position under existing time charters, without any specific clause to deal with the allocation of responsibility for the surrender of ETS allowances, such as BIMCO's Emission Trading Scheme Allowances for Time Charterparties clause (ETSA) 2022, will offer no prospect for the shipowner in recovering such allowances from the time charterer.[8] Indeed, a failure in two consecutive years to surrender allowances means

6 https://safety4sea.com/prepare-for-higher-shipping-costs-but-the-eu-ets-should-be-a-manageable-change/, accessed 1 February 2024.

7 https://ember-climate.org/data/data-tools/carbon-price-viewer/, accessed 1 February 2024.

8 Another part of the EU's "Fit for 55" maritime legislation is the FuelEU Maritime Regulation. This also recognises the polluter pays' principle, providing in art 23(8): "The company shall remain responsible for the payment of the FuelEU penalties, without prejudice to the possibility for the company to conclude contractual agreements with the commercial operators of the ship that provide for the liability of the commercial operators to reimburse the company for the payment of the FuelEU penalties, when the responsibility for the purchase of the fuel or the operation of the ship is assumed by the commercial operator. For the purposes of this paragraph, operation of the ship shall mean determining the cargo carried, the

a vessel sailing to a port in the EU would be at risk of detention, if an EU flagged vessel, or exclusion from the port. Such a vessel would probably be unseaworthy as a result and owners would be in breach of their obligations to maintain the vessel's efficiency during the time charter, as under cl 1 of NYPE 1946, which provides that the owners are obliged to exercise due diligence to maintain the ship's class and to keep her "in a thoroughly efficient state in hull, machinery and equipment for and during the service". It is likely that "efficiency" encompasses legal efficiency.[9]

Assuming that the EU is a permitted trading area, owners have no mechanism under the standard form time charters to recover these additional costs. For example, in NYPE 1946, there is no provision which would make charterers responsible for allowances surrendered by the shipping company in respect of voyages involving the EU. Clause 2 provides:

> That the Charterers shall provide and pay for all the fuel except as otherwise agreed, Port Charges, Pilotages, Agencies, Commissions, Consular Charges (except those pertaining to the Crew) and all other usual expenses except those before stated, but when the vessel puts into a port for causes for which vessel is responsible, then all such charges incurred shall be paid by the Owners.

Surrendered EU Allowances (EUAs) will not constitute "port charges" as these refer to all charges that a ship has to pay before she leaves a port, even if some of those charges relate to benefits which will accrue to the ship only after she has left the port.[10] However, surrender of allowances relating to the trip involving the EU would not be required until 30 September in the following calendar year. Nor would it fall under the umbrella of "all other usual expenses".[11] In *The Dimitris L (No 2)*[12] Christopher Clarke J rejected an argument that payments levied on owners under the US Gross Transportation Tax would fall within a similar clause which he held[13]

> [i]s designed to deal with the payments that need to be made to third parties (such as port authorities, canal operators, providers of fumigation services or dunnage equipment) to enable the vessel to be able to transport a cargo from port to port and to carry out the charter service; and not with a levy imposed on the contractual reward for the charter service, or a liability to reimburse someone higher in the charter chain in respect of that levy.

Nor could the costs of surrendered EUAs be recovered by way of an express or implied indemnity under the time charter, as these costs will be regarded as the natural costs of trading, as was the case in *The Dimitris L (No 2)*, where Christopher Clarke

route and the speed of the ship". There is a similar provision in art 23(9) with regard to contracts with fuel suppliers. Unlike the costs of surrendered ETS allowances, there is no provision for any statutory right of pass-through from the company to the time charterer of penalties in art 23(8) and (9).

9 Terence Coghlin, Andrew W. Baker, Julian Kenny, John D. Kimball, Tom Belknap, *Time Charters* (7th ed, Informa Law, 2014), at 11–16.

10 *Newman & Dale v Lamport & Holt* [1896] 1 QB 20.

11 Nor would surrendered EUAs fall under Baltime form clause 4, which expressly provides that the charterers are to pay "all dock, harbour and tonnage dues at the ports of delivery and redelivery (unless incurred through cargo carried before delivery or after redelivery)".

12 *Global Maritime Investments Ltd v STX Pan Ocean Co Ltd (The Dimitris L) (No 2)* [2012] EWHC 2339, [2012] 2 Lloyd's Rep 354.

13 Ibid. [54].

J held that the BIMCO US Gross Transportation Tax clause which was incorporated in a chain of charters only operated as regards reimbursement by the head charterer to the owner on whom the tax had been levied. He then considered that the disponent owner would not be able to recover by way of indemnity because the costs it had incurred under the head charter flowed from subcharterers' orders to proceed to the United States. He stated:[14]

> As to clause 8, in a broad sense the tax was incurred in consequence of the order to proceed to the US. But owners are not entitled to recover from charterers under the implied indemnity the ordinary expenses and losses of trading or those of which the owner has accepted the risk: *The Island Archon*, page 235; *Antiparos ENE v SK Shipping Co Ltd* (*The Antiparos*) [2008] 2 Lloyd's Rep 237, page 243. In the case of voyages to or from the USA USGTT is, as it seems to me, an ordinary expense of trading and not an unusual feature. In any event the risk of incurring or being liable for this very tax has been dealt with by clause 112 and, to the extent that the owners are not entitled to recover under that clause, the risk of having to bear the cost of the tax is one which they must be taken to have accepted.

On this analysis, with charters concluded after 1 January 2024 the cost of surrendered EUAs by reason of the time charterer's order to proceed to or from a port in the EU would be regarded as an ordinary expense of trading to a permitted area under the time charter. As such it would not be recoverable under the express or implied indemnity since the owner will have voluntarily accepted the risks of such trading. With a time charter concluded before 1 January 2024 these costs would still be regarded as a risk which the owners must be taken to have accepted as the extension of the ETS to shipping has been an imminent prospect since the EU Parliament initiated the legislative process in September 2020. Nor will there be an indemnity from the fact that the charterer is responsible for paying for the vessel's fuel during the currency of the time charter. True, the time charterer is responsible for paying for fuel, but there is no real choice as to the type of fuel as this will depend on the fuel used to power the vessel, something within the owner's province.

IV Avoiding the Pass Through

The right of pass-through against the time charterer granted by the ETS Directive cuts across the contractual agreement under most time charters. What will happen if the "shipping company" exercises its right to claim the costs of surrendered allowances in the courts of a Member State? If the "shipping company" is the shipowner, there is a clear conflict with the contractual position under the time charter. Assuming the charter is subject to English law and provides either for English Jurisdiction or London Arbitration, the time charterer's position will be similar to that facing the London P&I Club in a direct-action claim in Spain by both Spain and France in connection with pollution from the *Prestige* oil spill in 2002. In May 2003 the shipowner deposited with the Criminal Court in Corcubión, Spain, the limitation amount applicable to the *Prestige* under the 1992 CLC of approximately SDR 18.9 million, so constituting the limitation fund required under the 1992 CLC.

14 Ibid. [55].

That should have been the end of the matter as far as the Club was concerned. However, in a civil action commenced alongside criminal proceedings against the master and the owners of the *Prestige* under Article 117 of the Spanish Criminal Code, both Spain and France claimed against the Club up to the total limit of its cover for pollution damage of US$1bn, notwithstanding that under the CLC the liability insurer would not be liable for more than the amount of the established limitation fund. In 2016 the Supreme Court in Spain found the master guilty of a crime against the environment and that the Club had direct civil liability, up to the limit of the insurance policy of US$ 1,000 million, through the application of Spanish domestic law. In 2019 after quantum had been finalised, Spain sought to enforce its judgment against the Club in England.

The Club took no part in the Spanish proceedings, apart from making representations in the quantum proceedings following the judgment of the Spanish Supreme Court in 2016, but was very active before the English courts in proceedings aimed at forestalling any Spanish judgment from being enforced against it in the UK. Before any judgment had been issued in the Spanish proceedings, the Club commenced separate arbitration proceedings against Spain and France and the Commercial Court ordered that Mr Schaff be appointed as sole arbitrator in each arbitration. In 2013 Mr Schaff made awards in each of the arbitrations declaring that (1) Spain/France were bound by the arbitration clause in the Club's Rules to refer the civil claims being brought in Spain to arbitration; (2) actual payment of the insured liability by the insured member was a condition precedent to the Club's liability pursuant to the "pay to be paid" clause in the Club Rules; (3) in the absence of such prior payment the Club was not liable to Spain/France in respect of the claims; and (4) the Club's liability should, in any event, not exceed US$1bn. The Club subsequently converted the awards into judgments pursuant to s 66 of the Arbitration Act 1996, which Spain and France disputed, unsuccessfully.[15] However, the Club's subsequent attempt to claim damages or equitable compensation in respect of non-compliance with the declaratory award of Mr Schaff was unsuccessful, as the Court of Appeal ruled that failure to abide by the terms of a declaratory award did not give rise to a claim for damages.[16]

Following the decision of the Spanish Supreme Court in 2016 and the conclusion of the quantum proceedings in 2019, the Club applied to the court for an order for the appointment of a sole arbitrator under s 18 of the Arbitration Act 1996 against both Spain and France claiming coercive relief in the form of equitable compensation for breach of the obligation to arbitrate and to cover anything that was obtained by enforcing the Article 117 Spanish judgment in England or anywhere else, as well as claiming an anti-suit injunction to restrain the alleged breach of the equitable obligation to arbitrate, or damages in lieu pursuant to s 50 Senior Courts Act 1981 (SCA 1981). Henshaw J authorised the appointment of Sir Peter Gross as sole arbitrator in the arbitration against Spain, and Butcher J authorised the appointment

15 [2013] EWHC 3188 (Comm), [2014] 1 Lloyd's Rep 309. Spain's appeal to the Court of Appeal was dismissed. [2015] EWCA Civ 333, [2015] 2 Lloyd's Rep 33.

16 *The Prestige (Nos 3 and 4)* [2021] EWCA Civ 1589, [2022] 1 WLR 3434.

of Dame Elizabeth Gloster in the arbitration against France. Appeals were made to the Court of Appeal against the appointments but were unsuccessful.[17]

Shortly after obtaining the final award on quantum from the Provincial Court in Corunna on 1 March 2019, Spain applied to register its judgment in England which was done *ex parte*. The Club appealed against registration of the Spanish judgment on the grounds that under Article 34(3) of the Brussels Judgements Regulation No. 44/2001[18] the Spanish Judgment was irreconcilable with the English s 66 Judgments, and pursuant to Article 34(1) of the Regulation,[19] recognition of the Spanish Judgment would be contrary to principles of English public policy relating to *res judicata* by reason of the prior Schaff Award and the English s 66 Judgments ("the *res judicata* ground").[20]

The appeal was heard by Butcher J at the end of 2020. Shortly before the end of the Brexit implementation period on 31 December 2020,[21] he referred three questions to the CJEU as to the applicability of the exceptions in Articles 34(3) and (1) of the Brussels Regulation 2001 when the judgment in question arose out of the conversion of an arbitration award pursuant to s 66 of the Arbitration Act 1996. On 20 June 2022 the CJEU gave its judgment,[22] finding that a judgment entered in one Member State in the terms of an arbitral award was capable of constituting a "judgment", within the meaning of Article 34(3) of Regulation No 44/2001, which prevents the recognition, in that Member State, of a judgment given by a court in another Member State if those two judgments are irreconcilable.[23] However, this would not be the case where a judicial decision equivalent to the outcome of the converted award would have infringed the provisions and the fundamental objectives of the Brussels Judgment Regulation, as regards the relative effect of an arbitration clause included in an insurance contract and the rules on *lis pendens* contained in Article 27. Therefore, a judgment converting an arbitration award with that outcome could not prevent, in that Member State, the recognition of a judgment given by a court in another Member State.[24]

The Club's appeal against Spain's registration of the Spanish judgment returned to Butcher J in 2023 and was heard along with Spain and France challenging the awards of Sir Peter Gross[25] and Dame Elizabeth Gloster. On 6 October 2023 Butcher J

---

17 Ibid.

18 Now art 45(1)(c) of the Brussels Judgment Regulation (Recast) 2012.

19 Now art 45(1)(a) of the Brussels Judgment Regulation (Recast) 2012.

20 There was a third ground that pursuant to art 34(1) of the Regulation, recognition would be contrary to principles of public policy because the Spanish proceedings and Judgment involved a violation of the human rights of the Master, Owners and Club ("the human rights ground"). Butcher J subsequently dismissed the Club's appeal on this ground in a judgment in May 2021, [2021] EWHC 1247 (Comm).

21 After this time he would no longer have had the power to make a reference to the CJEU. The Court of Appeal subsequently found that in any event he had not had the authority to make the reference but only he had the power to recall the reference. By then it was too late as the CJEU quickly issued their judgment on the preliminary reference on 20 June 2022.

22 Case C-700/20.

23 Ibid at [53].

24 Ibid at [78].

25 In summary, Sir Peter Gross's second award of 23 March 2023 made the following remedial orders.

1. Spain in taking steps to enforce the Spanish judgment for non-CLC claims was in breach of its obligations not to pursue such Non-CLC Claims other than by way of London arbitration.

allowed the Club's appeal against registration on the grounds that on the grounds that the Spanish Judgment was irreconcilable with the English s 66 Judgments, and if that were wrong, recognition of the Spanish Judgment would be contrary to principles of English public policy relating to res judicata by reason of the prior Schaff Award.[26] He held himself not bound the finding of the CJEU that a s 66 judgment did not qualify as a judgment under Article 34(3) of the Brussels Regulation if the underlying award was such that, had it been a judgment, it would have conflicted with the scheme of the Regulation as regards arbitration clauses in insurance contracts and *lis alibi pendens*. These findings in paras 54–73 of the judgment were outside the scope of the three questions in the preliminary reference he had made to the Court. He also dismissed the challenges to the jurisdiction of the two arbitrators[27] and found that an arbitrator could award equitable compensation in the form of monetary compensation in the event of a breach of the equitable obligation to arbitrate, and this was not tied to the availability of an injunction.[28]

The *Prestige* litigation in the English High Court between 2013 and 2023 gives a useful outline of proceedings that would assist the time charterer in frustrating the eventual enforcement against it of any judgment in the court of a Member State awarding the "shipping company" the cost of surrendered emissions allowances referable to the vessel's voyages into, within, and out of the EU during the period of the time charter, from 1 January 2024. There are pre-emptive measures that the time charterer could take, such as seeking an anti-suit injunction and an arbitration award declaring that the shipowner by proceeding to claim reimbursement of emissions in allowance in the courts of an EU Member State was in breach of its obligation to refer all disputes to arbitration, and seek to convert the award into a judgment under s 66 of the Arbitration Act 1996.[29] There is also the reactive measure of challenging the registration of any "pass-through" judgment in the English Court.

There would be one advantage for the time charterer over the legal terrain staked out by the London P&I Club in its proceedings – and that is "Brexit". As of 1 January 2021 the Brussels Judgments Regulation 44/2001 and the Brussels Judgment Regulation (Recast) 1215/2012 both ceased to form part of the law of the United Kingdom.

2. Spain would also be in breach were it to take any further steps in Spain or England to enforce the Spanish judgment for the non-CLC claims.
3. If and when Spain obtains a final monetary judgment outside Spain against the Club it will in that jurisdiction by way of a final monetary award pay, give credit for and indemnify the Club in respect of an equal and opposite amount to that of the Further Execution Order obtained in its favour.
4. If and when the Spain obtains satisfaction (in whole or in part) in any country in respect of any amounts awarded to it by the Execution Order or any of the preceding judgments of the Spanish Courts, or any Further Execution Order which it may in future obtain, Spain shall pay to and indemnify the Club in an amount equal to the sum obtained.
5. Provision for Spain to pay resulting costs and to indemnify the Club to the extent not covered in a final order of costs made in respect of the proceedings in question.

26 [2023] EWHC 2473 (Comm).

27 [2023] EWHC 2474 (Comm) as regards France's appeal against the awards of Dame Elizabeth Gloster.

28 However, he found that the arbitrators had no power to order an injunction against a State due to s 13(2)(a) of the Sovereign Immunity Act 1978, and that they had no power to award damages in lieu of issuing an injunction against a State.

29 If the charter referred disputes to the jurisdiction of the English High Court then the time charterer could seek a judgment to that effect.

A Anti-suit Injunction

The first response of the charterer faced with a claim by shipowner for EA reimbursement against it in the courts of a Member State would probably be an application against the shipowner for an anti-suit injunction, something the English courts would have been precluded from ordering in the *Prestige* litigation which took place while The Brussels Regulation 2001 was in force, due to the decision of the Court of Justice in *The Front Comor*.[30]

The English courts have a discretion (under s 37(1) of the Senior Courts Act 1981) to grant an anti-suit injunction to restrain foreign proceedings. Where the foreign proceedings constitute the breach of a jurisdiction clause or a reference to arbitration in a contract between the parties, and the jurisdiction or arbitration clause covers the dispute in question, an anti-suit injunction will be granted unless there are strong reasons not to do so. This may be regarded as the contractual route. In making the claim in a foreign jurisdiction the defendant is in breach of its contract which submits disputes to arbitration or to jurisdiction of the English High Court. There is also the quasi-contractual route where there is no breach of contract in that there is no direct contract with the applicant, but the foreign proceedings are based on a derivative right under a contract which submits disputes to arbitration or to jurisdiction of the English High Court. Under the quasi-contractual route, such as a claim against an insurer under a foreign direct-action statute, a dispute would arise when the insurer rejects the claim against it in the foreign proceedings. From that moment on a dispute would have arisen which the insurer will claim should be referred to arbitration in accordance with the provisions of the contract between the insurer and its insured. This is due to the conditional benefit principle whereby third parties who seek to take the benefit of a contract, in this case the time charter, are subject to its burdens – in this case the requirement to arbitrate disputes. The contractual route would apply where the shipping company is the shipowner who is in direct contractual relations with the time charterer, and the quasi-contractual route when the shipping company is either the ship manager or the demise charterer who is not in contractual relations with the time charterer.

However, in both situations the key question will be how the foreign claim is to be characterised, which the Court will determine in accordance with English law, as the law of the contract. Is the foreign claim based on that contract in this case the time charter, or is it based on a free-standing provision of foreign law? This was the question before the Court in *The Prestige (No 2)*,[31] where Spain and France challenged the jurisdiction of the arbitrator appointed by the Court under s 18 of the Arbitration Act 1996 in respect of the Club's claims against them in response to their direct action claims in Spain against the Club. Hamblen J considered the characterisation of the right given under Article 76 of the Spanish 1980 Insurance Contract Act which provides:

> [Direct action against civil liability insurer and the insurer's right to action for recovery]
> The injured or aggrieved party or their heirs shall be entitled to a direct action against the insurer to demand of him the fulfilment of the obligation to compensate, without

30 *Allianz SpA and Generali Assicurazioni Generali SpA v West Tankers*. C-185/07. ECLI:EU:C:2009:69.
31 [2013] EWHC 3188 (Comm), [2014] 1 Lloyd's Rep 309.

> prejudice to the insurer's right to recover from the insured in the event that the damage or injury to the third-party was caused by the wilful misconduct of the insured. Direct action shall be exempt from the defences that the insurer may have had in respect of the insured. The insurer may, however, allege that the injured party is exclusively liable and may also raise the personal defences he may have in respect of the injured party. For the purposes of bringing direct action, the insured shall be obliged to inform the injured third party or their heirs of the existence of an insurance contract and the content of the same.

The legal mechanism by which the third party obtained its rights was not decisive. Hamblen J observed:[32]

> In all these cases both the law creating the right of direct action and the existence and validity of the contract made subject to the direct action will be essential prerequisites of the third party's right. Both are necessary to the existence of that right. In my judgment, in deciding whether or not the direct action right is "in substance" a claim to enforce the contract or a claim to enforce an independent right of recovery, what is likely to matter most is the content of the right rather than the derivation of that content. It is the content of the right which will be the most telling guide to what "in substance" that right is.

The substance of the right was contractual, notwithstanding that Article 76 provided that the right was "without prejudice to the insurer's right to recover from the insured in the event that the damage or injury to the third-party was caused by the wilful misconduct of the insured" and that "Direct action shall be exempt from the defences that the insurer may have had in respect of the insured". The former created a liability for an event which would not normally be insurable (damage caused by wilful misconduct) and the latter would disapply the "pay to be paid" and arbitration provisions in the contract of insurance between the shipowner and its P&I Club. Hamblen J then went on to conclude:[33]

> I agree with the Club (and the arbitrator) that the question is whether the extent of the exceptions is such as to change the essential nature of the right created so that it can no longer be regarded as being in substance a contractual right. Like the arbitrator, I do not consider that the exceptions go this far. Indeed, as already pointed out, in many cases they will be of no relevance and it is the contract alone which will matter. As the arbitrator observed, "the kernel of contractual obligation, as defined by the terms of the contract, remains at the heart of the claim". Indeed, if anything, it is far more than just the kernel.

Most direct action statutes would be characterised as contractual, although an exception would be the direct action provisions of the CLC under which the third party's rights against the insurer under the CLC arise from the mere fact of being an insurer, and the terms of the insurance contract are of no relevance.

With the statutory pass-through the characterisation of the right given to the "shipping company" under the ETS is arguably an independent right, as it is not a right to enforce the contract, under which the time charterer would not be obliged to reimburse the shipowner for what it has paid out by way of surrendered EUAs relating to periods of EU trading during the currency of the charter. Rather, it should be characterised as a statutory right which in most instances will be in contradiction to

32 Ibid. [87].
33 Ibid. [90].

the provisions of the charter, and apart from that right the statute has no concern with the provisions of the charter. Against that, the right is conditioned on the existence of a contract which provides for the charterer to pay for the vessel's fuel and to be able to direct its operations. Absent those provisions, there would be no statutory right of reimbursement for the shipping company against the charterer.

If the pass-through right is characterised as an independent right, the anti-suit injunction becomes more difficult to obtain. This will no longer be a case of a contractual or quasi-contractual ground, and the time charterer would have to show that the respondent's conduct is unconscionable, usually by showing the conduct is vexatious or oppressive or that it interferes with the English courts' due process, which will entail showing that England is the proper place for hearing the case.

B Arbitrate and Convert Award Into a Judgment

A second option for the time charterer would be to commence arbitration under the charter for a declaration that it is not liable to indemnify the shipowner for the costs of surrendered EU allowances incurred in relation to emissions during EU trading during the period of the time charter. Once obtained, the time charterer could then apply to convert the award into a judgment under s 66(1) and (2) of the Arbitration Act 1996, so as to establish its primacy over an inconsistent foreign judgment. In *The Front Comor* the Court of Appeal upheld the finding of Field J that the court had jurisdiction to make such an order, subject to its discretion.[34]

> Where, however, as here, the victorious party's objective in obtaining an order under section 66(1) and (2) is to establish the primacy of a declaratory award over an inconsistent judgment, the court will have jurisdiction to make a section 66 order because to do so will be to make a positive contribution to the securing of the material benefit of the award.[35]

A similar finding was made by Hamblen J in *The Prestige (No 2)*, again upheld by the Court of Appeal.[36]

There is no scope for a judgment for damages or equitable compensation in respect of non-compliance with a declaratory award.[37] However, the arbitration could also refer a question of a breach by owners in proceeding other than by way of arbitration in reference to a claim in relation to the charterparty. If the shipowner has not already commenced its EU allowances reimbursement claim before the courts of a Member State, the declaration sought could be coupled with a declaration that such claims would need to be brought by way of arbitration under the charter and a claim for equitable compensation were proceedings made otherwise than by way of arbitration.[38] Alternatively, a second arbitration could be commenced if

34 *West Tankers Inc v Allianz SPA* (*The Front Comor*) [2012] EWCA Civ 27, [2012] 1 Lloyd's Rep 398.

35 The judgment created from the award would create an issue estoppel or would provide a shield against enforcement of a subsequent inconsistent foreign judgment.

36 *The Prestige (No 2)* [2013] EWHC 3188 (Comm), [2014] 1 Lloyd's Rep 309. Spain's appeal to the Court of Appeal was dismissed. [2015] EWCA Civ 333, [2015] 2 Lloyd's Rep 33.

37 *The Prestige (Nos 3 and 4)* [2021] EWCA Civ 1589, [2022] 1 WLR 3434.

38 In *Rowland v Gulfpac Ltd* [1999] Lloyd's Law Rep (Banking) 86 at 97–98, Rix LJ made plain that the court has an equitable jurisdiction to grant *quia timet* relief to a party with the benefit of an indemnity

owners subsequently commenced reimbursement proceedings, claiming coercive relief – equitable compensation for the consequences of failing to proceed by way of arbitration. The doctrine of merger would not apply to preclude such a second reference to arbitration.[39] As with an application for an anti-suit injunction, this would again raise the issue of characterisation of the statutory right claimed by the shipping company against the time charterer in the Court of a Member State. Once the pass-through right is characterised as arising independently by the foreign statute, the time charterer's claim for equitable compensation against the shipping company falls away. There is no breach of contract by the shipowner under the time charter in making such a claim for reimbursement which is independent of the contract, *a fortiori* where the shipping company is not a party to the time charterer, as where it is the ship manager.

The pre-emptive remedy of an arbitration would need to be initiated as soon as it is clear that the shipowner/shipping company is intending to claim a statutory pass-through claim for reimbursement of the costs of emissions allowances incurred during the period of time charter. Time limits under the charterparty need to be considered. If, say, the charter provides for all disputes to be made within 12 months of the date of redelivery, the time charterer may find itself in difficulties if the shipowner commences its pass-through claim against it 13 months after the date of redelivery, assuming its claim is still within time under the implementing legislation in the Member State in which it intends to claim the statutory reimbursement. Bearing that in mind, the time charterer should consider commencing arbitration as soon as possible after the end of the time charterer. It would claim for a declaration of non-liability, coupled with a declaration that any claims against it for reimbursement in respect of EU emissions allowances should be made by reference to arbitration under the time charter, with claims for equitable compensation if such claims were made otherwise than by arbitration. Getting the arbitration in early would also have the advantage of being able to obtain an award before any pass-through judgment could be obtained by the shipowner, so creating a res judicata ground for non-recognition of any a resulting pass-through judgment in the English courts. The time charterer could also seek to enforce its s 66 Judgment in the Court of the Member State in which the pass-through claim was being heard.

C Resist Enforcement of Any Judgment in England

This would be unfeasible should the time charterer have assets in an EU Member State, due to the provisions of chapter 3 of the Brussels Regulation (Recast) 2012 which give a virtually automatic right for a judgment obtained in one Member State to be enforced in another Member State, subject to the limited exceptions in s 45 (formerly s 34 of the Brussels Regulation 2001).

before loss has occurred, and that there is an equitable right to create and preserve a fund to protect the party to be indemnified. The awards of Sir Peter Gross and Dame Elizabeth Gloster in *The Prestige* both gave such relief.

39 Ibid. [104–106] where the Court of Appeal referred to its decision in *Zavarco plc v Nasir* [2022] 2 WLR 261 that a cause of action does not merge in a declaratory judgment, which confirms the existing cause of action while leaving it intact, neither adding to it nor extinguishing it.

However, the English Courts no longer have to consider the provisions of the Brussels Judgment Regulation 2001 and the Brussels Judgment Regulation 2012 (Recast), both of which were repealed on 1 January 2021 at the end of the Brexit implementation period. For now, the relevant rules on the registration and enforcement of foreign judgments are the common law rules. Absent any reciprocal enforcement treaty, a foreign judgment will be registered if either (1) defendant was present in the foreign country at the time the claim was served or[40] (2) had submitted to the foreign country's jurisdiction, other than by challenging jurisdiction.[41] If either of those conditions are met, enforcement may still be challenged on various grounds, such as: the foreign court did not have jurisdiction according to the English rules; the proceedings were brought contrary to a jurisdiction or arbitration agreement; or inconsistency with a prior judgment on the same subject matter and between the same parties. The second and third for these would apply to an application to register a judgment of a Member State awarding the shipping company the costs of emissions allowances against the time charterer, but always depending on how that claim is to be characterised.

In the English litigation arising out of the sinking of *The Prestige*, Butcher J held on 6 October 2023 that the Club's Appeal against the Registration Order obtained by Spain succeeded on the grounds first that the Spanish Judgment was irreconcilable with the English s 66 Judgments, and secondly, if that were wrong, recognition of the Spanish Judgment would be contrary to principles of English public policy relating to res judicata by reason of the prior Award of Mr Schaff.[42] Butcher J noted that this would not be a case of cause of action estoppel, because he was not convinced that the entry of a s 66 judgment in terms of the Schaff Award and Spain's claim

40 Lord Collins of Mapesbury and Jonathan Harris, *Dicey, Morris & Collins on the Conflict of Laws* (16th Edn, Sweet & Maxwell, 2023) at 14–069: "In *Adams v Cape Industries Plc* [1990] Ch. 433, 530–544 the Court of Appeal held that in the case of corporations the test of jurisdiction is satisfied if the corporation is carrying on business at a definite and fixed place. The basic principle is that a trading corporation will be regarded as present within the jurisdiction of the courts of a foreign country if (a) it has established and maintained a fixed place of business and for more than a minimal time has carried on its own business there, *or* (b) its representative has for more than a minimal period of time been carrying on the corporation's business in that country at or from some fixed place of business. . . . In deciding whether a company is present in a foreign country as a result of the acts of a subsidiary present there, the court must consider whether the subsidiary was acting as agent, and if so, on what terms; it may also treat the subsidiary as the alter ego of the parent if special circumstances exist which indicate that there is a 'mere façade concealing the true facts'. If the local agent has authority to enter into contracts on behalf of the corporation without seeking the prior approval of the corporation, this is a powerful indicator that the corporation is present; if the agent does not have this authority, this fact points powerfully in the opposite direction".

41 Ibid. 14–075. "Section 33 [of the Civil Jurisdiction and Judgments Act 1982] provides that a judgment debtor shall not be regarded as having submitted by reason only of the fact that he appeared (conditionally or otherwise) in the foreign proceedings (a) to contest the jurisdiction of the court; (b) to ask the court to dismiss or stay the proceedings on the ground that the dispute in question should be submitted to arbitration or to the determination of the courts of another country; or (c) to protect, or obtain the release of, property seized or threatened with seizure in the proceedings. If the defendant in the foreign court fails on any of these issues, but nevertheless goes on to defend the case on the merits, he will be regarded as having submitted".

42 [2023] EWHC 2473 (Comm).

for recognition and enforcement of the Spanish Judgment, and the Club's Appeal against the recognition of that judgment, amounted to identical causes of action. However Hamblen J's decision did give rise to an issue estoppel to the effect that the jurisdiction-allocation provisions of the Regulation, and in particular its *lis pendens* and insurance provisions, were no good reason for the English s 66 Judgments not to have been entered because the Regulation is not applicable to arbitration, and this prevented Spain from contending to the contrary. In the context of a foreign pass-through judgment, it would not be possible to establish an issue estoppel where the right given by the legislation of the Member State whose Court had given the judgment was characterised as independent in nature, rather than based on the time charter contract.

By the time any pass-through litigation is likely to hit the English Commercial Court, it is almost certain that the Hague Judgments Convention of 2 July 2019 on the Recognition and Enforcement of Foreign Judgments in Civil or Commercial Matters (Hague 2019) will be in force in the UK. The Hague Judgment Convention 2019 came into force as of 1 September 2023, following the ratifications by the EU and Ukraine and entered into force on 1 October 2024. On 27 June 2024, the UK government ratified the Hague Convention of 2 July 2019. The Convention will take effect in the UK on 1 July 2025, and will apply to judgments made in proceedings that begin after that date.

Article 5(1) provides the bases for recognition and enforcement of judgments from Convention States in other Convention States, and expands on the common law bases for the enforcement of foreign judgments in England. The salient bases are (1) the person against whom recognition or enforcement is sought, in this case the time charterer, is not habitually resident in the State of Origin giving the judgment;[43] or (2) did not have a branch, agency, or other establishment without separate legal personality in the State of Origin when they became party to the proceedings and the judgment arises out of the operations of that branch, agency, or other establishment without separate legal personality in the State of Origin; or (3) did not expressly consent to judgment, nor argued on merits without contesting jurisdiction; and

---

43 Article 3(2) provides. "An entity or person other than a natural person shall be considered to be habitually resident in the State –

(a) where it has its statutory seat;
(b) under the law of which it was incorporated or formed;
(c) where it has its central administration; or
(d) where it has its principal place of business".

The definition is similar to that provided by Art 63 of the Brussels Regulation (Recast) 2012.

"Article 63 1. For the purposes of this Regulation, a company or other legal person or association of natural or legal persons is domiciled at the place where it has its: (a) statutory seat; (b) central administration; or (c) principal place of business. 2. For the purposes of Ireland, Cyprus and the United Kingdom, "statutory seat" means the registered office or, where there is no such office anywhere, the place of incorporation or, where there is no such place anywhere, the place under the law of which the formation took place".

(4) there is no contractual reference to the jurisdiction of that State of Origin.[44] Heading (g) provides:

> the judgment ruled on a contractual obligation and it was given by a court of the State in which performance of that obligation took place, or should have taken place, in accordance with (i) the agreement of the parties, or (ii) the law applicable to the contract, in the absence of an agreed place of performance, unless the activities of the defendant in relation to the transaction clearly did not constitute a purposeful and substantial connection to that State.

If the pass-through judgment can be considered a ruling on a contractual obligation, the performance of the obligation will not be regarded as taking place in the State of Origin as the agreement of the parties under the time charter will refer almost certainly have referred disputes to a different State or arbitration venue. That leaves the applicable law of the contract, which is very likely to refer to the law of a different State to the State of Origin, such as a reference to English law.

Article 7 provides discretionary grounds for Refusal of Recognition and Enforcement of which the salient grounds are due process failures; non-notification; fraud; manifest incompatibility with the public policy of the requested State; a reference to an agreement to hear the dispute in another Contracting State than the Contracting State of origin; or inconsistency with a judgment in court of requested state in dispute between same parties, or with a judgment in court of another state if the earlier judgment fulfils conditions necessary for recognition in the requested state. There may be a refusal or postponement if a Court of the requested State is first seised and the dispute has a close connection with the requested State.[45] Before an English court, at least, it is likely that these grounds would lead it to exercise its discretion not to recognise a pass-through judgment given by the court of an EU Member State.

---

44 "(a) the person against whom recognition or enforcement is sought was habitually resident in the State of origin at the time that person became a party to the proceedings in the court of origin;. . .

(b) the person against whom recognition or enforcement is sought is the person that brought the claim, other than a counterclaim, on which the judgment is based;
(c) the defendant maintained a branch, agency, or other establishment without separate legal personality in the State of origin at the time that person became a party to the proceedings in the court of origin, and the claim on which the judgment is based arose out of the activities of that branch, agency, or establishment;
(c) the defendant expressly consented to the jurisdiction of the court of origin in the course of the proceedings in which the judgment was given;
(d) the defendant argued on the merits before the court of origin without contesting jurisdiction within the timeframe provided in the law of the State of origin, unless it is evident that an objection to jurisdiction or to the exercise of jurisdiction would not have succeeded under that law;
(f) the judgment ruled on a contractual obligation and it was given by a court of the State in which performance of that obligation took place, or should have taken place, in accordance with (i) the agreement of the parties, or (ii) the law applicable to the contract, in the absence of an agreed place of performance, unless the activities of the defendant in relation to the transaction clearly did not constitute a purposeful and substantial connection to that State;
(g) the judgment ruled on a non-contractual obligation arising from death, physical injury, damage to or loss of tangible property, and the act or omission directly causing such harm occurred in the State of origin, irrespective of where that harm occurred".

45 "(a) recognition or enforcement would be manifestly incompatible with the public policy of the requested State, including situations where the specific proceedings leading to the judgment were incompatible with fundamental principles of procedural fairness of that State and situations involving infringements of security or sovereignty of that State;

Notwithstanding that the Convention excludes arbitration, as does the Brussels Judgments Regulation (Recast) 2012, it is likely that at least in England a s 66 Judgment will be considered a judgment falling under the Convention. It is also almost certain that the provisions on public policy, agreement to hear the dispute in another Contracting State of origin, and inconsistency with a judgment in the court of the requested dispute in a dispute between will not be construed in the way in which similar provisions in the Brussels Judgments Regulation 2001 were construed by the Court of Justice in its findings on the preliminary reference in *The Prestige* in June 2022. That judgment may also come to play a role as regards the enforcement in a Member State of any s 66 judgment from a converted arbitration award providing for equitable compensation in the event of breach of the shipowner's obligation to arbitrate all disputes arising under the charter. In a preliminary reference by the Greek Supreme Court in *The Alexandros T*[46] the CJEU decided that Article 34(1) of the Brussels Regulation No 44/2001 had to be interpreted as meaning that a court or tribunal of a Member State may refuse to recognise and enforce a judgment of a court or tribunal of another Member State on the ground that it is contrary to public policy, where that judgment impedes the continuation of proceedings pending before another court or tribunal of the former Member State. In this case the English judgment was regarded as a quasi–anti-suit injunction. For English proceedings commenced after 1 January 2021, the matter of recognition of a resulting judgment in the court of the Member State hearing the pass-through claim would be a matter for the domestic law of that State, as the Brussels Judgment Regulations have no provisions regarding the recognition and enforcement of judgments of courts of a non-Member State. For judgments in proceedings commenced after 1 July 2025 the Hague Judgments Convention 2019 will apply. A court of a Member State will have discretion to refuse recognition of such an English s 66 judgment in favour of the time charterer due to the public policy ground in Article 7 of the Convention.

V Contractual Approaches to ETS Emission Allowances

After the coming into force of the amended Emissions Trading Scheme Directive 2023/957 on 1 January 2024, contractual issues are increasingly likely to be at the forefront of the minds of owners and time charterers. Who will pay for acquiring the Emissions Allowances (EUAs) that will have to be surrendered for trading within the EU for calendar years 2024 and 2025 for CO_2 and, additionally, for methane and nitrous oxide for calendar years 2026 and onward?

BIMCO's Emissions Trading Scheme Agreement (ETSA) for Time Charterparties released on 31 May 2022 has a simple answer: the time charterer. The answer is entirely

(b) the proceedings in the court of origin were contrary to an agreement, or a designation in a trust instrument, under which the dispute in question was to be determined in a court of a State other than the State of origin;

(c) the judgment is inconsistent with a judgment given by a court of the requested State in a dispute between the same parties".

46 *Charles Taylor Adjusting Ltd, FD v Starlight Shipping Co., Overseas Marine Enterprises Inc.*, Case C-590/21 ECLI:EU:C:2023:633, 7 September 2023.

consonant with the pass-through in the Directive whereby Member States must legislate to provide a right for the shipping company to claim reimbursement for surrendered allowances from the time charterer. The clause is not explicitly limited to time charters, but its language is that of time charters with references to off-hire and redelivery. With voyage charters, the owner can calculate emissions costs in advance and take that into account in the freight rate. The clause deals with any emission scheme and is not limited to the EU scheme.[47] The obligation to acquire EUAs falls on the time charterer, who is then obliged to transfer them to the owners' nominated Emissions Account.[48] For this reason, the clause is not appropriate for inclusion in sub-charters to pass the cost of time charterer's transferred emissions allowances down the chain of charters. If this is desired, a simpler clause could be used requiring indemnification of the disponent owner in respect of the payments it has made in respect of EUAs surrendered to the account of the shipping company in respect of the vessel.

Co-operation between owners and time charterers is mandated in working out how to calculate the amount of EUAs that need to be surrendered for the period of the charter. Owners are to monitor and report GHG emissions, and not just CO_2 emissions, by an independent verifier. Charterers then have to provide and pay for emission allowances monthly. Within seven days of notification, the relevant amount of allowances must go into the owners' nominated Emission Scheme account. Provision is made for adjustment on redelivery if the actual quantity of allowances is higher or lower than that estimated. Charterers may offset allowances during any period of off-hire. The clause then provides owners' remedies for breach by the time charterers. Owners' obligations will be suspended without prejudice to other rights or claims owners may have under the charter, and the vessel will stay on hire. Owners will not be responsible for the consequences of exercising this right. Unlike many BIMCO clauses, there is no provision for incorporation into any bills of lading or waybills issued under the charter. This makes sense as ensuring the time charterers bear the financial consequences of acquiring ETS allowances required during the currency of the charter will not directly impact on third-party holders of bills of transport documents. This may happen, though, with delay due to owners operating their rights to suspend services under the clause. This will directly impact on third-party holders of bills of lading, and lead to liabilities for breach of the obligation to proceed to the discharge port with reasonable dispatch, and not to deviate. The clause enables owners able to be indemnified by charterers in respect of resulting liabilities incurred to such third parties by reason of suspending services under the charter, such as delaying discharge.

However, owners and time charterers are free to make other agreements as to the cost of surrendering allowances in respect of emissions during the period of the time charter. It would be prudent to ensure that these are reflected in owners' ship management agreement, or in a separate tripartite agreement between owners

47 "Emission Scheme" means a greenhouse gas emissions trading scheme which for the purposes of this clause shall include the European Union Emissions Trading System and any other similar systems imposed by applicable lawful authorities that regulate the issuance, allocation, trading or surrendering of Emission Allowances.

48 If the shipping company is the ship manager, the allowances would need to be surrendered to the ship manager's account.

and time charterers and owner's ship manager. Shipowners may also seek to modify their voyage operations to reduce emissions, something that can be done by slow-steaming and re-routing. This is fine if shipowners have contractual liberty to do so, but otherwise, they will find themselves in breach of express obligations under time charters to proceed on the route ordered by charterers and to meet the provisions of the speed and consumption warranties. For a voyage charter and the bill of lading, there will be a breach of the implied obligations to proceed with reasonable despatch and not deviate from a usual route on the voyage.

Ship managers will also be affected if there is a clear written delegation to them effective to constitute them as the "shipping company" under the ETS. This needs to be taken into account in the contract with the shipowner, not just regarding funding for the acquisition of allowances for vessels under their management trading to the EU, but also regarding penalties. Two years of non-compliance for one ship under their management could lead to detention of a ship in a Member State which is its flag ship or expulsion of any ship under the management when it attempts to enter a port in the EU, other than a ship under the flag of the Member State of the port in question. They will need to include provision in their management contract for dealing with reimbursement from the shipowner for emissions allowances they incur, which forms the subject of BIMCO's ETS – SHIPMAN Emission Trading Scheme Allowances Clause 2023.[49]

VI Conclusion

The statutory pass-through under the revised ETS Directive is litigation waiting to happen. Diverting though it may be to watch the battle of eminent counsel in the English courts re-running the arguments of the *Prestige* case, absent those relating to sovereign immunity, there is a better and cheaper way to deal with the pass-through. The sensible course for owners and time charterers, both under existing and under new charters, would be to agree how EUAs are paid for as between each other, and exclude completely any recourse to the statutory pass-through on the part of the shipowner and provide for the shipowner to indemnify the time charterer against all consequences of such a claim being made. The procedures discussed in Section III are subject to some uncertainty as to their effectiveness depending on how the English courts characterise the statutory pass-through right. Far better, to agree in advance under the time charter how such costs are to be apportioned, and then couple that with an express prohibition on making a claim of whatsoever nature in respect of such costs, other than under the arbitration or jurisdiction provisions of the charterparty.

If the shipowner has made the necessary delegation to another party, the ship manager or the demise charterer, to constitute them as the "shipping company" under ETS, the agreement should include that party, with the time charterer warranting that it will pay its proportion of the costs of surrendered emissions allowances agreed

49 www.bimco.org/contracts-and-clauses/bimco-clauses/current/ets-shipman-allowances-clause, last accessed on 1 February 2024. The clause is one of four ETS clauses published by BIMCO on 8 December 2023. The other three clauses relate to voyage charters: ETS – Emission Scheme Freight Clause for Voyage Charter; ETS – Emission Scheme Surcharge Clause for Voyage Charter Parties 2023; and ETS – Emission Scheme Transfer of Allowances Clause for Voyage Charter Parties 2023.

under the time charter directly to that other party. Both the shipping company and the shipowner should then warrant that the agreement will be the exclusive means of providing for paying the shipping company for the costs it has incurred in paying for and surrendering allowances in respect of emissions incurred by the vessel in voyages into, out of, and within the EU during the period of the time charter. A possible clause would read:

> The shipowner and the shipping company under the EU Emissions Trading Scheme under Directive 2003/87/EC as amended by Directive (EU) 2023/959 of the European Parliament and of the Council undertake that no claim or allegation whether arising in contract, bailment, tort or otherwise shall be made against the time charterer in respect of surrendered allowances for which the shipping company becomes liable in respect of emissions from the vessel during its employment on voyages from, to, and within the EU during the period of the time charter, otherwise than under this agreement. The shipowner and the shipping company warrant that if any such claim be made they will indemnify the time charterer against all consequences thereof.

CHAPTER 9

GA: London – An Examination of the Jurisdictional Bases for Claims in General Average

*Richard Sarll**

I Introduction

"We so rarely have to consider the law of general average that it is as well to remind ourselves of it", wrote Lord Denning MR.[1] At root, general average (GA) involves a system of risk transfer which pre-dates marine insurance and exists separately from it, but is nevertheless closely linked with it, since usual marine policies provide cover against general average losses. The founding principle has been enshrined in successive versions of the York-Antwerp Rules in Rule A:

> There is a general average act when, and only when, any extraordinary sacrifice or expenditure is intentionally and reasonably made or incurred for the common safety for the purpose of preserving from peril the property involved in a common maritime adventure.

Rule A marks the first of a series of lettered and numbered provisions which dictate how general average is to be adjusted. These rules – which first need to be incorporated by reference into contracts in order to have effect – are the product of a long-running law reform project that began in the 1870s. Their aim is to harmonise the adjustment of general average internationally, countering divergences in the laws of seafaring nations that had thitherto been left to develop independently since the pre-modern era.

It is not, however, the principles of adjustment, or the scope of any individual Rules, that is the focus of the present chapter. Instead, the aim is to identify the various means by which rights and liabilities in general average may arise – a topic of keen importance to both marine hull and marine cargo insurers who have indemnified their assureds in respect of general average sacrifices and expenditures, and are looking to make a subrogated recovery from net general average debtors.

In brief, if a party to the common maritime adventure should suffer a loss that is allowable in general average (such that the other parties to the adventure may be called upon to contribute to it), there exist no less than four jurisdictional "routes" by which that party's right of contribution might be recognised and enforced. These are (1) under the law maritime as interpreted by English courts; (2) under a contract of

* **Barrister, 7 King's Bench Walk. Co-author, *Carver on Charterparties, 2nd Edn; Co-editor, Lowndes & Rudolf, General Average and the York-Antwerp Rules,* 15th Edn; Associate Member of the Association of Average Adjusters.**

1 See *Australian Coastal Shipping Commn v Green* [1971] QB 456, 478.

DOI: 10.4324/9781032726243-11

carriage; (3) under an average bond; and (4) under an average guarantee. There may also be another route, i.e. (5) under bridging security.

So abundant is the armoury available to the net GA creditor that it is not always apparent which armament to choose. This chapter aims briefly to outline the jurisdictional routes that are available, identifying a number of incidental issues along the way – including some to which there is presently no clear answer.

II Under Maritime Law

The first route to be considered is the original one, but also the one that is today least likely to be encountered, i.e. maritime law. As will be seen, the reason why this route is no longer so important is because it is almost invariably the case that parties will, as a matter of contractual choice, select a version of the York-Antwerp Rules to govern their rights and liabilities, thereby displacing the law maritime.

Whereas it is tempting to refer to this route as existing "at common law", this would, strictly speaking, be a misnomer. General average has never formed part of English common law. Instead, rights and liabilities in general average used to be recognised in English courts on the basis that they formed part of the tradition of maritime law common to seafaring nations, having once been enshrined in Roman civil law.[2] Leaving that distinction aside, however, it is correct to say that rights in general average exist "at law", in the very same way that rights in e.g. bailment exist "at law". Such rights will exist, except in so far as a divergence from the position at law has been agreed upon in the parties' contract.

In former times, average adjusters would not infrequently have to adjust general average at law. But it was not necessarily English law that would be applied. Instead, English conflicts of law rules would select the law of the place where the voyage terminated as the law of the adjustment.[3]

Today, it is usual for the bill of lading or charterparty to contain a clause which makes express provision for the place of or the law governing general average, and such a provision is often combined with the express incorporation of the York-Antwerp Rules. By way of example, the GENCON 1994 form provides, "General Average shall be adjusted in London . . . according to York-Antwerp 1994 and any subsequent modification thereof".[4] The effect of such provisions will be considered further later. The point to note for present purposes is that, where contracts have been agreed which contain such terms, it is unnecessary to resort to the principles applicable at law – whether that may be English law or some foreign law. Rather, it is the contract which governs.

---

2 For example, in the oldest reported English decision, *Hicks v Palington* (1590) Moore 297, Dr Dale decided that parcels of cargo given as compositions to pirates should be allowed in general average for the reason that "*per le Civil ley average n'est due, si non que les biens sont pdus en tiel maner quod per ceo le residue en le Neife est saved*" ("according to the civil law, average is only due if the goods are lost in such a way that the remainder in the ship is saved").

3 In reflection of this principle, the leading textbook used to contain in its appendices a lengthy review of the principles of general average adjustment under foreign legal systems. See *Lowndes' General Average* (6th Edn, 1922), apps C to AA.

4 Clause 12.

There is nevertheless one scenario in particular where the position at law might still be relevant.[5] As noted in one leading commentary:[6]

> Whatever its basis in a contract context, an average obligation can arise where there is no contract on which it can possibly be based – as where it exists between cargo owners.

However, whilst that observation might on one reading suggest that there can never be a contract between cargo owners under which general average may be due, upon closer scrutiny this need not be (and would not ordinarily be) the case.

In issue is the relatively common situation where a cargo interest is a net GA creditor and is looking to recover contributions that are owed to it by the owners of other cargo who were also parties to the common maritime adventure. In earlier times, the prime example was jettison. Today, this is most frequently encountered in the form of the application of firefighting water, whereby the sacrifice of cargo through wetting is reasonably and intentionally made for the common safety, i.e. to prevent the fire from causing a total loss of ship and cargo.

Supposing there were no contractual nexus, it is clear from the decision in *Strang Steel & Co v A Scott & Co*[7] that a cargo interest could still claim a contribution in general average from another cargo interest at law. However, even if the existence of the rights might be clear, there would remain the challenge of finding some way in which an English Court could be seised with jurisdiction. Very often, the owners of the cargo owing a general average contribution will be foreign, and there may simply be no gateway for service out of the jurisdiction in such a case.[8]

Fortunately, there will in fact usually be a contractual nexus between cargo interests that also supplies the jurisdictional gateway, i.e. the average bonds and average guarantees which are routinely demanded by the shipowner as a precondition for the delivery of cargo after a general average event.

Typically, average security documents will be addressed to "the owners of the ship . . . and the other parties to the common maritime adventure as their interests may appear" – a form of words which has been adopted in the new standard form general average bonds and general average guarantees that have recently been approved for use by the Comité Maritime International (CMI), who are the custodians of the York-Antwerp Rules project.[9] It is perhaps debatable, when such manner of address is used, whether the average bonds and guarantees will constitute a single contract between the giver of the security and the shipowner (whose name a cargo interest might need to borrow against a suitable indemnity in order to bring proceedings against another

5 Whilst this article specifically considers inter-cargo claims, there are at least two other scenarios where the position at law could be relevant. The first is where a ship is sold and the new owner incurs general average losses but does not become party to the contracts of carriage. Another scenario is where a general average event occurs whilst a vessel is loading at berth and bills of lading have not yet been issued.

6 Jackson, *Enforcement of Maritime Claims* (4th Edn, 2005), para 26.158.

7 (1889) 14 App. Cas. 601.

8 Claims for general average are amongst those listed in s 20(2) of the Senior Courts Act 1981 as capable of being brought in rem against a ship. But that would not assist in a claim brought against cargo.

9 These may be found appended to the *CMI Guidelines on General Average* (2nd Edn) on the website of the CMI. These instruments have previously been known as "average bonds" and "average guarantees", no doubt in reflection of the fact that they secure not only general average, but two other forms of average, namely salvage and special charges.

cargo interest), or else whether they will constitute a bundle of contracts between the giver of the security and each of the other parties to the adventure (in which case the cargo interest could simply proceed directly against another cargo interest). But since the advent of the Contracts (Rights of Third Parties) Act 1999, that debate should prove futile. Addressing a bond or guarantee in the manner described earlier is likely to be understood as entitling creditors in the general average to bring a claim as a third party, whether because the contract expressly provides that they may, or else because its terms purport to confer benefits on them.[10] As for jurisdiction, average bonds and guarantees should include express choices of law and forum.[11]

It can therefore be seen that, as between cargo interests, the obligation to pay general average may indeed have a basis in contract, namely the average bond and/ or average guarantee. This being so, the next question that arises is this: are the rights and liabilities in general average to be adjusted according to the York-Antwerp Rules (which only have effect by dint of their incorporation into contracts of carriage) or are they to be adjusted according to the position at law? The distinction can prove important. For instance, whilst under English law the contributory values of cargo are to be assessed by reference to sound market values, under the various versions of the York-Antwerp Rules since 1974 the assessment is instead, for the sake of simplicity, to be based on the commercial invoice.[12]

No answer to this important question is to be found in the CMI-approved general average bonds and guarantees, which simply oblige the giver of the security to pay "any contribution to General Average . . . which may hereafter be ascertained to be properly and legally due in respect of the Secured Property". However, one very important suggestion in this regard is be found in the following commentary in *Lowndes & Rudolf*:[13]

> Where the cargo is carried under several bills of lading all incorporating the same version of the York-Antwerp Rules, it is the normal practice of British adjusters to treat that version of the Rules as governing all rights of contribution, not only between the shipowner and each cargo-owner, but between cargo-owners inter se. However, since it is not immediately obvious that there is any contract to that effect between the cargo owners, the question arises whether this practice can be justified, or whether rights of contribution between cargo-owners should be adjusted *e.g.* by the law of the place where the adventure ends, as suggested by some writers, however inconvenient that might be.
>
> . . . Having regard to the nature of general average, it is submitted that a merchant holding a bill of lading which provides "general average to be adjusted according to the York-Antwerp Rules 2016" would be likely to understand that provision as meaning that it was to be adjusted according to those Rules not only between him and the shipowner, but also between him and the other cargo owners; thus if his cargo were to be sacrificed, he would rightly expect to receive contribution assessed under the 2016 Rules not only from the shipowner, but also from other cargo-owners. If that is correct, it must follow that the holder of such a bill of lading assents to the shipowner contracting on the same terms

10 See the conditions set out in s 1 of the Contracts (Rights of Third Parties) Act 1999.

11 Severe problems may arise if they do not, as exemplified by *Mora Shipping Inc v Axa Corporate Solutions Assurance SA* [2005] EWCA Civ 1069; [2005] 2 Lloyd's Rep. 769; and *Galaxy Special Maritime Enterprise v Prima Ceylon Ltd (The Olympic Galaxy)* [2006] EWCA Civ 528; [2006] 2 Lloyd's Rep. 27.

12 See Rule XXVII.

13 See *Lowndes & Rudolf, General Average and York-Antwerp Rules*, 15th Edn, at para 30.32.

with other cargo-owners, and, since general average creates legal relations between cargo owners, gives the shipowner authority to do so.

This ingenious analysis has never come up for judicial consideration, but it is certainly persuasive. One problematic situation which it cannot, however, readily resolve is the one where multiple bills of lading have been issued, some of which incorporate one version of the York-Antwerp Rules whilst others incorporate another. That situation is, regrettably, not entirely uncommon.

Before leaving the topic of rights under maritime law in the absence of any contract, it is as well to revisit the point made earlier that English conflict of law rules would select the law of the place where the voyage terminates as the law of the adjustment. Whilst that used to be the proper analysis on occasions where the entitlement to a contribution did not arise in contract, nowadays a court would have to apply Rome II Regulation,[14] a European law instrument governing the identification of the applicable law in cases of non-contractual obligations that has been retained following Brexit. Suffice it to say that the Rome II Regulation is not well attuned to rights and liabilities in general average and its proper operation in such instances is hard to predict.[15]

III Under a Contract of Carriage

If maritime law is the least used of the four "routes" for enforcing rights in general average, then the pursuit of rights arising under a contract of carriage is the second least used. That might seem surprising, and it is convenient to explain the reasons for this before descending further into the legal detail.

A Modalities of Claims for General Average

Having suffered a loss that is allowable in general average, a shipowner's immediate aim will be to "go after the money". Provided the cargo has been insured, the entity with money to pay the claim will most obviously be any marine cargo insurers who have given an average guarantee. Furthermore, enforcement against the insurers is usually easier than enforcement against the cargo interest itself. Hence, it is usually the average guarantee which constitutes the route of most interest to the GA creditor. Typically, an average guarantee will expressly select High Court jurisdiction, rather than London arbitration, albeit this need not be the case.[16]

14 Formally, Regulation (EC) No 864/2007 of the European Parliament and of the Council of 11 July 2007 on the law applicable to non-contractual obligations.

15 As explained in *Lowndes & Rudolf, General Average and York-Antwerp Rules*, 15th Edn, at para 30.15 the Regulation distinguishes, in general, between torts/delicts on the one hand, and on the other hand, obligations arising from other sources including unjust enrichment and *negotiorum gestio* (which concerns acts performed without due authority in connection with the affairs of another). In case of both *negotiorum gestio* and unjust enrichment, the place where this occurred may provide the connecting factor. But in incidents of general average, a unitary place may prove difficult to identify, especially if the events took place on the high seas. For further analysis, see J. Kruit, *General Average, Legal Basis and Applicable Law* (2017) at para 6.5.3.2.4.

16 A prominent example of a casualty in which the average security documents selected arbitration rather than court is the case of *Ever Given*, the container ship which famously blocked the Suez Canal.

Secondly, inasmuch as average guarantees may be designed for use in conjunction with average bonds, it would seem precautious (whether or not it is strictly necessary[17]) simultaneously to bring claims under the average bond, which will typically have been given by the consignee or receiver of the goods at the same time as the average guarantee was given. An average bond will usually also select High Court jurisdiction rather than arbitration, albeit that, once again, this need not be the case. It is a relatively straightforward thing to bring claims in court under both an average bond and an average guarantee within the same set of proceedings. Indeed, where multiple bills of lading have been issued (as will invariably be the case in container ship casualties where there could be hundreds or thousands of bonds and guarantees), there is no particular procedural difficulty in bringing claims against multiple defendants. All such claims can be determined together, without any of the problems regarding confidentiality or the joinder of multiple parties that are associated with arbitration.

By contrast with average bonds and guarantees which typically contain a choice of forum in favour of the High Court, bills of lading and voyage charterparties will very often select arbitration. There is no ready way of bringing proceedings under a bill of lading containing an arbitration agreement simultaneously with a claim under an average guarantee that contains a High Court jurisdiction clause. Fortunately, this should not prove necessary. Since the shipowner's aim is to "go after the money", claims will typically be brought in court under the average guarantee and (if only out of precaution) under the average bond. As for a claim in arbitration under the bill of lading, this option will usually be left by the wayside and not pursued.[18]

None of this is to say that an identification of the rights under the relevant contract of carriage is unimportant. On the contrary, that exercise is essential. It is just that the process of identifying those rights is not usually undertaken within a claim under the contract of carriage itself. Instead, it is conducted within the parameters of claims under the average bonds and average guarantees which, in the CMI-approved standard forms, require the giver of the security to pay "any contribution to General Average . . . which may hereafter be ascertained to be properly and legally due in respect of the Secured Property". At least where the basis of the obligation is in contract,[19] that

The use of arbitration clauses in that case presumably reflects the fact that much of the cargo originated in China, a jurisdiction in which arbitral awards are readily enforceable thanks to China's membership of the New York Convention on the Recognition and Enforcement of Foreign Arbitral Awards. Historically, English court judgments have, by contrast, not readily been enforced in China, but perhaps that may change following the decision of the Hubei Court in *Spar Shipping AS v Grand China Logistics Holding (Group) Co Ltd* [2022] 2 CMCLR 35.

17 The question of whether an average guarantee is a distinct contract in its own right, or else only operates in conjunction with a bill of lading or average bond, is considered further later.

18 In this regard, a court would not ordinarily impose a case management stay in favour of prior resolution in arbitration, not least because of the status of average bonds and guarantees as new contracts (see further later). For a similar case in which a parent company guarantee was given and a case management stay was refused, see *Classic Maritime Inc v Lion Diversified Holdings bhd* [2009] EWHC 1142 (Comm); [2010] 1 Lloyd's Rep. 59.

19 What, however, is the position where the basis of the obligation is not in contract, as for instance where a ship is sold and the new owner incurs general average losses but does not become party to the

promise leads one back to an analysis of the rights and liabilities under the relevant contract of carriage.

With that lengthy introduction of the modalities of these sorts of claims, the discussion can now return to a consideration of the manner in which contracts of carriage engender rights relating to general average. Given the preceding explanation of the practicalities, it will be appreciated that the comments in the next paragraphs should not be of direct relevance when claims are brought under average bonds and guarantees. But the subsequent comments under the headings "Current Issues" are of potential relevance in that context, given the promises by the givers of such security to pay whatever GA is "properly and legally due".

B Charterparties

The legal liability to contribute in general average falls, *prima facie*, upon those persons who, at the time of the general average act, were the owners of the property imperilled in the common adventure – namely ship, cargo, bunkers, and freight at risk. The categories of those who are liable may, however, be altered or extended by contract.[20] In the GENCON 1994 form it is stated, "Proprietors of cargo to pay the cargo's share of general average expenses". Consistently with that statement, the provisions in that form which relate to general average are not understood as rendering the charterer liable to contribute in respect of cargo not owned by him.[21]

It is nevertheless still possible for a charterer to attract liability under such provisions, even if it was not the owner of the goods at the relevant time, but any such liability would only arise indirectly, in this way. The effect of such a requirement for general average to be adjusted according to the York-Antwerp Rules is considered to be twofold: (1) to provide that any claim in general average arising between shipowner and charterer shall be governed by the York-Antwerp Rules and (2) to agree between shipowner and charterer that the rights and liabilities in general average of any other parties to the adventure shall be governed by the Rules.[22] Hence, if a charterer failed to issue bills of lading in the form prescribed by the charterparty, it could become liable for the consequences.

---

contracts of carriage? In the case of an average bond on the Lloyd's Average Bond form, the answer is to be found in the express term to pay whatever general average is ascertained to be due under an adjustment prepared "in accordance with the law and practice of the place where the common maritime adventure ended" – such a formula having the effect of putting the English conflict of law rule (see earlier) on a contractual footing. Such language is not, however, to be found in the new CMI-approved general average bond or general average guarantee, which simply provide that "any contribution to General Average . . . which may hereafter be ascertained to be properly and legally due in respect of the Secured Property". Whilst it will be necessary for the purposes of such an ascertainment to identify the applicable law, the new standard forms do not explain how this is to occur, whether by reference to Rome I Regulation or Rome II Regulation (as to which see earlier).

20 See *Hain SS Co Ltd v Tate & Lyle Ltd* (1936) 41 Com. Cas. 350, 356.

21 Cooke et al., *Voyage Charters* (5th Edn, 2022), para 20.56.

22 Ibid.

C Bills of Lading

At least where it is anticipated that ownership in the goods will be transferred under a contract of sale, seaborne carriage will also typically involve the issuance of a bill of lading. In CONGENBILL 1994 form, for example, it is stated on its reverse:

> General Average shall be adjusted, stated and settled according to York-Antwerp Rules 1994, or any subsequent modification thereof, in London unless another place is agreed in the Charter Party.
>
> Cargo's contribution to General Average shall be paid to the Carrier even when such average is the result of a fault, neglect or error of the Master, Pilot or Crew.

Regarding the first sentence of these clauses, it was held by the House of Lords in *The Potoi Chau*[23] that a provision in a bill of lading that general average shall be adjusted in accordance with the York-Antwerp Rules would transfer to a subsequent indorsee a contractual obligation to contribute, even if it was not the owner of the goods at the time of the sacrifice or expenditure. Since *The Potoi Chau*, however, Parliament has enacted the Carriage of Goods by Sea Act 1992, a statute which regulates the rights and liabilities of holders of bills of lading. It was argued in *The Lehmann Timber*[24] that s 3(1)(a) of the 1992 Act imposed a liability on the consignee to pay whatever general average was due by reason of their having presented bills of lading to request delivery. That seems correct, even if it was considered unnecessary in that case to resolve the question. Hence, the liability to pay general average may transfer to a subsequent indorsee a contractual obligation to contribute, either by operation of the common law (as per *The Potoi Chau*) or else by statute (the Carriage of Goods by Sea Act).

i Current Issues: "Or Any Subsequent Modification Thereof"

Before leaving the topic of contracts of carriage, there are two incidental questions which arise out of the drafting of CONGENBILL 1994 that are of interest.

The first issue relates to the words, "according to York-Antwerp Rules 1994, or any subsequent modification thereof". The issue is whether it is the York-Antwerp Rules 1994 that are incorporated, or else the latest version, i.e. York-Antwerp Rules 2016. In other words, does this formula take effect as an automatic updating mechanism capable of prescribing the use of the latest edition of the Rules? Or is each edition of the Rules stand-alone, and not a modification of the last?

Until recently, one would very often find a statement in the narrative section of an average adjustment explaining that the York-Antwerp Rules 2016 were not considered to be a modification of the York-Antwerp Rules 1994, but instead a new set of rules altogether; and that, since the York-Antwerp Rules 1994 were never themselves amended, those rules applied to the adjustment.

However, even if such statements were very often found in average adjustments, it remained in doubt whether they were legally correct. In successive editions of *Lowndes*

23 See *Castle Insurance Co v Hong Kong Shipping Co (The Potoi Chau)* [1984] AC 226, 235.

24 See *Metall Market OOO v Vitorio Shipping Co Ltd (The Lehmann Timber)* [2014] QB 760 at [38].

& Rudolf it was noted that such formulae were "ambiguous" and that it would be "best to avoid them".[25]

In 2023, the question finally came up for judicial scrutiny. In *The Star Antares*,[26] it was held that the words "according to York-Antwerp Rules 1994, or any subsequent modification thereof" were reasonably to be seen as intended to select the most recent version, i.e. York-Antwerp Rules 2016. As such, the decision is consistent with the treatment of updating mechanisms in other contractual contexts.[27]

ii Current Issues: "When Such Average Is the Result of a Fault, Neglect or Error of the Master, Pilot or Crew"

The second incidental question of some interest relates to wording in the second paragraph of the CONGENBILL form as set out earlier. The issue is whether the express obligation upon cargo to pay a contribution to general average even "when such average is the result of a fault, neglect or error of the Master, Pilot or Crew" could apply to crew errors that are committed before the commencement of the voyage and which render a vessel unseaworthy. The most notable error of this nature (and one which has garnered enormous attention since the decision in *The CMA CGM Libra*[28]) is deficiencies in passage planning.

One's initial reaction would be to think not. First, in *The CMA CGM Libra*, a deficiency in passage planning through the crew's failure to update nautical charts was found to have rendered the vessel unseaworthy in breach of Article III r. 1 of the Hague Rules as incorporated into bills of lading. It was held that the cargo interests therefore had a defence to the carrier's claim for a general average contribution by reason of an actionable fault. Secondly, Article III r. 8 of the Hague and Hague-Visby Rules contains certain "repugnancy provisions" whose effect is to strike down clauses in contracts of carriage that lessen the liability of the carrier. Would not those provisions nullify the second paragraph of the CONGENBILL form as set out earlier, in so far as it purported to impose an obligation to contribute even if the Vessel was initially unseaworthy due to some navigational error by the crew? Perhaps surprisingly, there are two reasons why this might well not be the case.

The first reason relates to the wording of Article III r. 8, which provides:

> Any clause, covenant or agreement in a contract of carriage relieving the carrier or the ship from liability for loss or damage to or in connection with goods arising from negligence, fault or failure in the duties and obligations provided in this Article or lessening such liability otherwise than as provided in these Rules, shall be null and void and of no effect.

---

25 See e.g. *Lowndes & Rudolf, General Average and the York-Antwerp Rules* (15th Edn, 2018), para 30.30.

26 *Star Axe I LLC v Royal and Sun Alliance Luxembourg SA* [2023] EWHC 2784 (Comm), [2024] 1 Lloyd's Rep. 342.

27 Reference was made in the judgment in *The Star Antares* to cases involving incorporation of the Hague-Visby Rules, rather than the Hague Rules, namely *The Marinor* [1996] 1 Lloyd's Rep. 301 and *The Vechschroon* [1982] 1 Lloyd's Rep. 301. A similar treatment has also been given to a provision relating to the Inter Club Agreement which referred to the ICA of "1970 and reprints of May 1984 and any amendments thereto" – see *London Arbitration 10/22* [2022] LMLN (3 March 2022).

28 See *Alize 1954 v Allianz Elementar Versicherungs AG (The CMA CGM Libra)* [2021] UKSC 51; [2022] 2 All ER 479; on appeal from [2020] EWCA Civ 293; [2020] 2 All ER (Comm) 1072 (CA) and [2019] EWHC 481 (Admlty); [2019] 2 All ER (Comm) 679 (Admiralty Court).

The reference to "liability for loss or damage to or in connection with goods" is significant. Similar wording can be found in the time-bar in Article III r. 6 of the Hague Rules, which discharges the carrier from "all liability in respect of loss or damage unless suit is brought within one year after delivery of the goods or the date when the goods should have been delivered". In *Goulandris Bros v Goldman*,[29] it was held that the time-bar did not apply to claims for general average. Unless the meaning of "loss or damage" is now to be reconsidered,[30] it is perhaps hard to see why Article III r. 8 should be capable of nullifying the second paragraph of the CONGENBILL form.[31]

The second reason relates to Article V of the Hague-Visby Rules, which provides:

> Nothing in these Rules shall be held to prevent the insertion in a bill of lading of any lawful provision regarding general average.

In this regard, successive editions of *Lowndes & Rudolf* have commented:

> Although the purport of the word "lawful" in art.V is unclear, if the words of the article are given their ordinary meaning it is difficult to resist the conclusion that no provision of the Rules, including art.III r.8, may be invoked in order to invalidate a "provision regarding general average" which would otherwise be lawful.[32]

Ultimately, Article V is rather obscure, and it is hard to comment more extensively in the absence of any reported case in which its effect has been considered.[33]

At the symposium at which this paper was first presented, the view amongst delegates was that the words "even when such average is the result of a fault, neglect or error of the Master, Pilot or Crew" were simply not aimed at unseaworthiness and for this reason did not qualify the obligation in Article III r. 1, where a fault of the master etc. is to blame for this. That may indeed be so.[34] Yet it requires one to overlook that the words themselves do not contain any such express limitation.

IV Under an Average Bond

Average bonds represent "one half" of the reasonable security which a shipowner is entitled to demand from the receiver of the goods as a precondition of delivery.

29 [1958] 1 QB 74.

30 It has in the past been suggested that the decision in *Goulandris Bros v B Goldman* is incorrect in this regard. But where would this lead? Might the result not then be that the package limitation in art IV r. 5 of the Hague-Visby Rules should also apply, given its stipulation that "neither the carrier nor the ship shall be or become liable for any loss or damage to or in connection with goods in an amount exceeding 666.67 units of account per package" etc.?

31 This is the view expressed in *Lowndes & Rudolf* (15th Edn, 2018), para 00.54, and it had previously appeared in successive editions.

32 *Lowndes & Rudolf* (15th Edn, 2018), para 00.53. See also Cooke et al, *Voyage Charters* (5th Edn, 2022), para 66.484.

33 In so far as the *travaux préparatoires* are concerned, it appears the intention behind art V of the Hague Rules was the notion that "nothing in these rules has to interfere with general average". As Mr Franck, the Chairman of the conference, intriguingly explained, "These rules are limited to their object. They are restrictions to the freedom of contract and such restriction is not to be construed in an extensive way; so, general average stands entirely independent from this". See *The Travaux Préparatoires of the Hague Rules and of the Hague-Visby Rules* (available on the website of the CMI) at pp 429, 430, and 639.

34 Compare *The Carron Park* (1890) 15 P.D. 203, and see the commentary in *Lowndes & Rudolf* (15th Edn, 2018), paras D.04 to D.08.

(The other half is the average guarantee or cash deposit, considered later.) Unless and until reasonable security has been provided, the shipowner is entitled to withhold possession of goods in exercise of a possessory lien that arises upon the accrual of rights and liabilities in general average.

The average bond is usually given by the receiver of the goods, as is reflected in the first line of the principal obligation ("delivery . . . to us"). But another entity – for instance, a parent company – could potentially give the average bond, provided this is acceptable to the shipowner.

The latest standard form is the one that has been approved by the CMI.[35] The principal obligation is as follows:

> In consideration of the delivery in due course of the Secured Property to us or to our order, on payment of the freight due, I/we . . . hereby agree to pay to the owners of the ship named in box 1 or the Adjuster on behalf of the various parties to the common maritime adventure, as their interests may appear, any contribution to General Average and/or Salvage and/or Special Charges which may hereafter be ascertained to be properly and legally due in respect of the Secured Property.[36]

As explained in *The Potoi Chau*,[37] the effect of an average bond is that it is a "fresh agreement which stands on its own independently of the bill of lading and is for fresh consideration on either side".[38] Given that, for reasons explained earlier, a consignee will usually be liable to pay general average already – whether because of section 3(1)(a), Carriage of Goods by Sea Act 1992 or else common law – it has been argued that an average bond should no longer be required as part of the package of reasonable security which a shipowner is entitled to demand. In *The Lehmann Timber*,[39] however, the Court of Appeal gave this (not entirely unreasonable) suggestion short shrift. As explained by Rix LJ, who took a conservative view of the matter:[40]

> It may be perfectly true that, in the circumstances, by the time, whenever that was, that the bills came into the consignee's hands, and the consignee presented them to the owner, a bond might not have added in any practical way to the sources of its liability to the owner. However, the very refusal by the consignee to provide its bond would have given the owner pause for thought, and in my judgment rightly so. In any event, the bond would probably have clarified the consignee's liability very helpfully. Moreover, it would have postponed the running of the limitation period considerably,[41] which in the context of

35 Available on the website of the CMI, appended to the *CMI Guidelines on General Average*, (2nd Edn).

36 By contrast, the standard form which has hitherto been most commonly in use (the Lloyd's Average Bond) requires the giver to pay the proper proportion of any general average etc. which may be ascertained to be due "in accordance with the provisions of the contract of affreightment governing the carriage of goods or, failing any such provision, in accordance with the law and practice of the place where the common maritime adventure ended and which is payable in respect of the goods by the shippers or owners thereof".

37 *Castle Insurance Co v Hong Kong Shipping Co (The Potoi Chau)* [1984] 1 AC 226.

38 See [1984] 1 AC 226 at 239.

39 *Metall Market OOO v Vitorio Shipping Co Ltd (The Lehmann Timber)* [2013] EWCA Civ 650; [2015] QB 760 at [39].

40 See [2013] EWCA Civ 650; [2015] QB 760 at [39].

41 Under York-Antwerp Rules 2004 or 2016, this would not necessarily be the case. This is because of r. XXIII of those rules which provides, "Any rights to general average contribution *including any rights to claim under general average bonds and guarantees*, shall be extinguished unless an action is brought by the party claiming such contribution within a period of one year after the date upon which the general average adjustment is issued. However, in no case shall an action be brought after six years from the date

> the lengthy delays which can overtake the settlement of a general average adjustment can be of substantial importance (as the facts of the *Potoi Chau* illustrate). There were other advantages which the bond would have given, such as the right to a payment on account. In my judgment, the clarity and certainty of the obligations undertaken by the consignee under the bond are a sufficient justification, were any needed, for the owner's continuing request for one.

However, even if shipowners may be entitled to request average bonds, this is not to say that they will necessarily do so. In cases involving a large number of interests (and/or a relatively low percentage rate of contribution from each interest) it may be decided not to request average bonds from receivers who are insured, in order to reduce the cost and paperwork involved in the security collection. Instead, only average guarantees will be taken from insured receivers.[42] Such an approach is premised on the understanding that an average guarantee gives rise to primary liability and is not in any way dependent on the existence of an average bond – an issue that is considered further later.

V Under an Average Guarantee

As remarked earlier, it is the average guarantee which represents the "jurisdictional route" of most interest to the net GA creditor.

The average guarantee represents the "other half" of the package of reasonable security which a shipowner is entitled to demand as a precondition of the relinquishment of its possessory lien. Unlike the average bond which will usually be given by the receivers, the average guarantee will be given by insurers. As an alternative to an average guarantee, a cash deposit may be given on account of general average. Cash deposits will be demanded in those cases where the cargo is uninsured, or where a general average guarantee offered by insurers is considered unsuitable.[43]

As with the word "bond", the nomenclature "guarantee" is somewhat confusing. Rather than being triggered only in case of non-payment by the net GA debtor, standard form average guarantees have been interpreted as instruments of primary liability. As explained by Lord Diplock in *The Potoi Chau*:[44]

> The letters of guarantee given by the various insurers were not in identical terms. . . . Although the expression "we hereby guarantee" appears in each of the forms the verb "guarantee" is used loosely, as meaning "agree" or "undertake" and not in its strict legal sense of agreeing to answer for the debt, default or miscarriage of another. By each of the forms of letters of guarantee the insurers assume a primary liability to pay a sum of money on the happening of a defined event.

---

of termination of the common maritime adventure". In the CMI General Average Guarantee and General Average Bond, it is provided that "any period of prescription/limitation . . . shall commence to run from the date upon which the general average adjustment is issued, *unless otherwise provided in the applicable York-Antwerp Rules*" [emphasis supplied].

42 Even if an average bond is not required, it may still be necessary for the cargo owner to put up separate security to salvors, as remarked in the *CMI Guidelines relating to General Average* (2nd Edn), p 13.

43 *Lowndes & Rudolf* (15th Edn, 2018), para 30.60. For rules on the treatment of cash deposits, see r. XXII of the York Antwerp Rules 1994 and successive editions.

44 *Castle Insurance Co v Hong Kong Shipping Co (The Potoi Chau)* [1984] 1 AC 226, 241–242.

Notwithstanding that explanation, the status of the average guarantee has occasionally been the subject of some confusion. For instance, in *The Lehmann Timber* at first instance, Popplewell J conjectured, as reasons why an average bond should be required, that the

> legal analysis might be that the guarantee is to be construed as a secondary liability guaranteeing only such liability as was undertaken under a GA bond by the consignees; or it might be that the circumstances indicated that the provision of a GA bond was a condition precedent to liability under the guarantee.[45]

In the Court of Appeal, however, Rix LJ distanced himself from those remarks, albeit perhaps not quite as affirmatively as one might like. Having explained why an average bond was required (see the quotation set out earlier), he continued:[46]

> I say that on the assumption, which I am prepared to make in light of *The Potoi Chau*, that the insurer's guarantee may well have been sufficient security on its own without the presence of any liability on the part of the consignee, whether derived from an average bond or from the bills of lading. I am willing to make that assumption despite the arbitrators' and the judge's views that the guarantee was conditional on the consignee's liability, and I am prepared to assume that those views were mistaken.

In view of those comments, it seems likely that an average guarantee will impose a primary liability on the insurer. But it will be apparent from Rix LJ's choice of words why one might, at least out of precaution,[47] commence proceedings both under an average bond and an average guarantee. Ideally, the shipping community would embrace the BIMCO Average Bond Clause 2018 which puts the issue beyond all doubt by providing that the furnishing of an average bond is unnecessary on presentation of a bill of lading, provided an average guarantee or deposit is supplied.[48]

The preceding observations have served to show that an average guarantee is probably a distinct contract in its own right. Next, it is necessary to enquire into the nature of the obligation that is undertaken by the insurer. In this regard, the principal obligation in the CMI-approved general average guarantee is in similar terms to the bond. In both cases, the giver of the security promises to pay "any contribution to

---

45 *Metall Market OOO v Vitorio Shipping Co Ltd (The Lehmann Timber)* [2012] EWHC 844 (Comm); [2012] 2 All ER (Comm) 577 at [30]. See also *Navalmar UK Ltd v Ergo Versicherung AG (The BSLE Sunrise)* [2019] EWHC 2860 (Comm); [2020] 1 Lloyd's Rep. 355, in which HHJ Pelling QC stated at [5]: "I infer that the second defendant's Average Guarantee was issued by way of security for Iteco France's liabilities under its Average Bond". It does not, however, seem from the judgment that the Court of Appeal's decision in *The Lehmann Timber* was referred to him.

46 *Metall Market OOO v Vitorio Shipping Co Ltd (The Lehmann Timber)* [2013] EWCA Civ 650; [2015] QB 760 at [39].

47 Maintaining proceedings under both the average bond and average guarantee might nevertheless prove so impractical as to make this course not worthwhile. Given the difficulty and delay that can be involved in serving a claim on the giver of a boner in e.g. China, one might simply get the proceedings under the guarantee underway and see whether any point is taken about non-service upon the giver of the bond.

48 As noted in *Lowndes & Rudolf* (15th Edn, 2018), para 30.61, BIMCO's Documentary Committee has drafted a recommended wording for insertion into the contract of carriage with the intention of making the collection of an average bond unnecessary in all cases. The wording was drawn up in consultation with the Association of Average Adjusters, but it has yet to come into wide use. Whether or not an average bond will be required will usually be made clear in the declaration of general average.

General Average and/or Salvage and/or Special Charges which may hereafter be ascertained to be properly and legally due in respect of the Secured Property".

Whilst that formula might appear straightforward, it conceals a number of points of potential complexity.

First, as already alluded to, the requirement to pay whatever is general average is "properly and legally due" will usually prompt an examination of the rights and liabilities arising under the respective contract. But the question might arise, which contract? For instance, in the case of a container ship casualty, there will usually be a multiplicity of contracts. The registered owner will typically let the vessel on time charter to a liner operator. The liner operator will then issue charterers' bills of lading, containing general average provisions. Sometimes, the charterers' bills of lading will be issued to freight forwarders, who may issue their own house bills of lading covering carriage by sea and by land.

On such occasions, the practice of average adjusters is to understand the principal obligation in the average bonds and guarantees as referring to the requirements under the charterers' bills of lading. But in doing so, one has to ignore the fact that the contribution in general average is not properly and legally due *to the shipowner* who is taking the guarantee, but instead to the charterer. In defence of this approach, it is not stated in the CMI-approved average bonds and guarantees *to whom* the general average must be due; the promise is to pay whatever general average is due *in respect of* the goods.

Secondly, what is the proper analysis where the liability does not, for whatever reason, arise under contract? In the course of discerning whatever GA is legally due, it may in those circumstances be necessary to apply the conflicts of law rules in Rome I or Rome II Regulation, whose operation, in the context of general average claims, is difficult to predict.[49]

VI Under Bridging Security

Bridging security is frequently but not invariably used in cases of container ship casualties with a view towards keeping the containers moving. Rather than the shipowner exercising its possessory lien over the containerised goods unless and until reasonable security is provided, the liner operator will provide the shipowner with an interim agreement. Whilst the nature of these agreements vary, often they will permit the liner operator to transship and forward cargoes aboard other vessels without average security having first been furnished. In case average security is not ultimately supplied at the respective ports of destination, the liner operator may agree itself to pay whatever general average is ascertained to be properly and legally due.

Only one such agreement has so far come before the courts. In *The Maersk Neuchatel*,[50] it was held that, upon the true construction of the agreement, the liner operator was obliged to pay whatever sum was ascertained to be due and owing,

49 See supra note 19.

50 *St Maximus Shipping Co Ltd v AP Moller-Maersk A/S (The Maersk Neuchatel)* [2014] EWHC 1643 (Comm); [2014] 2 Lloyd's Rep. 377.

without any right of challenge. This was because the obligation to pay general average had not been qualified by the usual qualification regarding what was "legally and properly" due.

VII Unjust Enrichment?

Having detailed five jurisdictional "routes" for the pursuit of general average claims, could there yet be a sixth? Some commentators have observed that an explanation of general average may lie in the law of unjust enrichment.[51] Suffice it to say that there is not yet any reported case in which the principles of unjust enrichment have been directly transposed to a general average situation. In general terms, however, the chances of applying such principles without any recourse to the law and practice of general average are likely to be slim, given the latter's distinct development.

VIII Conclusion

General average is a field in which old principles butt into new modes of transport, with little intermediation in the form of recent case law. Unfortunately, the dearth of case law only adds to the mystique with which the practice and principles of general average adjustment are shrouded. It is hoped that this inspection of the battery of artillery that is available to the net GA creditor will be of assistance to the prospective general average litigator.

51 *Goff and Jones' Law of Unjust Enrichment* (10th Edn, 2022), para 18–37; F.D. Rose, "General Average as Restitution" (1997) 113 LQR 569.

CHAPTER 10

The 2005 Choice of Court Convention – Accomplishments and Perspectives

*Marta Pertegás Sender**

I Introduction

In this chapter, I intend to present the status of the 2005 Choice of Court Convention as at early 2024. More precisely, I shall examine its relevance for current international commercial disputes, both from the perspective of continental Europe and the United Kingdom.

The chapter is divided into three parts. The first describes the applicability requirements of the 2005 Convention and stresses its limited significance for international shipping disputes. The chapter then turns to the Convention's accomplishments so far by reviewing its operation in practice. By reference to past or pending cross-border litigation in different jurisdictions, the significance of the Convention's application for the outcome of the underlying disputes is made clear. In the third and last part, I try to assess the Convention's perspectives in the current post-Brexit era. While international litigation in England and Wales is different without the civil justice instruments that apply on the Continent (also referred to as the "Brussels regime"), some points of convergence remain, and this Convention is one of them. The 2005 Choice of Court Convention ensures uniform rules on forum selection clauses on both sides of the Channel. On a broader perspective, the incremental benefits the Convention may produce will depend on its ability to attract a higher number of Contracting States in the years to come.[1]

II The Scope of Application of the 2005 Choice of Court Convention

Compared to the overall jurisdictional regime applicable in a given EU Member State or in England and Wales, the 2005 Choice of Court Convention fulfils a limited, yet essential goal: it affirms party autonomy with regard to forum selection in international commercial transactions.

* **Full Professor, Maastricht University (The Netherlands) and University of Antwerp (Belgium); Visiting Professor, University of Johannesburg (South Africa); and Adjunct Professor, IE University (Spain).** I am thankful to student assistant José Duron Julià (Maastricht University) for his diligent research assistance.

1 On 15 August 2024, the Convention was applicable in 35 Contracting States. On its mid-term prospects, see e.g. M. Pertegás & L.E. Teitz, "Prospects for the Convention of 30 June 2005 on Choice of Court Agreements", in Permanent Bureau (ed.) *A Commitment to Private International Law. Essays in Honour of Hans van Loon*, Intersentia (Antwerp), 2013, 465–476.

DOI: 10.4324/9781032726243-12

The 2005 Convention applies to any *exclusive choice of court agreement*, in which the designated court is located *in a Contracting State*. Furthermore, the underlying agreement must refer to *civil and commercial matters*, and the agreement must have been concluded after the Convention's entry into force.

Let us examine these applicability requirements in reverse order.

A Temporal Requirement

The Hague Convention applies to choice of court agreements concluded on, or after, 1 October 2015. However, views diverge about the date of entry into force of the Convention for the UK.

One view is that the Convention has remained in force since it entered into force to date. This view takes into consideration that the UK was an EU Member State when the EU approved the Convention.[2] As a result, the UK was bound by this approval from the date of entry into force (1 October 2015) until the end of the transition period further to Brexit (31 December 2020). After that date, the EU Council Decision that led to the Convention's application in EU Member States was no longer applicable in the UK and, as a result, the Convention would theoretically cease to apply there from 1 January 2021.

However, the UK had already expressed its intention to accede to the Convention in its own right and completed the ratification procedure in time to ensure that the Convention "continued" to apply on 1 January 2021 and beyond.

This view prevails in the UK.[3] Importantly, the status table of the Convention on the HCCH website lists 1 October 2015 as the date of entry into force of the Convention for the UK.

Conversely, the Convention's Depositary, the Ministry of Foreign Affairs of The Netherlands, lists 1 January 2021 as the date of entry into force for the UK.[4] In litigation pending before EU courts, the prevailing view is indeed that the UK is only bound by the Convention as from 1 January 2021 – i.e. the date that the ratification of the Convention became effective. For instance, the President of the Amsterdam Court has decided that the Convention was not applicable to a case that involved a choice of court agreement concluded on 21 August 2018, where the summary proceedings

2 See 2014/887/EU: Council Decision of 4 December 2014 on the approval, on behalf of the European Union, of the Hague Convention of 30 June 2005 on Choice of Court Agreements [2014] OJ L353/5

3 J. Harris, "Civil Jurisdiction and Judgments in England and Wales after Brexit" (4th IBA Litigation Committee Conference on Private International Law, 15 September 2023) slide 8 https://www.ibanet.org/medias/IBA-Milan-15-September-2023-Jonathan-Harris.pdf?context=bWFzdGVyfENvbmZlcmmZlcmVuY2UtbWF0ZXJpYWxzfDQ5NjQ0MnxhcHBsaWNhdGlvbi9wZGZ8YURjMUwyZzNOUzg1TURReE5qTXdNRE0xT1RrNEwwbENNRUzBnVFdsc1lXNHRJREUxSUZObGNIUmxiV0psY2lBeU1ESXpMU0JLYjI1aGRHaGhiaUJJWVhKeWFYTXVjR1JtfDNhNWNjY2U3YTIxMzE3NGNkODgyZjQyYzk5YTEzN2RkMzNkOTVjNDJhMjZkYjIyMzUzZGYxNjU2OTkzZDVmNjg&attachment=true, accessed 27 December 2023.

4 See https://verdragenbank.overheid.nl/nl/Verdrag/Details/011343?expand-table=partijtabel, accessed 12 January 2024.

(*kort geding*) were filed in Amsterdam despite a forum selection clause in favour of the courts of England and Wales.[5]

The practical relevance of this matter should not be underestimated. If this latter view is right, courts in EU Member States will not be inclined to apply the obligation (set out in Article 8 of the Convention) to recognise and enforce a judgment from an English court designated in an exclusive choice of court agreement concluded between 2015 and 2021.

B Substantive Requirements

The Choice of Court Convention applies to *international* cases relating to *civil and commercial matters*.

i International Cases

The Convention only applies to *international* cases. Elaborating on the point of internationalism, Article 1 makes a distinction between jurisdiction, and recognition and enforcement. For the former, a case cannot be qualified as international if (1) the parties are resident in the same Contracting State and (2) the relationship of the parties and all the relevant elements of the dispute are connected only with that state. However, parties can still choose a court in a Contracting State for the purposes of the Hague Convention being applied even if neither is domiciled in such a state. For instance, if a contract between a Chinese seller and a US buyer contains a choice of court clause in favour of "the courts of England and Wales, to the exclusion of all other courts", the Convention applies. Similarly, the international requirement is met, and the Convention applies, in a mainly domestic situation whereby parties have agreed upon a choice of court jurisdiction in favour of a foreign court (of a Contracting State) provided there is a relevant element to the dispute located elsewhere.[6]

For issues of recognition and enforcement, the Convention is only applicable in cases between courts in Contracting States (i.e. where both the court of origin and the requested court are in Contracting States, for instance the enforcement of an English order in Singapore).

ii Civil and Commercial Cases

The term "civil and commercial matters" is habitual in other HCCH instruments, such as the Evidence or Service Conventions. However, the applicability to such cases of the 2005 Choice of Court Convention is limited by a long list of excluded matters set out in Article 2. Indeed, the 16 sub-paragraphs of this article on "excluded matters" make clear that there are considerable limitations to the Convention's application to civil and commercial disputes.

5 See ECLI:NL:RBAMS:2022:1453 [2022] (Rechtbank (Court of First Instance), Amsterdam).

6 The CJEU has rendered a decision on this same issue (i.e. is the case international when the only foreign element is a choice of court agreement in favour of a foreign court?) in the context of the Brussels I Regulation: see CJEU, 8 February 2024, case *Inkreal sro v Dúha Reality sro* (Case C-566/22) ECLI:EU:C:2024:123.

To start with, the Convention is not applicable to consumer contracts and contracts of employment.

In addition, the Convention enumerates a number of excluded matters for varying reasons. In some cases, there are more specific international agreements for certain areas of maritime law, although they may not contain specific provisions on choice of court agreements. In other cases, the Convention drafters sought alignment with other international instruments (e.g. with the Brussels I Regulation on the tenancies of immovable property). Very importantly, no agreement could be reached during the negotiations on a number of matters such as most intellectual property disputes. The combined effect of these three factors is a rather heterogeneous list of excluded matters, ranging from international family disputes to litigation related to liability from nuclear damage.

For those active in the international shipping legal sector, the most important subject matter exclusions are disputes relating to the carriage of passengers and goods; and disputes relating to marine pollution, limitation of liability for maritime claims, general average, and emergency towage and salvage. Where such matters excluded from the Convention are brought to courts in England and Wales, jurisdiction will be ruled by the common law.

iii Selected Court in a Contracting State

The third condition for the Convention to apply is based on Article 3 of the 2005 Convention. The chosen court has to be "the court of one Contracting State or one or more specific courts of one Contracting State to the exclusion of the jurisdiction of any other courts". In other words, the Convention is only relevant if the chosen court is in a Contracting State.

As London remains one of the preferred dispute resolution hubs in the world, the 2005 Choice of Court Convention is a helpful tool for the recognition and enforcement of English judgments in other Contracting States (e.g., the European Union, including Denmark; Mexico, Montenegro, Ukraine, and Singapore). The more Contracting States join the Convention, the more uniform standards develop with regard to the validity and effects of choice of court clauses.

iv An Exclusive Choice of Court Agreement

The last applicability requirement relates to the exclusive formulation of the forum selection clause. It must designate a court or courts in a Contracting State, to the exclusion of all other courts. The exclusivity requirement is meant to avoid problems associated with parallel proceedings (*lis pendens*), which as such are not addressed by the Convention.

The Convention contains a rebuttable presumption of exclusivity. In other words, unless expressly otherwise stipulated by the parties, a choice of court clause is presumed to be exclusive under the Convention.

The position as regards asymmetrical jurisdiction clauses is difficult to assess in practice. Given that they allow one of the parties to file proceedings elsewhere than in the chosen court, Dutch courts seem to take the view that the exclusivity requirement is not met. For instance, an Amsterdam court considered that the following clause was non-exclusive, as it was limiting the forum shopping options of the Guarantor but not the Beneficiary: "14.2 For the exclusive benefit of the Beneficiary and Juno Holdings, the Guarantor irrevocably agrees that the courts of England are to have exclusive jurisdiction to settle any dispute".[7] Conversely, the same Amsterdam court ruled that the following clause was exclusive, despite the literal meaning of the formulation used in the contract:

> 25.2 The Parties submit to the non-exclusive jurisdiction of the courts of England and Wales as regards any claim, dispute or matter arising out of or relating to this Agreement or any of the documents to be executed pursuant to this Agreement, with the potential exception of claims or disputes regarding the Property which due to its locality may fall to be adjudicated on by courts within which the Property is situated.

As England was the law of the chosen court, the Amsterdam court relied on an expert opinion of an English QC. According to this legal opinion, this clause is to be read as an exclusive clause.[8]

III The Operation of the Convention: Recent Applications

The operation of the Convention is still a work in progress, as the case law develops in the States bound by the Convention and ratification procedures continue in other States. The Permanent Bureau of the HCCH keeps track of case law relating to the Convention, and all those working with the Convention should be invited to share recent developments in their respective jurisdictions with the Permanent Bureau.[9]

In a nutshell, the application of the Convention leads to three main legal effects. First, the chosen court must hear the case. The case law makes clear that, when applying the Convention, the chosen court no longer possesses a discretion to consider whether a stay of proceedings should be ordered on the basis of a choice of court clause.[10] On the other hand, the chosen court must also consider, as set out by Article 5(1), whether the agreement is null and void under the law of the law of the chosen state. Hence, the designated court must rely on its domestic law, choice of law rules included, to assess the material validity of the parties' agreement. If the clause is valid, the chosen court is bound to accept jurisdiction: it has no discretion to stay the proceedings or set them aside on jurisdictional or *forum non conveniens* grounds.

Conversely, a non-chosen court will in principle dismiss the case, unless one of the rather exceptional situations listed in Article 6 applies. It remains to be seen whether the application of Article 6 will lead to the desired effects. In line with Article 5(1), Article 6(a) also states that the non-chosen court shall assess whether the agreement is null and void under the law of the state of the court seised. This solution cannot give rise to situations where one of the parties intentionally institutes proceedings in a forum whose law may be less inclined to consider a jurisdiction agreement valid, unlike a conflict rule applying the law of the court seised. However, the law of the court seised

7 ECLI:NL:RBAMS:2022:7521 [2022] (Rechtbank (Court of First Instance) Amsterdam).

8 ECLI:NL:RBAMS:2022:1453[2022] (Rechtbank (Court of First Instance) Amsterdam.

9 See www.hcch.net/en/instruments/specialised-sections/choice-of-court/case-law-coca. Ideally, the Permanent Bureau should seek external assistance to develop a database with the relevant case law and summaries in at least one of the HCCH's official languages.

10 See the Singapore decision in *6DM (S) Pte Ltd v AE Brands Korea Ltd and others* [2021] SGHC 257.

is still to play a residual role in the assessment of two other exceptions: in order to assess whether there is a lack of capacity by the party who concluded the agreement and in order to assess whether the agreement "would lead to a manifest injustice or would be manifestly contrary to the public policy of the state of the court seised". Most importantly, all exceptions are to be interpreted restrictively.

The third main legal effect of the Convention relates to the recognition and enforcement of judgments rendered by the chosen court. As set out in Article 8, the judgment rendered by the chosen court circulates under the Convention. For instance, a Singapore court granted an application against a Singapore company seeking the recognition and enforcement of a summary judgment made by the English High Court with reference to the 2005 Hague Convention.[11] In the same vein, the Rotterdam Court applied the Convention to the recognition and enforcement in The Netherlands of an order rendered by the London Commercial Court on 9 May 2022.[12] Interestingly, Article 8 does not cover the recognition and enforcement of judgments rendered by a non-chosen court in breach of a jurisdiction clause. This issue falls outside the scope of the Convention and will therefore be governed by the otherwise applicable domestic rules. At common law, there is a defence or ground for refusal under s 32 of the Civil Jurisdiction and Judgments Act 1982:

> a judgment given by a court of an overseas country in any proceedings shall not be recognized or enforced in the United Kingdom if the bringing of those proceedings was contrary to an agreement under which the dispute in question was to be settled otherwise than by proceedings in the courts of that country.

Conversely, no corresponding ground for refusal exists in the Brussels I Regulation.

In addition to these three main legal effects under the Convention, a study of the first applications on the Convention yields at least five points of attention.

First, there is the principle of severability, set out in Article 3(d) of the Convention, according to which the validity of the choice of court clause must be assessed separately from the rest of the contract. The nullity of the underlying contract does not automatically affect the clause's validity. However, there may be validity issues raised about the specific clause (e.g. in case of a forged contract or a contract induced by misrepresentation) that specifically compromise the forum selection clause.

Secondly, the reach of the choice of court agreement beyond the nominal parties to the contract is always a source of contention. I may refer to three conjoined joined cases that led to a judgment by the CJEU where this question was determined in the context of Article 25 of the Brussels I Regulation. The main proceedings concern an insurance company subrogated to the rights of the insured in a claim for damages brought against a maritime transport operator (Maersk).[13] The insured party was the consignee of the goods that were transported. In the corresponding contract of carriage, there was a bill of lading with a jurisdiction clause on the document's reverse. The CJEU was asked to determine whether, under Article 25 of the Brussels I

11 See *Ermgassen & Co Ltd v Sixcap Financials Pte Ltd* [2018] SGHCR 8.

12 ECLI:NL:RBROT:2023:9354 [2023] (Rechtbank (Court of First Instance) Rotterdam.

13 See CJEU, 25 April 2024, *Maersk A/S v Allianz Seguros y Reaseguros, SA*, cases C-345/22 to 347/22, ECLI:EU:C:2024:349.

Regulation, this jurisdiction clause impacts the determination of jurisdiction in the main proceedings. While the *Maersk* case refers to insurance and carriage of goods and, as such, would be excluded from the 2005 Convention's substantive scope of application, I believe that a CJEU ruling on the question of third-party effect can be influential for cases falling under the Convention relating to third-party effects of choice of court agreements. Indeed, the CJEU distinguishes the question of third-party effectiveness of a choice of court agreement from the agreement's validity.

A third recurrent issue relates to the reference in the requirement set out in Article 3(a) of the Convention, according to which the choice of court clause shall be "in connection with a particular legal relationship". It is expected that courts in Contracting States will accept a broad interpretation whereby the choice of court clause encompasses both contractual and non-contractual claims.

Fourthly, the case law will have to consolidate how the formal requirements set out by Article 3(c), in particular in the context of digital communications. The clause must either be in writing, or documented "by any other means of communication which renders information accessible so as to be usable for subsequent reference". In *Ebury Partners Belgium SA/NV v Technical Touch BV*,[14] Jacobs J in the English Commercial Court referred to the conclusion of agreements by using online application forms that included a link to general conditions that most parties (including judges!) failed to read before agreeing to them by ticking a box. As he phrased it,

> in e-commerce, it is now commonplace for a person to agree to another person's terms and conditions by ticking the appropriate box when completing an on-line application form. Equally commonplace, at least speaking personally, is for a person to fail to do so and then to receive a reminder that the box must be ticked in order for the transaction to proceed.

The terms and conditions, including the jurisdiction clause, were considered valid under the Choice of Court Convention.[15]

Finally, and most importantly, the substantive requirements of the law of the chosen court apply. In the aforementioned *Ebury* judgment, English law determined such requirements given the formulation of the clause: "each party irrevocably agrees that the courts of England shall have exclusive jurisdiction to settle any dispute or claim arising out of or in connection with this Agreement or its subject matter or formation, interpretation, performance and/or termination (including non-contractual disputes or claims)" and the governing law clause in favour of "the laws of England and Wales".

IV The Convention Perspective

Litigation on choice of court agreements is often perceived as delaying procedural tactics. The 2005 Choice of Court Convention, which will reach its tenth year of application in 2025, is a helpful tool to prevent or at least discourage such tactics, by offering litigants a predictable and straightforward legal framework. A choice of court agreement in favour of a court in a Contracting State is a sound forum selection

14 [2022] EWHC 2927 (Comm); [2023] 1 Lloyd's Rep. 575.

15 See *Ebury Partners Belgium SA/NV v Technical Touch BV & Anor* [2022] EWHC 2927 (Comm); [2023] 1 Lloyd's Rep. 575 at [1], [131].

strategy, not only for cases related to Contracting States, but also for those involving parties in States where the Convention is set to be applicable soon (the United States, China, and other significant trade partners of the UK and the EU being among the Convention's signatory States).[16]

That said, the operation of the Choice of Court Convention is a "work in progress" as case law develops, and as the Convention's longevity and the number of States bound by it increase. Furthermore, the Convention does not operate in a vacuum: it is part of the procedural framework in each Contracting State, and its functioning partially relies on the procedural rules of the chosen jurisdiction.

The aforementioned case law analysis yields some interesting preliminary results. While the three main legal effects of the Convention's operation seem to be confirmed, some differences arise. For instance, a technical issue such as the date of entry into force of the Convention for the UK may give rise to unexpected hurdles – based on the domestic rules on recognition and enforcement of foreign judgments – for the enforcement of UK judgments in continental Europe. My view on this, as indicated earlier, is that the Convention should be seen as having applied in the UK since 1 October 2015 without interruption. However, the discussions during the 18th International Colloquium on Commercial Disputes and reported case law in the Netherlands made clear that the views are divided on this matter.

16 In 2023, the London High Court decided *Pantheon International Advisors Ltd v Co-Diagnostics, Inc* [2023] EWHC 1984 (KB), a case between an English and a Utah-based US company. The Convention was not applicable to the case because the United States, albeit a signatory, is not bound by the Convention yet. For a comprehensive study of the Convention's perspectives, see A. Mammadzada, *Enhancing Party Autonomy under the Hague Convention on Choice of Court Agreements 2005: Comparative Analysis with the 2012 EU Brussels Recast Regulation and 1958 New York Arbitration Convention*, PhD dissertation defended at the University of Southampton (on file with the author), chs 4 and 8.

CHAPTER 11

Navigating Parallel Proceedings

The Hague Judgments Convention and Non-exclusive (Asymmetrical) Jurisdiction Agreements

*Aygün Mammadzada**

I Introduction

In an increasingly interconnected global economy, businesses engage in cross-border transactions that often give rise to disputes requiring resolution through different means including litigation. However, navigating the complexities of international commercial litigation, particularly in terms of the recognition and enforcement of judgments across borders, has been a longstanding challenge. When disputes arise, obtaining a judgment in one jurisdiction may not suffice if enforcement is necessary in another jurisdiction. The process of recognition and enforcement of judgments across borders presents complex challenges, ranging from differences in legal systems to issues of sovereignty and enforcement mechanisms. Divergences in service of process, evidence rules, and limitation periods can hinder the enforcement process and create opportunities for strategic manoeuvring by parties seeking to put off enforcement.

The 2019 Hague Judgments Convention, or HJC, represents a significant milestone, aiming to enhance legal certainty and thereby facilitate cross-border trade and investment. It was adopted as the 41st instrument of the Hague Conference[1] and will have the effect of enhancing access to justice and promoting international co-operation and harmonisation. Indeed, the HJC is the only global convention providing free circulation of judgments in cross-border commercial dispute resolution. By addressing challenges associated with legal, jurisdictional, procedural, and practical complexities of the recognition and enforcement of judgments, it has become a game-changer in the landscape of international commercial dispute resolution. In short, the HCCH is right to greet the Convention as a means to increase certainty and predictability, promote the better management of transaction and litigation risks, and shorten timeframes for the cross-border recognition and enforcement of judgments.

The HJC is a complementary instrument to its sister instrument, the HCCCA, not only originating from the same project,[2] but also sharing the same objectives and ideals.

---

* **Member of the Institute of International Shipping and Trade Law, Swansea University.**

1 Statute of the Hague Conference on Private International Law, art 1.

2 The original project was derived from the proposal of Edwin Williamson, who was the Legal Adviser at the US Department of State to the Secretary-General of The Hague Conference on Private International Law in May 1992, to negotiate a multilateral convention on the recognition and enforcement of judgments throughout the world, which brought up the United States' initiative. See Letter of May 5, 1992, from

DOI: 10.4324/9781032726243-13

It is however wider, for example in that it covers judgments given on the basis of non-exclusive jurisdiction agreements, which are excluded from the scope of the HCCCA unless there is a declaration made by a Contracting State.[3] Hence a judgment is eligible for recognition and enforcement if it was given by a court designated in an agreement concluded or documented in writing or by any other means of communication which renders information accessible so as to be usable for subsequent reference, other than an exclusive choice of court agreement.[4] By this provision, the HJC adds to party autonomy and ensures respect for their non-exclusive designations. This can only be a good thing. Non-exclusive jurisdiction agreements allow parties to select multiple fora for dispute resolution. Such agreements ensure flexibility in international commercial litigation and enable parties to bring their claims where it might be more convenient for obtaining favourable outcomes. However, such agreements might lead to further complex issues, for instance, if parties initiate parallel proceedings in multiple jurisdictions. This is an issue dealt with later.

The key difference between the HCCCA and HJC is that the HJC, while giving effect to final judgments decided on the basis of non-exclusive jurisdiction agreements, does not give such agreements any derogative effects. By contrast, the HCCCA states that a court of a Contracting State other than that of the chosen court shall suspend or dismiss proceedings to which an exclusive choice of court agreement applies.[5] The absence of any protection given to non-exclusive agreements brings a serious threat of parallel proceedings and inconsistent judgments, with the result that party autonomy and legal certainty principles are jeopardised. This risk is particularly elevated due to the diverse approaches to non-exclusive jurisdiction agreements in national laws.

II Non-exclusive Jurisdiction Agreements

Contracting parties often formulate exclusive jurisdiction agreements to resolve their disputes. Also, there is a strong tendency in both legal theory and practice towards presuming exclusivity of choice of court agreements.[6] Most legal systems uphold parties' expressed will for choice of court, and the principles applicable in this regard are extensively designed for maintaining a unique forum for the exclusion of any other court.[7] Yet, sophisticated and well-informed parties and their lawyers may also designate different forms of complex and multi-faceted dispute resolution agreements.

Edwin D. Williamson, Legal Adviser, US Department of State to Georges Droz, Secretary General, The Hague Conference on Private International Law (May 5, 1992). See R. Brand & P. Herrup, *The 2005 Hague Convention on Choice of Court Agreements: Commentary and Documents* (Cambridge University Press, 2008), 6; A. Schulz, "The Hague Convention of 30 June 2005 on Choice of Court Agreements" (2006) 2 Journal of Private International Law, 243, 244–246.

3 HCCCA, art 22.

4 HJC, art 5.1(m).

5 HCCCA, art 6.

6 Dicey, Morris & Collins on the Conflict of Laws (16th Edn, 2022), para 12–072; R. Fentiman, *International Commercial Litigation* (2nd Edn, OUP 2015), para 2.52. See too *Credit Suisse First Boston (Europe) Ltd v MLC (Bermuda) Ltd* [1999] 1 All ER (Comm) 237 and *Bank of New York Mellon v GV Films Ltd* [2009] EWHC 3315 (Comm); [2010] 1 Lloyd's Rep. 425.

7 M. Keyes & B. Marshall, "Jurisdiction agreements: exclusive, optional and asymmetrical" (2015) 11 Journal of Private International Law 345.

In fact, non-exclusive jurisdiction agreements are commonly used in international commercial contracts to allow parties to bring disputes before multiple courts. In other words, they create jurisdiction in a nominated forum but do not prevent a party from commencing proceedings elsewhere.

The Hartley/Dogauchi Report attached to the HCCCA[8] confirmed that "non-exclusive agreements are quite common".[9] According to Briggs, regardless of its type, " 'non-exclusive' defines solely a jurisdiction agreement that is not 'fully, bilaterally and immediately exclusive' ".[10] Parties might agree that Party A could bring proceedings before the English courts, whereas Party B could bring proceedings before the courts of any other State, or that Party A had to bring proceedings in the courts of England or Wales while Party B had to sue in the courts of France. They could also agree that proceedings under the contract could be brought before the English courts, but without excluding the jurisdiction of any other courts, thus allowing each party to bring proceedings before the courts of the State of their residence. Or they could simply agree that the French courts should have non-exclusive jurisdiction under their contract.

National laws and practices demonstrate different approaches to the nature and validity of jurisdiction agreements. For instance, the Australian courts showed an inclination towards presuming the exclusivity of jurisdiction agreements.[11] Canadian courts by contrast held that "when both parties articulate their commitment to a forum, absent the express intention to render that forum one of exclusive jurisdiction, such a clause will be interpreted as necessarily conferring concurrent (i.e. non-exclusive) jurisdiction".[12] Likewise, courts in the United States are not usually inclined to presume the exclusivity of choice of court agreements, unless an agreement designating one forum contains specific language to clearly exclude jurisdiction elsewhere. For instance, where the clause was read as "jurisdiction for all and any disputes arising out of or in connection with this agreement is Munich. All and any disputes arising out of or in connection with this agreement are subject to the laws of the Federal Republic of Germany", the court concluded that "is Munich" did not sufficiently imply "is only Munich". Moreover, it was stated that "where venue is specified (in a forum selection clause) with mandatory or obligatory language, the clause will be enforced; where only jurisdiction is specified (in a forum selection clause), the clause will generally not be enforced unless there is some further language indicating the parties' intent to make the venue exclusive".[13]

---

8 Many Hague Convention instruments have semi-authoritative reports from legal experts attached to them. For the HJC the report was written by F. Garcimartín and G. Saumier; that for the HCCCA was composed by T. Hartley and M. Dogauchi. The latter can be found at https://assets.hcch.net/docs/0de60e2f-e002-408e-98a7-5638e1ebac65.pdf (as at May 2024).

9 Hartley/Dogauchi Report, para 843.

10 A. Briggs, *Civil Jurisdiction and Judgments* (7th Edn, Informa Law from Routledge, 2021), para 4.19.

11 V. Nanda, "The Landmark 2005 Convention on Choice of Court Agreements" (2007) 42 Texas International Law Journal 773, 779.

12 See *Old North State Brewing Company Inc v Newland Services Inc* [1999] 4 WWR 573 at [36]; *BC Rail Partnership v Standard Car Truck Co* [2003] BCCA 597; (2003) 20 BCLR (4th) 1; and *B.A. Blacktop Ltd v Gencor Industries Inc* [2008] BCSC 231.

13 *K&V Scientific Co., Inc. v BMW*, 314 F.3d 494, 499 (2002) (10th Circuit); R. Brand & P. Herrup, *The 2005 Hague Convention on Choice of Court Agreements: Commentary and Documents* (Cambridge University

The English courts have constantly demonstrated their inclination to give effect to parties' autonomy and intention of the rational businessmen and enforced asymmetrical jurisdiction clauses. In practice, the mandatory jurisdiction of the English court was upheld regardless of the non-exclusive nature of the jurisdiction agreement.[14]

Besides national variations, there is equally no established academic consensus on these agreements. In this vein, it was claimed that what matters is individual promises in an agreement, and as long as parties have agreed on their promises, the nature of a clause should not prevent its enforcement.[15] Others remark that choice of court agreements should be enforced as they are contractual, and contracts should be enforced.[16] In this regard, non-exclusive asymmetrical jurisdiction agreements have brought additional controversies in both academia and practice. While including such clauses in their commercial contracts, parties should carefully consider the risk of varying interpretations and approaches.

III Asymmetrical Jurisdiction Agreements

As part of non-exclusive designations, asymmetrical clauses, also known as one-sided jurisdiction agreements, are frequently used in international commerce and especially financial relations. This designation determines an exclusive choice for only one party and the other party is entitled to seise different courts – i.e. a borrower can sue in a particular court while a lender or bank may sue anywhere.[17] Accordingly, a claimant has the flexibility to commence proceedings wherever a defendant's assets are and prevent difficulties regarding freezing of assets without initiating substantive proceedings.[18] Despite the words "non-exclusive" or "asymmetrical" not always being found as such in a jurisdiction agreement, it may well be clear from the language and structure of an agreement that parties intended to specify exclusivity in favour of only one party.[19] This asymmetry in the allocation of jurisdictional rights and obligations between the parties has presented complexities in practice and unique challenges in their legal regulation.

National courts have shown different approaches to enforcing asymmetrical jurisdiction agreements, having regard to their fairness and reasonableness. While some jurisdictions have upheld asymmetrical jurisdiction agreements as valid and

Press, 2008), 42. See also L. Silberman, "The Impact of Jurisdictional Rules and Recognition Practice on International Business Transactions: The U.S. Regime" (2004) 26 Houston Journal of International Law 327, 348, 351; Hartley/Dogauchi Report, para 39.

14 *Mauritius Commercial Bank Ltd. v Hestia Holdings Ltd. & Sujana Universal Industries Ltd* [2013] EWHC 1328; [2013] 2 Lloyd's Rep. 121. See also *Perform Content Services Ltd v Ness Global Services Ltd* [2021] EWCA Civ 981; [2021] 1 WLR 4146.

15 For more on the related discussions see L. Merrett, "The future enforcement of asymmetric jurisdiction agreements" (2018) 67 ICLQ 37.

16 A. Briggs, *Agreements on Jurisdiction and Choice of Law* (OUP, 2008), 531–532.

17 For the related discussions see the Hartley/Dogauchi Report, para 249.

18 R. Fentiman, *International Commercial Litigation* (2nd Edn, OUP, 2015), 44.

19 Ibid. 62.

enforceable, others have scrutinised their terms and conditions more rigidly, considering them unconscionable or contrary to public policy.

For instance, in 2012, the French Supreme Court decided that asymmetrical jurisdiction clauses were void.[20] The case was concerned with a jurisdiction clause between a Spanish client and a Luxembourg bank. According to the asymmetrical jurisdiction agreement, the Luxembourgish courts had exclusive jurisdiction for the client, yet, the bank could bring the proceedings anywhere. The court stated that the jurisdiction agreement was inequitable, and unenforceable because it embodied a "potestative condition";[21] that is a condition for which satisfaction was completely within the power of one party, with no mutuality of obligation.[22] The same reasoning brought the invalidity of an asymmetrical jurisdiction agreement between a French company and a Swiss bank in another decision of the French Supreme Court in the *Crédit Suisse* ruling.[23] In contrast, having reconsidered the same question in 2015, the French Supreme Court concluded that as long as asymmetrical jurisdiction clauses complied with the foreseeability requirement, they were valid under French law and each party could identify the competent jurisdictions before commencing the proceedings.[24] Indeed, such a contrasting line of cases led the French court to refer several questions about the validity of asymmetrical jurisdiction agreements and substantive validity rule to the CJEU.[25]

Among other legal domains, Brexit has had various implications for asymmetrical jurisdiction agreements and enforcement of resulting judgments. Further, as the European legal framework ceased to apply to the UK post-Brexit, the Hague Conventions and in particular, the HJC have gained momentum in the reshaped legal landscape. Indeed, the HJC is the only global instrument giving effect to judgments resulting from non-exclusive jurisdiction agreements. Yet, challenges might arise due to the absence of any uniform provision applicable to these agreements.

The following discussion sheds light on the way the English courts dealt with asymmetrical jurisdiction agreements involving EU Member States before the UK's withdrawal from the Union and how the approach might differ in the changed judicial realm in light of the HJC.

---

20 *La Société Banque Privée Edmond de Rothschild Europe v Mme X* (Cass Civ 1,11–26.022), 26 September 2012.

21 Ibid.

22 According to the then article 1170 of the French Civil Code, "A potestative condition is one which makes the execution of the agreement depend upon an event that one or the other of the contracting parties has the power to bring about or to prevent". Further, Article 1174 provided: "Any obligation is null when it has been contracted subject to a potestative condition on the part of the party who binds himself". Since the changes in the French law of contract of 2016 the relevant provision has been contained in art 1304–2: "An obligation is void if contracted subject to a condition the fulfilment of which is dependent solely on the will of the obligor. This ground of ineffectiveness cannot be relied on when the obligation has been performed in the knowledge of the facts".

23 Cass., civ. 1, 25 March 2015, No. 13–27.264.

24 For more on the discussion of these cases see Mary Keyes, *Jurisdiction in International Litigation* (Federation Press, 2005).

25 See Cass civ 1, 13 April 2023, 22–12.965. See also 22/85 *Rudolf Anterist v Crédit lyonnais* [1986] ECR 1951; [1987] 1 CMLR 333, where the CJEU held in the context of Article 17 of the 1968 Brussels Jurisdiction Convention that jurisdiction clauses conferring a benefit on one party were valid.

IV Before HJC

The English courts have demonstrated an inclination towards the extensive interpretation of exclusive jurisdiction agreements and reasserted a strong presumption of exclusivity. This disposition has also been demonstrated while validating asymmetrical jurisdiction agreements. Before Brexit, English courts typically upheld these agreements under the previously applicable Brussels Recast Regulation (BRR) for the objective of ensuring parties' autonomy.

In *Etihad Airways PJSC v Flother*,[26] the Commercial Court decided that an asymmetrical jurisdiction agreement was exclusive for the purposes of the BRR. It was underlined that the issues should be determined not by applying labels but by identifying the parties' agreement.[27] This judgment affirmed the emphasis that has traditionally been placed on party autonomy, wide liberty, and flexibility that have been upheld in English law and practice. The Court reiterated its conclusion by emphasising the significance of the academic discussions. As stated by Fentiman, the agreement "is exclusive against a counterparty".[28] Similarly, Merrett argues that asymmetrical agreements should not be considered "as a whole", but each obligation could be considered separately.[29]

In similar decisions, the courts highlighted the significance of the contractual bargain between the parties while enforcing asymmetrical jurisdiction agreements. In *Mauritius Commercial Bank Ltd v Hestia Holdings Ltd*,[30] the Commercial Court enforced an asymmetrical jurisdiction clause in a loan agreement which gave exclusive jurisdiction to the English courts on the side of a debtor but did not prevent the lender from bringing proceedings in any other courts. In *Commerzbank AG v Liquimar Tankers Management Inc*,[31] the High Court also concluded that an asymmetric jurisdiction clause could not be treated as non-exclusive under BRR. Cranston J asserted that where a clause conferred exclusive jurisdiction on the courts of a Member State when one party sued, the clause would still be exclusive for the purposes of Article 31(2). That reasoning was in line with a related CJEU judgment, in which the Court asserted that the reciprocal clause was exclusive in effect even though which court had exclusive jurisdiction turned on which party sued.[32]

The case law also highlighted the EU's accession to the HCCCA and building coherence with the Brussels regime. Indeed, as it was held before Brexit, the English

---

26 [2019] EWHC 3107 (Comm); [2020] QB 793.

27 The court related this reasoning to the aims of the BRR. Recital 19 ensured party autonomy, and Recital 22 stated that there needed to be an exception to the general *lis pendens* rule to enhance the effectiveness of exclusive jurisdiction agreements and to avoid abusive tactics: see at [183]. The judge also referred to similar cases where art 31(2) had been applied to asymmetrical jurisdiction agreements, such as *Codere SA v Perella Weinberg Partners and others*, Spanish Judgment of 10 February 2016; *Perella Weinberg Partners UK LLP & Anor v Codere SA* [2016] EWHC 1182 (Comm); and *Commerzbank Aktiengesellschaft v Liquimar Tankers Management Inc* [2017] EWHC 161 (Comm); [2017] 1 WLR 3497.

28 R. Fentiman in U. Magnus & P. Mankowski (eds), *European Commentaries on Private International Law* (Sellier, 2015), vol 1, 751–753.

29 L. Merrett, "The future enforcement of asymmetric jurisdiction agreements" (2018) 67 ICLQ 37.

30 [2013] EWHC 1328 (Comm); [2013] 2 Lloyd's Rep. 121.

31 [2017] EWHC 161 (Comm); [2017] 1 WLR 3497.

32 See *Firma Meeth v Glacetal Sarl* [1979] CMLR 520 (decided in the context of Article 17 of the 1968 Brussels Jurisdiction Convention).

court based its decision on the EU law and referred to the HCCCA as part of it.[33] Furthermore, the court referred to the Hartley/Dogauchi Report, which proposed that there should be express wordings for a precise exclusion that "Such an agreement must be exclusive irrespective of the party bringing the proceedings", but it was not done.[34] Yet, it was explicitly noted that the HCCCA was not relevant in that scenario since it excluded all non-exclusive types of agreements.[35]

On the other hand, having regard to the Hartley/Dogauchi Report, Henderson LJ in the Court of Appeal in *Etihad*, contrary to the first instance decision, inferred that the HCCCA might not apply to asymmetrical jurisdiction clauses.[36] Accordingly,

> It was agreed by the Diplomatic Session that, to be covered by the Convention, the agreement must be exclusive irrespective of the party bringing the proceedings. So, agreements of the kind referred to in the previous paragraph (i.e. asymmetric agreements) are not exclusive choice of court agreements for the Convention.[37]

The case law shows that the following factors have influenced English courts: (1) the intense partisanship of the party autonomy principle; (2) the deficiency as described earlier of the international regulation of asymmetrical (non-exclusive) jurisdiction agreements; and (3) the need for uniform interpretation of the law (the Brussels regime and HCCCA). Considering the statements of the judges are *obiter*, and there has not yet been any specific ruling on the applicability of the HCCCA to asymmetrical jurisdiction agreements, interpretative challenges might still be possible. On the other side of the coin, contrary to the recent past, the international legal domain now contains the HJC which formalises the firm distinction between exclusive and non-exclusive jurisdiction agreements and establishes a provision on the recognition and enforcement of final decisions given following asymmetrical jurisdiction agreements. Yet, the prospects of uniformity in the treatment of these designations are likely to be reduced by the unique formulation of the respective provisions of the HJC and potential applications of the national rules. Possible application of the Brussels rules

---

33 See *Commerzbank AG v Liquimar Tankers Management Inc* [2017] EWHC 161 (Comm); [2017] 1 WLR 3497 at [38].

34 *Commerzbank AG v Liquimar Tankers Management Inc* [2017] EWHC 161 (Comm); [2017] 1 WLR 3497 at [38]–[39].

35 Although Cranston J in *Commerzbank* alleged the existence of some good arguments showing that asymmetric jurisdiction clauses fell within the definition given to the exclusive jurisdiction clauses under art 3(a) of the HCCCA, he did not go into more details. He submitted no further comments on this matter, stating the distinction between this issue and characterisation of jurisdiction clauses for the purposes of art 31(2) of the Recast Regulation. See Cranston J in *Commerzbank*, at [71]–[74]. Similar to Cranston J and Merrett's view, Jacobs J, in the first instance decision in *Etihad*, referred to earlier, discussed divergences and overlaps between the HCCCA and BRR and highlighted the point that the Council Decision referred to the coherence of the instruments. It was stated that there were good arguments showing the application of the HCCCA to asymmetrical clauses. Yet, since the matters concerned applying the BRR rather than the HCCCA, the latter was not assessed further. See EU Council Decision on the approval, on behalf of the European Union, of the Hague Convention of 30 June 2005 on Choice of Court Agreements, 4 December 2014, 2014/887/EU.

36 See *Etihad Airways PJSC v Flother* [2020] EWCA Civ 1707; [2022] QB 303 at [215]–[217].

37 Henderson LJ further noted that the BRR did not refer to the HCCCA. It thus did not have any express requirement about the consistent interpretation of the instruments; hence this remained only a desirable general objective.

might pose further challenges, particularly upon the commencement of the proceedings in an EU Member State.

V In the Aftermath of the HJC

As mentioned earlier, the HJC adopts a variation of jurisdictional filters, including non-exclusive jurisdiction agreements. For the international circulation of judgments in all Contracting States on the basis of agreed jurisdiction, a judgment must be given by a court designated, albeit non-exclusively. In fact, by this provision, the HJC draws a distinct line in its application scope, compared to the complementary HCCCA which gives effect to exclusive jurisdiction agreements.

The English judgments discussed earlier illustrate the legal position towards asymmetrical jurisdiction agreements concluded and respective legal proceedings commenced before the UK's withdrawal from the EU. English courts based their decisions on the EU law and made reference to the HCCCA only in their *obiter dicta*, non-binding statements irrelevant to the facts or issues of the cases. Indeed, the HCCCA applies to exclusive jurisdiction agreements, and with the adoption of the HJC legal scene has altered.

The ramifications of the HJC for asymmetrical jurisdiction agreements may be defined by the elimination of questions in regard to the application domain of the HCCCA. Indeed, the HJC has made a sharp distinction between exclusive and non-exclusive jurisdiction agreements which has further been amplified by the Explanatory Report. Accordingly, asymmetrical clauses are not considered exclusive under the HCCCA and therefore fall within the scope of the Convention.[38] With the adoption of the HJC, there should not be any further concerns about whether asymmetrical choices could be considered exclusive. Yet, the formulation of the respective filter of the HJC leaves additional difficulties.

The HJC is a single convention determining rules for the recognition and enforcement of judgments with no direct grounds.[39] Article 5 defines only indirect jurisdictional grounds with implications for the effects of judgments given by particular courts. Likely, Article 5.1(m) provides a mandatory rule for the Contracting States to recognise and enforce judgments given by non-exclusively designated courts without any provisions on non-exclusive (including asymmetrical) jurisdiction agreements as a specific jurisdictional ground in that regard. Unlike the HJC, the HCCCA is a double convention giving effect to both exclusive jurisdiction agreements and the resulting judgments. In fact, while Article 5 of the HCCCA determines a mandatory obligation of the Contracting States to give effect to exclusive jurisdiction agreements and therefore, the exclusively chosen court shall have jurisdiction, Article 6 prevents any other court than the court chosen to continue proceedings. The derogative effect of an exclusive jurisdiction agreement compels any other court (even if first

38 See the Garcimartín/Saumier Report, para 217 (available at https://assets.hcch.net/docs/a1b0b0fc-95b1-4544-935b-b842534a120f.pdf (as at May 2024)). See also the Hartley/Dogauchi Report, paras 32, 106, and 249.

39 Unlike a double convention determining both jurisdictional grounds and recognition and enforcement rules, this single convention provides only recognition and enforcement rules.

seised) to decline jurisdiction. The latter leaves a certain risk of multiple or parallel proceedings. Indeed, the absence of *lis pendens* rules in the HCCCA might also be a significant point while interpreting its scope and exclusion of non-exclusive jurisdiction agreements.

Since the HJC does not contain any provision on non-exclusive (asymmetrical) jurisdiction agreements, there is not any such protection for parties. This leaves a real risk of parallel proceedings that are brought before different courts between the same parties and on the same subject matter.

Further dilemmas arise from the relatively new realities of Brexit. Post-Brexit and post-transition, the Brussels regime has ceased to apply to proceedings involving the UK and EU (and EFTA) Member States. When the EU Commission opposed the UK's request to join the Lugano Convention, its view was that the Hague Conventions should be used for relations between the EU and third States.[40]

The BRR and the Lugano Convention still apply to proceedings initiated before the end of the transition period.[41] If a borrower commenced proceedings in an EU Member State in breach of an asymmetrical jurisdiction agreement in favour of English courts, the Brussels Recast Regulation would not prevent the court first seised on any possible jurisdictional ground from continuing the proceedings.[42] Indeed, Article 31(2) of the Brussels Recast Regulation gives priority to the exclusively chosen court regardless of which court first seised. In this regard, the Lugano Convention also gives priority to the first seised court even if parties have agreed on an exclusive jurisdiction agreement.[43] The latter means that if a party brings proceedings in an EFTA state in breach of an asymmetrical jurisdiction agreement, the Lugano Convention would not prevent parallel proceedings and any possible irreconcilable judgment.

The provisions of the BRR applicable to the *lis pendens* proceedings and related actions in third states give discretion to the courts of the Member States. Indeed, in the case of parallel proceedings between the same parties and on the same cause of action, it is up to the court of the Member State to stay the proceedings if such a stay is necessary for the proper administration of justice, and provided that the court of the third State will give a judgment capable of recognition and, where applicable, of enforcement in that Member State.[44] Where there are related actions in a third State, it is again up to the court of the Member State to stay the proceedings if it is expedient to hear and determine the related actions together to avoid the risk of irreconcilable judgments resulting from separate proceedings. In that case, it is expected that the court of the third State will give a judgment capable of recognition and, where applicable, of enforcement in that Member State and the court of the Member State is satisfied that a stay is necessary for the proper administration of justice.[45]

---

40 See Communication from the Commission to the European Parliament and the Council, "Assessment on the application of the United Kingdom of Great Britain and Northern Ireland to accede to the 2007 Lugano Convention", COM (2021) 222 final.

41 See UK Government Guidance, "Cross-border civil and commercial legal cases: guidance for legal professionals from 1 January 2021", 30 December 2020.

42 BRR, art 29.

43 Lugano Convention, art 25.

44 BRR, art 33.1.

45 BRR, art 34.1.

Apart from the discretionary nature of possible stays, the Brussels regime does not provide any express provisions on jurisdiction agreements in favour of non-Member State courts.[46] Recital 24 states that the assessment of the proper administration of justice while deciding upon possible stays may include consideration of the question whether the court of the third State has exclusive jurisdiction.[47] The latter means that the discretion of the Member State courts will yet depend on a set of conditions even where there is a jurisdiction agreement giving exclusive jurisdiction to the courts of third states. Therefore, asymmetrical jurisdiction agreements designating the courts of third states will not prove relevant here.

Now the focus of the discussion must go back to the HJC as the only instrument applicable to non-exclusive and asymmetrical jurisdiction agreements post-Brexit. As mentioned earlier, the treaty applies only to the recognition and enforcement of the resulting judgments without preventing the risk of parallel proceedings in different states over the same matter. In this regard, the HJC states that a court may refuse to recognise or enforce a judgment if the proceedings in the court of origin were contrary to an agreement, or a designation in a trust instrument, under which the dispute in question was to be determined in a court of a State other than the State of origin.[48] By this refusal ground, the HJC aims to ensure parties' exclusive jurisdiction agreements: however, it is of limited relevance to asymmetrical jurisdiction agreements.

Furthermore, parallel proceedings may lead to different judgments reached in the same or different jurisdictions. In this context, the HJC takes steps to prevent inconsistent judgments from becoming enforceable elsewhere. Accordingly, the requested court may refuse to recognise or enforce a judgment that is inconsistent with an earlier judgment given by the court of the requested State in a dispute between the same parties. Further, the requested court may refuse to recognise or enforce the judgment that is inconsistent with an earlier judgment given by a court of another State between the same parties on the same subject matter.[49] Recognition or enforcement may also be postponed or refused if proceedings between the same parties on the same subject matter are pending before a court of the requested State which was seised before the court of origin, and there is a close connection between the dispute and the requested State.[50]

The aforementioned provisions demonstrate that the HJC aims at avoiding any risk of inconsistent judgments to be given effect without any clause preventing parallel proceedings. In fact, even if an inconsistent judgment is refused recognition or enforcement, the possible parallel proceedings at different courts upon an asymmetrical jurisdiction agreement may well still cause a serious waste of time and expense. Further, the risk could be augmented by strategic delays and fraudulent tactics.

46 For instance, where a French seller and a German buyer negotiate a jurisdiction agreement favouring the Brazilian court, that clause will not get any protection under BRR, art 25. In comparison, if these parties negotiate a choice of law clause selecting Brazilian law, that will be given effect according to the Rome I Regulation. See the Rome I Regulation, Recital 13.

47 BRR, Recital 24.

48 HJC, art 7.

49 HJC, art 7.1(f).

50 HJC, art 7.2.

Another important factor to highlight is that the HJC is not in force for the UK yet. Indeed, the UK ratified the HJC only recently – on 27 June 2024. Once ratified, the Convention comes into force only after the expiration of 12 months.[51] And, of course, it only applies to the recognition and enforcement of judgments if, at the time the proceedings were instituted in the State of origin, the Convention had effect between that State and the requested State.

The UK government considers that the HJC by asserting that it would be "an important vehicle to drive the UK's PIL Strategy".[52] Apart from the harmonisation of the global recognition and enforcement rules, by ratifying the HJC, the UK government would also provide a shield for the parties' asymmetrical jurisdiction agreements and the effectiveness of the resulting judgments.[53] Yet, the questions of parallel proceedings and remedies are left open that will be dealt with by the national laws.

VI Parallel Proceedings and Remedies

Upon breaches and parallel proceedings, the nature of a jurisdiction agreement would determine the consequences and possible remedies. While breaching an exclusive jurisdiction agreement might usually result in a stay, grant of an anti-suit injunction, and damages, non-exclusive jurisdiction agreements do not automatically render similar rights and protection to the parties. The possibility of remedies is up to the applicable national law and the circumstances of each case.

As discussed earlier, English courts have shown their sympathy for parties' choices. As an important basis of jurisdiction, English law has thus upheld asymmetrical jurisdiction agreements. Yet, unlike exclusive jurisdiction agreements, much scepticism has been expressed in academia and practice about whether non-exclusive choice of court clauses could be subject to breach in the same way as exclusive jurisdiction clauses.[54] While some commentaries relied on the absence of any negative effects of non-exclusive jurisdiction agreements while justifying the impossibility of granting any stay or anti-suit injunctions, others presented opposing views.[55] Relevantly, in *Perform*

51 HJC, arts 24(2) and 28.

52 The Consultation paper, para 1.3, *Consultation on the Hague Convention of 2 July 2019 on the Recognition and Enforcement of Foreign Judgments in Civil or Commercial Matters (Hague 2019)* (www.gov.uk/government/consultations/hague-convention-of-2-july-2019-on-the-recognition-and-enforcement-of-foreign-judgments-in-civil-or-commercial-matters-hague-2019 (as at May 2024)).

53 For the related discussions see A. Mammadzada, "Multilateralism Post-Brexit: Do The Hague Conventions Preserve The Status Quo of Judicial Cooperation?" [2024] JBL [forthcoming].

54 According to the decision in *Royal Bank of Canada v Cooperative Centrale Raiffeisen-Boorenleenbank Binding Authority* [2004] EWCA Civ 7; [2004] 1 Lloyd's Rep. 471, if the agreement stipulates for a rights of a party to commence proceedings in any other forum than a particular one (England), that act will not count as a breach. For more on the discussion of the relevant issues see M. Ahmed, *The Nature and Enforcement of Choice of Court Agreements: A Comparative Study* (Hart, 2017), 59.

55 See A. Briggs, *Agreements On Jurisdiction and Choice of Law* (OUP, 2008), 376. See also J. Fawcett, "Non-exclusive jurisdiction agreements in private international law" [2001] LMCLQ 234, 260. Accordingly, courts occasionally refused to apply the principles relevant to exclusive designations and their breach, to non-exclusive jurisdiction agreements based on the irrelevance of their exceptional nature. See e.g. *E.D. & F. MAN Ship Ltd. v Kvaerner Gibraltar Ltd (The Rothnie)* [1996] 2 Lloyd's Rep. 206. See also *BNP Paribas v Anchorage Capital and others* [2013] EWHC 3073 (Comm), [93], where Males J refused to grant an anti-

Content Services Ltd v Ness Global Services Ltd,[56] the English Court of Appeal held that Article 25 of the BRR conferred mandatory jurisdiction on the courts designated in an exclusive or non-exclusive jurisdiction agreement.

Indeed, non-exclusive clauses express parties' will and hold a positive effect; therefore, they should be recognised by much more effective means than that of the discretionary common law doctrine as some contended them to be a factor in assessing the possible application of the *forum non conveniens* doctrine.[57] Parties to large commercial contracts who are usually rational and sophisticated businessmen would prefer impartiality to convenience. Therefore, it is fair to assume that parties will be seen as acting vexatiously and oppressively if they pursue parallel proceedings in a non-contractual court despite having agreed on a non-exclusive choice, as long as there are no exceptional reasons that were not foreseeable at the time of contracting.[58] The latter justifies granting, respectively, stays and anti-suit injunctions in favour of a non-exclusive designation upon apparent vexation or oppression resulting from parallel proceedings.[59] Relevantly, it has been suggested that

> by drafting a non-exclusive jurisdiction clause, parties have anticipated and accepted the possibility of parallel proceedings, and as a result, only foreign proceedings which are vexatious and oppressive for some reason and independent of the mere presence of the non-exclusive clause will be restrained by injunction.[60]

Likewise, as mentioned by Waller LJ, parallel proceedings elsewhere upon commencement of the proceedings in the non-exclusively designated court could not be consistent with the parties' intention unless there was an exceptional reason for doing so.[61]

According to English law and practice, courts will likely grant stays and anti-suit injunctions if there are vexatious and oppressive parallel proceedings in breach of an asymmetrical jurisdiction agreement. Another point worth emphasising here is that with the UK's withdrawal from the European Union, English courts are no longer bound by mutual trust and hence the prohibitions on granting anti-suit injunctions in the EU context have been lifted.[62] Post-Brexit anti-suit injunctions have revived and

suit injunction against the ongoing New York proceedings since a breach of the non-exclusive English jurisdiction clause was not shown.

56 [2021] EWCA Civ 981; [2021] 1 WLR 4146.

57 See M. Keyes & B. Marshall, "Jurisdiction agreements: exclusive, optional and asymmetrical" (2015) 11 Journal of Private International Law 345, 363.

58 See *British Aerospace plc v Dee Howard Co* [1993] 1 Lloyd's Rep 368; *Mercury Communications Ltd v Communication Telesystems International* [1999] 2 All ER 33.

59 See *Sabah Shipyard (Pakistan) Ltd v Islamic Republic of Pakistan* [2002] EWCA Civ 1643; [2003] 2 Lloyd's Rep. 571; *Highland Crusader Offshore Partners LP v Deutsche Bank AG* [2009] EWCA Civ 725; [2010] 1 WLR 1023, per Toulson LJ at [105]–[110]. See also *Amoco (UK) Exploration Co Ltd v Teesside Gas Transportation Ltd* [2001] UKHL 18; [2001] 1 All ER (Comm) 865.

60 T. Raphael, *The Anti-Suit Injunction* (OUP, 2008), para 9.12. See also *Cheshire, North and Fawcett: Private International Law* (15th Edn, OUP 2008), 474.

61 *Sabah Shipyard (Pakistan) Ltd v Islamic Republic of Pakistan* [2002] EWCA Civ 1643; [2003] 2 Lloyd's Rep. 571 at [36].

62 It has been said that "a truly European Area of Justice can only work if there is trust in each other's justice systems . . . and the whole EU legal system . . . is based on mutual trust". See T. Hartley, "The Brussels I Regulation and Arbitration" (2014) 63 ICLQ 843; M. Weller, "Mutual Trust: In Search of the Future of European Private International Law" (2015) 11 JPIL 64. See also *Allianz SpA v West Tankers Inc*

English courts have already granted anti-suit orders against vexatious and oppressive proceedings in the EU Member States.[63] In fact, the Hague Conventions as the legal frameworks applicable to civil judicial co-operation post-Brexit do not contain mutual trust or any other similar constraints over anti-suit measures. Moreover, interim measures do not qualify as judgments under the Conventions;[64] therefore, their enforcement depends on the applicable national laws.

VII The Future

Hopes rest on the Hague Conference. With the conclusion of the HJC, the organisation has shifted its focus to the Jurisdiction Project. The latest discussions following the Diplomatic Session in 2019 have been assessing the necessity, desirability, and feasibility of a new international instrument harmonising, or coordinating, the legal framework dealing with parallel proceedings and related actions. Indeed, the Experts' Group at the Permanent Bureau as mandated by the Council drafted the provisions on parallel proceedings for future discussion. The draft document has prioritised parties' autonomy stating that if the parties to the proceedings in both or all courts have agreed prior to the dispute that one or more courts shall have jurisdiction over the dispute, and only one of the courts seised is designated under such agreement as having jurisdiction, then that court shall proceed with adjudication of the dispute unless such agreement states that it does not deprive any other court or courts of jurisdiction. Any other court shall suspend the proceedings.[65] Further, the draft has also emphasised the possible need to address non-exclusive jurisdiction agreements with purely prorogatory effect.

Only time will tell whether a convention on parallel proceedings will be achieved. If so, it might bring extra protection for asymmetrical jurisdiction agreements and legal certainty for the parties. If such an instrument were concluded, it would complement the HCCCA and HJC and fill the gap left for the effectiveness of asymmetrical jurisdiction agreements. Indeed, the three conventions might serve as a triad of legal illumination, casting light upon the murky waters of international commercial litigation, and guiding stakeholders towards clarity, certainty, and effective resolutions. Meantime, to avoid potential risks, parties might reconsider their agreements with careful thought and renegotiate exclusive jurisdiction or arbitration agreements which have more certainty with regard to the applicable legal frameworks.

(Case 185/07) [2009] ECR I-00663 and *Turner v Grovit (Case 159/02)* [2004] ECR I-3565; in addition A. Mammadzada, "Arbitral Anti-Suit Measures: Implications of Mutual Trust" (2023) 3 Italian Review of International & Comparative Law 28.

63 See A. Mammadzada, "The Rebirth of the European 'Anti-Suit Injunction' Issue Post-Brexit", in B. Soyer & A. Tettenborn (eds), *Damages, Recoveries and Remedies in Shipping Law* (Informa Law from Routledge, 2023), 226. See also *QBE Europe SA NV v Generali España de Seguros y Reaseguros* [2022] EWHC 2062 (Comm); [2022] 2 Lloyd's Rep. 481; *Ebury Partners Belgium SA v Technical Touch BV* [2022] EWHC 2927 (Comm); [2023] 1 Lloyd's Rep. 575.

64 HCCCA, arts 4 and 7; HJC, art 3.

65 Revised draft of the provisions on parallel proceedings for future discussion, art 7, Working Group on Jurisdiction: Report of 2024 (Prel. Doc. No 2 of February 2024) (available at https://assets.hcch.net/docs/dc1c8d98-6303-438e-8f16-b1013ef71bdc.pdf (as at May 2024)).

PART 3

CHOICE OF LAW – APPLICABLE LAW ISSUES

CHAPTER 12

The Rome Convention on the Law Applicable to Contractual Obligations – Past, Present, and Future

*John A. Kimbell**

I Introduction

Boris Johnson's book *The Churchill Factor* starts by taking the reader back to Tuesday, 28 May 1940, and a small meeting room in the House of Commons. The Belgian army has just surrendered and the evacuation of the British Expeditionary Force from Dunkirk is just beginning. The subject under discussion is a potential peace offer from Hitler. The French are in favour of engaging with it, as are Lord Halifax, the Foreign Secretary, and Neville Chamberlain, who until two weeks earlier had been PM. The only person firmly against engaging in any talks with the Führer was the new PM, Winston Churchill. His view ultimately prevailed (but only just).

However, Boris Johnson uses this meeting as a springboard to describe a counterfactual history without Churchill. In this version of events, it is Lord Halifax who succeeds Neville Chamberlain as PM and the British sue for peace in May 1940. Johnson describes how on this scenario, we would have had to hand over Gibraltar and Malta and would have ultimately ended up with a Nazi EU. According to Boris Johnson, this would have been realisation of a plan drawn up in 1942 by Dr Walther Funk of the Nazi *Reichsbank* for something he called the *Europäische Wirtschaftsgesellshaft* – i.e. a German-dominated European Economic Community.

It is not an accident that in a book published in 2015 Boris Johnson is suggesting that the EEC was an idea first dreamt up by the Nazis. It was part of a narrative leading up to the Brexit referendum in which being a member of the EU was equated with a loss of sovereignty and a subjugation to rule from Brussels and Berlin which Brexit would reverse. The question I want address in this chapter, though, is not whether Brexit was a wise choice for the country or even its private international law, but rather whether the conflict of laws rules for contractual obligations with which we have now ended up are appropriate in a post-Brexit UK.

II The Origins of the Rome Convention

There cannot be any serious doubt about the fact that our conflict-of-laws rules became fully Europeanised as a result of the accession by the UK to the European Economic Community. However, the door to European law in this area was not (initially at least)

* **Barrister, Quadrant Chambers.**

DOI: 10.4324/9781032726243-15

s 2(1) of the European Communities Act 1972. Prior to 1 May 1999,[1] the Community lacked jurisdiction to pass laws in relation to private international law. It also lacked the competence to enact laws on the mutual recognition of judgments. However, that did not stop the original six Member States of the European Community from entering into the Brussels Convention in 1968 on jurisdiction and mutual recognition of judgments and the Rome Convention on the Law Applicable to Contractual Obligations in 1980.

The Rome Convention of 1980 was conceived as a "natural sequel" and companion to the Brussels Convention of 1968.[2] Work began on what became the Rome Convention as long ago as 1967. The project was led by the governments of Belgium, the Netherlands, and Luxembourg.[3] In 1975 it was decided to limit the draft convention to rules for contractual obligations. The convention was finally agreed and signed by all the members of the European Community by December 1981.

The connection and joint aim of the Brussels Convention and the Rome Convention is made clear in the preamble of the Rome Convention itself. This states:

> The High Contracting Parties to the Treaty establishing the European Economic Community [are] anxious to continue in the field of private international law the work of unification of law which has already been done within the Community in particular in the field of jurisdiction and enforcement of judgments.

The Lord Chancellor said this in 1994:

> Although the Rome Convention is not strictly a piece of Community legislation, it is related to Article 220 of the Treaty of Rome, the treaty which established the European Economic Community.[4]

III The Aim of the Rome Convention

The object of the Rome Convention has been said to be:

> To establish common rules to identify the applicable law for contractual obligations in order to increase predictability in international commercial transactions and to promote the development of the Community's internal market.[5]

Richard Plender was in my view also right to say that the Rome Convention formed part of the Community legal order.[6] The Rome Convention entered into force in the United Kingdom on 1 April 1991. The mechanism for incorporation was the Contracts (Applicable Law) Act 1990.

Although the Rome Convention affirmed the basic principle that parties to a contract were free to choose the applicable law (which had long been the fundamental

---

1 This is the date on which the Amsterdam Treaty came into force.

2 See R. Plender, *The European Contracts Convention* (2001), para 1–04, citing p 5 of the Guiliano-Lagarde Report. The UK acceded to the Brussels Convention in 1978. It became part of English law in 1987 via the Civil Jurisdiction and Judgments Act 1982.

3 See R. Plender, op. cit., para 1–25.

4 HL Deb 18 July 1994 vol 557 col 104.

5 R. Plender, op. cit., para 2–02.

6 R. Plender, op. cit., para 1–05.

rule at common law),[7] the Convention in the form introduced in 1990 contained a number of innovations, including:

1 an applicable-law rule based on identifying the *country* (rather than a legal system) having the closest connection to the contract;
2 a series of presumptions to identify the relevant country, the main one being that it was the law of the country in which the person whose performance was "characteristic of the contract" habitually *resided* that ought to apply;
3 an escape clause based on weighing "all the circumstances" to identify the relevant country (if it was appropriate for the presumptions to be disregarded).
4 the use of an official report written by two professors of law (Prof Mario Giuliano from Italy and Prof Paul Lagarde from France) as the primary aid to interpretation of the Convention;[8]
5 the concepts used in the Convention were to be given an autonomous European meaning and interpreted in accordance with general principles of European law;[9]
6 a mechanism to obtain a ruling from the ECJ on a point of interpretation of the Convention.[10]

The idea of anchoring choice of law to the *place of residence* of the person whose performance was *characteristic* of the contract was entirely alien to English law. It was not even taken from the law of any of the EC states, but was instead borrowed from the private international law of a non–Member State, Switzerland.[11]

The new rule was, however, relatively easy to understand and apply in civil law countries whose law of contracts was based on Roman law. Such systems tended in their respective codes to identify certain types of contract and to have prescribed obligations for each party depending on the particular type of contract, and the primary method of enforcement was to seek specific performance. By contrast, English law fundamentally had a unitary law of contract and the most common form of enforcement was to claim damages for breach. Arguments about the correct categorisation of a contract are very rare in English courts; they very common in civil law countries such as Germany.

Perhaps because the approach of the Rome Convention appeared rather alien, the English courts tended to be all too willing to discard the presumptions in Article 4 and instead made liberal use of the "escape clause" in Article 4(5), which was far closer to the common law approach.[12] This manner of proceeding was not that sanctioned by the Giuliano-Lagarde report, and was not the one taken by the courts of the most of the other Member States who applied the presumptions first and foremost. Thus while the rules were uniform, the courts' approach and the outcomes were anything but.

7 See e.g. *Vita Food Products Inc v Unus Shipping Co Ltd* [1939] AC 277, 289–290.
8 This was such a novelty that a special provision had to be inserted in the 1990 Act to allow it – s 3(a).
9 See art 18.
10 This was separately agreed in the Brussels Protocol reproduced as Schedule 3 to the 1990 Act.
11 See now art 117 of the Swiss Private International Law Act of 1987.
12 See e.g. *Crédit Lyonnais v New Hampshire Insurance Co Ltd* [1997] 2 CMLR 610.

The Rome Convention applied to a wide range of civil and commercial matters. It did not cater at all, however, for floating choice-of-law clauses, used for example by banks. It did not apply at all to arbitration agreements, contracts of insurance or a number of other categories of legal relationships. It did however contain particular rules for consumers and employment contracts.

The Rome Convention operated for just under 20 years until it was replaced by Regulation (EC) 593/2008, usually known as the Rome I Regulation, and applying to contracts concluded after 17 December 2009.

IV The Rome I Regulation

Unlike the Rome Convention, the Regulation applied directly and automatically in the UK. It had no fewer than 46 Recitals. Among them was the following:

> (1) The Community has set itself the objective of maintaining and developing an area of freedom, security and justice. For the progressive establishment of such an area, the Community is to adopt measures relating to judicial cooperation in civil matters with a cross-border impact to the extent necessary for the proper functioning of the internal market.

Recital (7) emphasised how the Rome I Regulation was part of a package that also included the Brussels Regulation and the Rome II Regulation. It said this:

> The substantive scope and the provisions of this Regulation should be consistent with Council Regulation (EC) No 44/2001 of 22 December 2000 on jurisdiction and the recognition and enforcement of judgments in civil and commercial matters (Brussels I) and Regulation (EC) No 864/2007 of the European Parliament and of the Council of 11 July 2007 on the law applicable to non-contractual obligations (Rome II).[13]

The Rome I Regulation continued to give full effect to the principle of freedom of choice. Like the Rome Convention it also permitted implied choice of law provided that the implied choice could be "clearly demonstrated".[14] Like the Rome Convention it excluded arbitration agreements; unlike the Convention it brought within its scope insurance and re-insurance.

One significant change in the Regulation was to the structure of rules in the absence of an express or implied choice by the parties. The Regulation laid down rules for seven categories of contract:

No.	Category of contract	Applicable law
1	A contract for the sale of goods	The law of the country where the seller had their habitual residence
2	A contract for the provision of services	The country where the service provider had their habitual residence
3	A contract relating to a right *in rem* in immovable property	The law of the country where the property was situated

(*Continued*)

13 See also Recital 17.

14 The words in the Convention are "demonstrated with reasonable certainty". Prof Briggs suggested in *Conflict of Laws* (2013) that the test in the Regulation might be if anything slightly more stringent.

(Continued)

No.	Category of contract	Applicable law
4	A tenancy of immovable property concluded for temporary private use for a period of no more than six consecutive months	The law of the country where the landlord had their habitual residence (provided that the tenant was a natural person and had their habitual residence in the same country)
5	A franchise contract	The law of the country where the franchisee had their habitual residence
6	A distribution contract	The law of the country where the distributor had their habitual residence
7	A contract for the sale of goods by auction	The law of the country where the auction took place, if such a place could be determined

Special rules applied for consumer, insurance and carriage contracts – see Articles 5–7.

But otherwise, if a contract did not fall within one of the seven categories listed in Article 4 or fell into more than one of the categories (as many complex commercial contracts do), the Regulation returned again to the idea of identifying the party required to effect the characteristic performance of the contract and stipulating that the contract was governed by the law of the country where that person had their habitual residence.

The Rome I Regulation was in operation for less than seven years before Brexit referendum result on 24 June 2016.

V The Initial Approach

The UK Government's initial stated intention following the Brexit referendum was to seek to continue "close cooperation" with the EU in the form of a "partnership framework" in relation to the legal trio of the Brussels Regulation, the Rome I Convention, and the Rome II Convention.[15]

The UK government followed up that stated intention of remaining close to existing frameworks of co-operation by applying to join the Lugano Convention on 8 April 2020. Switzerland, Iceland, and Norway quickly gave their consent. After all, the UK was a major trading nation physically located within the European Economic Area and its jurisdictional laws were already aligned with the Lugano rules, because they very closely modelled on those of the Brussels Convention.

However, the European Commission vetoed the UK's application. The Commission said that the Lugano Convention was a flanking measure to promote the EU internal

15 Providing a cross-border civil judicial co-operation framework: a future partnership paper, 22 August 2017, www.gov.uk/government/publications/providing-a-cross-border-civil-judicial-cooperation-framework-a-future-partnership-paper, last accessed 5 July 2024.

market. The Commission had come to the conclusion that the UK had decided it no longer had any interest in promoting the development of the internal market. The Commission also said that the Lugano Convention was based a high level of "mutual trust" which in the aftermath of Brexit was no longer present in the relationship between the UK and the EU.

The failure of UK's application to join Lugano meant that on 31 December 2021 the entire Brussels Convention edifice (as it applied in the UK) disappeared in a puff of smoke. The English courts had no choice but to fall back on their pre-Brussels Convention rules to decide upon their own jurisdiction. This meant a return overnight to jurisdiction by means of service of a claim form within the jurisdiction or service outside the jurisdiction with permission of the court combined with the common law principle of *forum non conveniens*. The sky did not fall in. So far as I am aware, there has not been a decline in the number of claims commenced in the UK, nor a noticeable shift of any legal business from the UK to the EU.

VI Rome I Post-Brexit

But what has happened to the Rome I Regulation since Brexit? It has experienced a two-stage facelift. First it became "retained" EU law, and now it is about to become "assimilated". But what do these two descriptions actually mean? And is assimilation a satisfactory outcome?

Retained law is what is created by s 3(1) of European Union Withdrawal Act 2018, as amended by the European Union (Withdrawal Agreement) Act 2020:

> Direct EU legislation, so far as operative immediately before [implementation completion day], forms part of domestic law on and after exit day.

The effect of this provision was to retain the entirety of the Rome I Regulation by relabelling it as English domestic law with effect from 11 pm on 31 December 2020.

By means of a statutory instrument, SI No 834/2019, Parliament amended the newly domesticated provision, but only very slightly. The name of the new domestic English law is somewhat surprisingly very European sounding:

> Regulation (EC) No 593/2008 (www.legislation.gov.uk/eur/2008/593/contents) of the European Parliament and of the Council of 17 June 2008 on the law applicable to contractual obligations (Rome I).

As to the substance of the provisions, almost nothing is changed. So for example "the United Kingdom" is substituted for "a Member State" and "retained EU law" replaces "Community law implemented in the Member State of the forum". There are just over a dozen changes to the wording of the Regulation. The bare minimum was done in order to transplant the Rome I rules and allow them to function as a piece of domestic English law.

Although references to the Court of Justice of the European Union on issues of interpretation are not possible in any case commenced in a UK court after 1 January 2021, the Withdrawal Act retained all the accumulated EU case law on Rome I and decisions of the CJEU and its predecessor the status of decisions of the UK Supreme Court.

The reason for the minimal changes would appear to have been that the government planned a two-stage approach. Stage One was nothing more than taking a snapshot of EU law immediately before exit day in order to ensure a functioning statute book.[16] What was then supposed to follow was a Stage Two. Depending on where you stood in the Brexit-supporting continuum, this was to be either a careful and objective assessment of whether to keep the newly domesticated law in whole or in part, or a bonfire of EU law. What actually happened did not match either of these descriptions.

A potential mechanism for a large-scale bonfire of EU law was written into the Retained EU Law (Revocation and Reform) Bill 2023 in the form of a general sunsetting of retained EU law. Until very recently, the intended structure was to sunset all retained EU law at the end of 2023 unless a positive decision had been taken to keep it. Any law that we decided to keep would then be upgraded from mere retained law to "assimilated law".

However, in May 2023, the government announced a U-turn. Instead of a general sunset with exceptions for law assessed worthy of assimilation, the Bill was amended to provide instead for a general rule of retention. A new schedule in the form of a spreadsheet listed just 591 laws that were to be sunsetted. The schedule included the "Habitat (Salt Marsh) (Amendment) Regulations 1995" and the "Commission Decision of 22 November 2010 on the withdrawal of Georgia as regards education, training and certification of seafarers for recognition of certificates of competency".

So instead of a careful selection of laws which were to be hand-picked as worthy of the upgrade in status from retained to fully assimilated, the entirety of the retained EU law (save for the 591 provisions listed in the schedule) was automatically upgraded to become assimilated law.

VII The Nature of Assimilated Law

Three points are important about assimilated law (in contrast to retained law):

1. All UK courts will be obliged to interpret the "assimilated law" in accordance with the case law of the CJEU as it stood on 31 December 2020. This case law will now be referred to as "assimilated EU case law".
2. However, the status of decisions of the CJEU/ECJ is downgraded from being treated as a decision of the Supreme Court to being treated as just a decision of a "foreign court", of which it may take account. A UK court invited not to follow a decision of the CJEU or ECJ on Rome I is required to "have regard to any changes of circumstances which are relevant to the retained EU case law and the extent to which the retained EU case law restricts the proper development of domestic law". It remains to be seen how this rather opaque test is interpreted.
3. There is also a revised rule of precedent for previous UK court decisions on assimilated law. According to section 6(5ZA) of the 2023 Act, a UK court will be permitted to depart from its own "assimilated domestic case law" (which means UK case law on "assimilated law" and not the assimilated case law of the CJEU) without the usual domestic restrictions on deviation from

16 See L. Merrett, "International Employment Cases Post Brexit: choice of law, territorial scope, Jurisdiction and Enforcement" (2021) 50 ILJ 346.

> domestic precedent. When deviating from its own case law, a UK court will have to consider "the extent to which the assimilated domestic case law is determined or influenced by assimilated EU case law from which the court has departed or would depart; any changes of circumstances which are relevant to the assimilated domestic case law; and the extent to which the assimilated domestic case law restricts the proper development of domestic law".

What is clear is that the scope for departure from both previous decisions of the CJEU/ECJ on Rome I and domestic law decisions is intended to be much wider than it was for Rome I in the form of retained law under the 2018 Act. However, given how little change has been made to the substance of the Rome I Regulation in its assimilated form, it remains to be seen how ready and willing the UK courts will be to go it alone and depart from their own and previous EU case law.

As to the Rome I Regulation in its assimilated form:

1 The name remains unchanged. It is still called the "Regulation (EC) No 593/2008 of the European Parliament and of the Council of 17 June 2008 on the law applicable to contractual obligations (Rome I)".

2 It still starts with the following recitals, which is rather baffling for a domestic law provision:

> (1) The Community has set itself the objective of maintaining and developing an area of freedom, security and justice. For the progressive establishment of such an area, the Community is to adopt measures relating to judicial cooperation in civil matters with a cross-border impact to the extent necessary for the proper functioning of the internal market.
>
> . . .
>
> (6) The proper functioning of the internal market creates a need, in order to improve the predictability of the outcome of litigation, certainty as to the law applicable and the free movement of judgments, for the conflict-of-law rules in the Member States to designate the same national law irrespective of the country of the court in which an action is brought.
>
> (7) The substantive scope and the provisions of this Regulation should be consistent with Council Regulation (EC) No 44/2001 of 22 December 2000 on jurisdiction and the recognition and enforcement of judgments in civil and commercial matters ((Brussels I) and Regulation (EC) No 864/2007 of the European Parliament and of the Council of 11 July 2007 on the law applicable to non-contractual obligations (Rome II).

3 The only change of real substance is that "Member States" become "relevant states", defined as "the UK and states where Rome I applies".[17]

17 In art 1(4).

In other words, the previous European law recitals, aims and substance is in reality simply cut and pasted into domestic law, including the full civil law categorisation of contract types and the characteristic performance and residence tests.

Does it make sense to retain the Rome I rules in this way? It is certainly true that most academics regard the Rome I rules as a whole as a workable or even "sensible"[18] set of rules. It might also be said that over the course of the past 30 years a whole generation of practitioners have become familiar with the Rome Convention and then the Rome I Regulation.

However, there remain reasons to doubt whether an assimilated Rome I is the right approach, for four main reasons:

1. Rome I's inspiration and reason for coming into being (as described earlier) has little or no relevance now in the UK. The adoption of the Rome Convention and then the Rome I Regulation was part of a project to facilitate and promote the operation of a single internal European market where goods, services, and professionals were able to circulate with minimum obstruction.[19] Following the decision to leave the EU and to adopt a "hard" version of Brexit, the English legal system has no further interest in promoting this unification project and the EU's internal market mission. The recitals to the Rome I Regulation are as alien to English law now as Justinian's Code.
2. By freezing and assimilating Rome I as it happened to be on 1 January 2021, the UK obtain the appearance of control. True the English courts are not bound by CJEU decisions, but how real is that freedom to depart? The CJEU is and always was best placed to interpret the Convention in the context of its own particular aims and as part of the Community legal order (as per the Recitals). The decisions of that court are going to remain highly persuasive for the foreseeable future, notwithstanding the theoretical legal power of the UK courts now have not to follow it.
3. More fundamentally, the UK is left in the position of law-taker in relation to its own private international law rules without any influence over future law reform or its interpretation in the CJEU. The UK no longer has a judge at the CJEU, no longer has a voice in the Parliament or Commission. It is a feature of EU law that it is regularly reviewed. When the EU moves on to Rome I "bis" or Rome I "recast", the UK will either have to make do with the old model or will have to assimilate whatever the EU introduces, without any insight or influence over what that is.
4. Finally, there always was and remains a home-grown, fully developed, tried-and-tested alternative set of common law rules.

18 See A. Briggs, *The Conflict of Laws* (3rd Edn, 2013), p 239.

19 When the 1990 Act was introduced in Parliament it was said to be "part of a beneficial exercise in harmonisation with our partners in the European Community" (HL Deb 12 December 1989 vol 513 col 1260 (Lord Fraser of Carmyllie)). See too the Lord Chancellor in 1994 who said of the Rome Convention: "This is a convention made between member states of the European Community, the purpose of which is to harmonise their private international law rules on contract" (HL Deb 18 July 1994 vol 557 col 103).

VIII The Home-Grown Alternative to the Assimilated Rome I Regulation

When the Rome Convention was introduced in 1990, it was not because the common law rules were considered to be outdated or in a mess. The *Law Quarterly Review* of July 1991 published an article by Dr F A Mann in the form of an obituary:

> The Contracts (Applicable Law) Act 1990 came into force on April 1 1991, a day which many lawyers and traders will remember with sadness and resignation so as to render a tribute in the nature of an obituary appropriate.
>
> The Act replaces one of the great achievements of the English judiciary during the last 140 years or so, an achievement which produced an effective private international law of contracts, was recognized and followed in practically the whole world and has not at any time or anywhere led to dissatisfaction or to a demand for reform.

The common law rules had been developed largely by reference to commercial contracts, especially international trade contracts. The leading cases were the decisions of the House of Lords in *Amin Rasheed Shipping Co v Kuwait Insurance Co*[20] and of the Privy Council in *Bonython v Commonwealth*.[21]

The common law approach was to seek to identify the proper law of the contract. Rule 180 in the 11th edition of *Dicey & Morris* (1987)[22] defined the proper law of a contract as:

> The system of law by which the parties intended the contract to be governed, or, where their intention is neither expressed not to be inferred from the circumstances, the system of law with which the transaction has its closest and most real connection.

English law thus operated a three-tiered hierarchy. It first looked to see whether the parties to a contract had expressly chosen a "system of law"[23] to govern the contract. If they had, that choice was generally enforced. Secondly, in the absence of an express choice, the common law looked to see if there was an implied or inferred choice based on factors such as language of the contract, the use of law terms of art in it, and any jurisdiction clause.[24] Thirdly, in the absence of any implied choice by the parties, the proper law was determined by weighing up connecting factors such as the place of performance of the contract and the nature and purpose of the contract.

The approach of English law summarised previously was fully explained in a little over 24 pages in Dicey & Morris. Each of the three limbs set out earlier was illustrated and explained by dozens of examples, drawn it must be said from commercial cases but widely – from England, Australia, New Zealand, and other Commonwealth legal systems.

It is true that there was a lively debate in academic circles in particular about the nature of and relationship between the second and third limbs of the test. However,

---

20 [1984] AC 50.

21 [1951] AC 201

22 See vol II, p 1161.

23 That chosen system did not need to have anything to do with the residence or domicile of either of the contracting parties.

24 See e.g. *Tzortzis v Monark Line A/B* [1968] 1 WLR 406. This case involved the sale of a ship by a Swedish seller to a Greek buyer and contained a London arbitration clause. It was held that English law applied.

by the time it was supplanted by the Rome Convention, 150 years or so of case law had resolved itself into a rich, nuanced and essentially pragmatic three-part formula for determining the applicable law in particular in respect of commercial contracts.

Those common law rules and the case law from which they were drawn and explained were not abolished or even frozen in 1990. The rules and case law I have described have continued to be discussed, developed, and applied to new types of commercial contracts and new commercial contexts in the course of the past 30 years in the courts and law journals of the common law world, in particular in Australia, New Zealand, and Canada.

IX Conclusion

In conclusion, there are good reasons to consider that simple assimilation option which has been chosen as a result of Brexit is less than ideal. Despite having had seven years to think about it, what the UK legislature has achieved is little more than an emergency cut-and-paste combined with a modified rule on precedent. The decision to adopt the Rome Convention in the first place was part of the price to be paid for being part of a single market in people, services, goods, and judgments. If we had been permitted to remain in the EEA and become a party to Lugano different considerations may have applied, but as the UK has been firmly excluded and is therefore likely to remain a third country on the periphery of the EU internal market for the foreseeable future, there is much to be said for re-embracing the flexible and pragmatic common law rules. To do so would amount to a decision to re-connect and re-engage with the living legal tradition of the Commonwealth. It might be thought that this is a better path then seeking to cling on desperately to concepts and rules that only really make sense as part of the grand European project of which we are no longer part.

CHAPTER 13

The Challenges and Limitations of Choice of Law Clauses in International Commercial Agreements

*Daniel Wand**

I Introduction

This chapter is concerned with choice of law clauses and provisions in international commercial agreements. More specifically, it aims to consider the challenges and limitations of choice of law clauses in practice and to what extent the autonomy of parties to select the law which governs their agreement and any disputes arising therefrom is limited or curtailed. It also identifies some of the challenges and pitfalls of using choice of law clauses.

The topic of choice of law agreements is seemingly under-researched and analysed within the existing literature and appears to have been somewhat overlooked. This is likely because such clauses rarely give rise to significant disputes between contracting parties and, therefore, there is little litigation, which provides rich subject matter for academic analysis. Furthermore, from a practical perspective, choice of law provisions are often a very small part of large, complex international agreements where the focus of the parties is predominantly on the substance of the relationship and bargain between the parties rather than on the provisions which anticipate disputes between the parties arising and particularly on questions as where disputes shall be adjudicated and what law shall be applied. During the course of presenting this paper, an audience member familiar with these types of agreements and clauses pointed out that choice of law clauses are usually one of the last points to be considered by the parties concluding an agreement, and the clauses incorporated are often boilerplate with little serious thought given to them.

Whilst it is entirely understandable commercial parties would wish to focus upon the substance of their agreement, choice of law clauses are a fundamental constituent part of any agreement. They can have a significant effect on how contractual provisions are interpreted and applied and on the outcome of disputes arising from the agreement. This is particularly so in the context of the rapid growth of international commercial relationships and transactions over the preceding decades. As a result, choice of law clauses merit greater consideration than they have seemingly been afforded to date. This chapter seeks to make a small contribution to that endeavour.

It should be noted that this work does not attempt to provide a comparative analysis in respect of the treatment of choice of law clauses in different jurisdictions around the globe. This would be far beyond the scope of this short chapter. Rather, this chapter seeks to identify some of the broad issues that exist in this area and provides a general

* **Barrister 4KBW.**

DOI: 10.4324/9781032726243-16

analysis of the limits of choice of law agreements with a slight focus on Europe and England and Wales. However, references are made to other jurisdictions. The chapter provides a nod to further potential research, but a detailed analysis of the issues raised herein is beyond the scope of the chapter and for another day.

The chapter is structured as follows. It begins with a brief explanation of choice of law clauses and then identifies relevant international legal instruments endorsing and adopting the ability of the parties to a contract to choose their governing law. The chapter goes on to consider the theoretical underpinning of choice of law agreements being the principle of party autonomy. It then considers three potential limitations in respect of choice of law, namely (1) jurisdictional nexus and mandatory rules; (2) public policy considerations; and (3) the absence of choice of non-state law as the governing law. Finally, some concluding remarks are given.

The argument and conclusion of this article are that whilst there are some limitations imposed upon the ability of parties to choose the law which governs their contractual relations and any disputes arising therefrom, and the extent of the application of the choice of law, the limitations are rather limited and apply only in quite exceptional circumstances such that the principle of party autonomy is preserved to a very significant degree. That being said, the fact that parties are restricted to choosing a state law to govern their contract could be said to represent a not insignificant and quite substantive limitation on party autonomy. However, such a limitation is perhaps arguably academic at present in the absence of a wholly sufficient non-state body of rules and principles sufficient to govern an international commercial contract and the adjudication of any dispute arising therefrom.

II Choice of Law Agreements

A Nature and Purpose

A choice of law clause, also known as a choice of law agreement, is a provision contained in an international commercial agreement by which the parties to the agreement decide what law should govern the application and interpretation of the agreement and the litigation of disputes arising out of the agreement. It shall be noted that the choice of law made by the parties is not the same as the choice of how any disputes arising should be resolved and/or in what state any dispute should be litigated, although the jurisdiction and choice of law will often be the same i.e. the courts of England and Wales and English law.

The choice of law agreement should be clearly expressed in a written clause within the contract. It should be drafted in such a way so that there is no room for dispute as to what law has been chosen and to what part of the agreement, if not the whole, it is intended to apply, given that it is possible for a contract to provide for a choice of law applicable to only part of an agreement. It is possible for a court, at least in England and Wales, to imply a term into a contract providing for a choice where this was the intention of the parties from the contract and the circumstances surrounding it. Still, it is, of course, very far from ideal for parties to have to rely upon a court adjudicating whether a choice of law has been made.

The primary purpose of choice of law clauses in commercial agreements is to give flexibility and certainty to parties. The parties are able to mutually choose the governing law that is most appropriate to govern their contractual relationship. Furthermore, with a clear and well-drafted choice of law provision, the parties can be confident as to the law that shall be applied to the agreement and, therefore, how the terms of the agreement will or may be interpreted by a court and how disputes will or may be resolved. Such certainty and predictability are highly valuable for commercial entities, including because it allows them to make associated decisions and plan contingencies. As has been argued by Born and Kalelioglu, "[a] choice of law clause . . . provides enhanced predictability, security and efficiency in the interpterion and enforcement of the parties' right and obligations, which are critical to commercial parties".[1]

Such a clause also allows the parties to avoid a dispute about what is the law to be applied to the agreement in the absence of a choice of law which can be costly and distract parties from the efficient resolution of the substantive dispute. In the absence of a choice of law clause or any subsequent agreement between the parties, the contract will be governed by the law of the state that is most closely connected to the transaction, and this may not be particularly appropriate or beneficial for the parties and/or their transaction. In light of the benefits of using choice of law clauses in commercial agreements, such clauses are now widely used in such international agreements.

B Recognition of Choice of Law Agreements

The use and application of choice of law agreements are recognised worldwide and have presumptive validity.[2] As stated by Girsberger et al., "[i]n a global perspective, the vast majority of jurisdictions recognise the principle of party autonomy with respect to choosing the law applicable to international commercial contracts".[3] In light of the extent of the state practice with respect to the recognition of the validity of choice of law agreements, it is said that the norm of a choice of law governing agreements can be considered to have achieved the significant status of customary international law.[4] The consequence of such recognition is the significant use of such clauses in commercial agreements, as explained by Mills: "[t]he use of such clauses is ubiquitous, flourishing as an apparent international consensus around at least certain core questions of their validity and effectiveness has emerged and consolidated".[5] In a 2019 empirical study

1 Gary Born and Cem Kalelioglu, "Choice of Law Agreements in International Contracts" (2012) 50 Georgia Journal of International Law 44, 45, 47 ("Born and Kalelioglu").

2 Ibid., 46.

3 Daniel Girsberger, Thomas Kadner Graziano and Jan L Neels, *Choice of Law in International Commercial Contracts* (OUP, 2021) 34 ("Girsberger").

4 Born and Kalelioglu, note 1, 46. See also Andreas F Lowenfield, "International Litigation and the Quest for Reasonableness" (1994) 245 Rec des Cours 1, 256.

5 Alex Mills, "Conceptualising Party Autonomy in Private International Law" (2019) 2(2) Revue Critique de Droit International Privé 417–426 (Mills).

of 157 international supply agreements, Coyle and Drahozal found that 99% of the agreements contained a choice of law clause.[6]

While it is somewhat trite to note, the Court of Appeal of England and Wales explained in *Vita Foods Products Inc v Unus Shipping*:[7]

> [i]t is now well settled that by English law . . . the proper law of the contract "is the law which the parties intended to apply". That intention is objectively ascertained, and, if not expressed, will be presumed from the terms of the contract and relevant surrounding circumstances . . . where there is an express statement by the parties of their intention to select the law of the contract, it is difficult to see what qualifications are possible.

Subsequently, the ability of parties to choose the governing law of their contractual agreements has been endorsed by and incorporated into a number of international legal instruments. In the Convention on the Law Applicable to Contracts for the International Sale of Goods, concluded in 1986, although not in force, Article 7(1) provides that "[a] contract of sale is governed by the law chosen by the parties".

Article 3(1) of the Rome Convention provides that "[a] contract shall be governed by the law chosen by the parties . . . By their choice the parties can select the law applicable to the whole or a part only of the contract".[8] It is stated in the report on the Convention prepared by Professors Giuliano and Lagarde that this article of the Convention "reaffirms a rule currently embodied in the private international law of all of the Member States of the Community and of most other countries".[9]

Similarly, in EC Regulation 593/2008 (Rome I),[10] it is recorded at recital 6 that "[t]he proper functioning of the internal market creates a need, in order to improve the predictability of the outcome of litigation, certainly as to the law applicable", and further recital 11 states that "[t]he parties' freedom to choose the applicable law should be one of the cornerstones of the system of conflict-of-law rules in matters of contractual obligations". Article 3 goes on to provide that "[a] contract shall be governed by the law chosen by the parties".

Article 7 of the Inter-American Convention on the Law Applicable to International Contracts ("Mexico Convention") provides that "[t]he contract shall be governed by the law chosen by the parties. . . . Said selection may relate to the entire contract or to a part of same".[11] It must be noted, however, that the Mexico Convention has only been ratified and put into force by two states, Mexico and Venezuela.[12] Therefore its

6 John F Coyle and Christopher R Drahozal, "An Empirical Study of Dispute Resolution Clauses in International Supply Contracts" (2019) 52 Vanderbilt Journal of Transnational Law 327.

7 [1939] AC 277, 289.

8 Convention 80/934/EEC on the law applicable to contractual obligations opened for signature in Rome on 19 June 1980 OJ L 266, 9.10.1980, 1–19. ("Rome Convention").

9 Mario Giuliano and Paul Lagarde, *Report on the Convention on the law applicable to contractual obligations* (C-282, 31/10/1980) 15, https://eur-lex.europa.eu/legal-content/EN/TXT/PDF/?uri=CELEX:31980Y1031(01), last accessed 18 December 2023 ("Giuliano and Lagarde report").

10 Regulation (EC) No 593/2008 of the European Parliament and of the Council of 17 June 2008 on the law applicable to contractual obligations OJ L 177, 4.7.2008, 6–16 ("Rome I").

11 Inter-American Convention on the Law Applicable to International Contracts signed at Mexico, D.F., Mexico, on 17 March 1994, at the Fifth Inter-American Specialized Conference on Private International Law (CIDIP-V).

12 See Signatories and Ratifications, Inter-American Convention on the Law Applicable to International Contracts. www.oas.org/juridico/english/sigs/b-56.html, last accessed 18 December 2023.

significance is perhaps rather limited, albeit the fact that it was concluded represents an acceptance, at least in principle, of the freedom of parties to make a choice of law.

The non-binding Hague Principles on Choice of Law in International Commercial Contracts (the "Hague Principles"), which are said to be "an illustration of how a comprehensive choice of law regime for giving effect to party autonomy may be constructed and as a guide to 'best practices' in establishing and refining such a regime", provide in Article 2(1) that "[a] contract is governed by the law chosen by the parties".[13] The Hague Principles reflect the establishment of an almost universal recognition of the validity of choice of law agreements in international commercial contracts.

C Party Autonomy

As has already been mentioned, the underpinning normative basis for choice of law clauses is the principle of party autonomy. This is the idea that just as parties are free to choose to enter into contractual relationships, as well as the nature, scope and extent of those relationships, the parties should be similarly free to determine how the contract should be governed and where disputes arising out of the contract shall be adjudicated. In the Preamble to the Hague Principles – which are underpinned by the objective of promoting party autonomy in private international law – it is stated that:

> [p]arty autonomy, which refers to the power of parties to a contract to choose the law that governs that contract, enhances certainty and predictability within the parties' primary contractual arrangement and recognises that parties to a contract may be in the best position to determine which set of legal principles is most suitable for their transaction. Many States have reached this conclusion and, as a result, giving effect to party autonomy is the predominant view today.

Furthermore, it has been said that "party autonomy has become, or at least is in the process of becoming, close to universal and incontestable as a 'unifying principle' of modern private international law" and that it is the entire foundation of such a body of law.[14]

III Limitations of Choice of Law Agreements

While the concept of party autonomy is well established as a grundnorm of private international law, there remain several limits upon the application of choice of law agreements created by parties to a contract; the freedom of parties is not wholly absolute. This is even recognised within the Hague Principles with it being stated in the Preamble that "[w]hile the aim of the Principles is to promote the acceptance of party autonomy for choice of law, the principles also provide for limitations on that autonomy".

13 Hague Conference on Private International Law, Principles on Choice of Law in International Commercial Contracts (19/05/2015). www.hcch.net/en/instruments/conventions/full-text/?cid=135, last accessed 18 December 2023.

14 Mills, note 5, 3.

The limits on choice of law represent the nation-state continuing to assert some level of control over the regulation of parties' contractual relationships and, particularly, the use of a state's law in order to resolve disputes arising out of the contractual agreement. Whilst the ongoing and deepening entrenchment of the principle of party autonomy represents the continued evolution of a variegated supranationalised international society within which the governance of private relationships and transactions can take place within and beyond the state, and such mechanisms of governance are constantly evolving, including with the growth of soft law, there are various limitations imposed which demonstrate the continued and vital role of the nation-state.

In this section, we shall consider some of the potential limitations to the freedom of parties to choose the governing law of their contract and the application of it and the extent to which they can be considered to impose a limitation upon party autonomy. More specifically, we shall consider three particular matters: (1) the jurisdictional nexus and mandatory rules; (2) the role of public policy; and (3) the requirement that the choice of law be state law.

A Jurisdictional Nexus/Mandatory Rules

Notwithstanding the principle of choice of law, there was traditionally a need for a relationship to exist between the parties to a contract or its substance for a particular state's law to be applied in the resolution of a dispute, which is known as the jurisdictional nexus. The reason for such an approach was potentially to ensure that parties to a contract which was very clearly associated with and connected to only one state did not seek to avoid any particular rules and laws of that state by choosing the law of another jurisdiction. It would have also ensured that the state with the closest connection to the matter maintained control over the parties and the transaction. It is also likely the product of the fact that in the past, far fewer contracts would have been truly international in their nature as compared to today, where rapid globalisation has permitted and fostered transnational commence on a substantial scale to such an extent that agreements may have little to do, if anything, with any particular nation-state.

As a consequence, the position has moved on and in most jurisdictions, albeit not all, the need for a jurisdictional nexus is no longer a requirement for a court to uphold and apply the parties' choice of law. This clearly represents an enhancement of party autonomy and more specifically, the freedom of parties to choose the state law which is best suited to the parties' needs and/or is most convenient. Article 2(4) of the Hague Principles provides that "[n]o connection is required between the law chosen and the parties or their transaction", and this reflects the wide adoption of this position.

It should be noted, however, that some states, including the United States, continue to require a jurisdictional nexus. The United States retains a requirement that there must be a "substantial relationship" between a transaction or the parties to a transaction and the chosen law which governs the rights and duties of the parties in order for the courts to uphold and apply the choice of law clause. It is said that "[t]he requirement of a 'substantial relationship' is fulfilled if a designated State is one where the contract was formed or to be performed or where the parties had their domicile or establishment when the contract was made".[15]

There is no jurisdictional nexus requirement in the Rome Convention. However, it is important for there to be consideration of Article 3(3) of the Convention, which does impose a form of limitation on the parties' choice of law, and the extent of that limit merits detailed consideration. Article 3(3) states:

> The fact that the parties have chosen a foreign law, whether or not accompanied by the choice of a foreign tribunal, shall not, where all the other elements relevant to the situation at the time of the choice are connected with one country only, prejudice the application of rules of the law of that country which cannot be derogated from by contract, hereinafter called "mandatory rules".

The successor to the Rome Convention, Rome I, contains a similar provision to the foregoing, also in Article 3(3):

> [w]here all other elements relevant to the situation at the time of the choice of law are located in a country other than the country whose law has been chosen, the choice of law of the parties shall not prejudice the application of provisions of law of that other country which cannot be derogated from by agreement.

While the language differs slightly from the Rome Convention, recital 15 of Rome I explains that "no substantial change is intended as compared with Article 3(3) of the 1980 Convention".

In respect of the inclusion of Article 3(3) in the Rome Convention, it was explained in the Giuliano and Lagarde Report that:[16]

> This solution is the result of a compromise between two lines of argument which have been diligently pursued within the Group: the wish on the one hand of certain experts to limit the parties' freedom of choice embodied in this Article by means of a correcting factor specifying that the choice of a foreign law would be insufficient per se to permit the application of that law if the situation at the moment of choice did not involve another foreign element, and on the other the concern of other experts, notably the United Kingdom experts, that such a correcting factor would be too great an obstacle to the freedom of the parties in situations in which their choice appeared justified, made in good faith, and capable of serving interests worthy of protection. In particular these experts emphasized that departures from the principle of the parties' freedom of choice should be authorized only in exceptional circumstances, such as the application of the mandatory rules of a law other than that chosen by the parties; they also gave several examples of cases in which the choice of a foreign law by the parties was fully justified, although there was apparently no other foreign element in the situation.

The purpose of the provision is to prevent parties, by way of a choice of law, from avoiding important mandatory provisions of the law of a state which would, but for the choice of law agreement, govern the contractual agreement. In *Banco Santander Totta SA v Companhia Carris de Ferro de Lisboa SA* ("*Banco Santander*"),[17] a case in which the application of Article 3(3) of the Rome Convention was considered in detail

15 Girsberger note 3, 36–37.
16 Giuliano and Lagarde Report, note 9, 18.
17 [2016] EWHC 465 (Comm).

and which will be looked at further later, Blair J explained that the "underlying policy is to prevent the parties avoiding internally mandatory rules" in a purely domestic case.[18]

In this case, Portuguese public sector companies had entered into long-term interest rate swaps agreements with the claimant bank, Banco Santander, which were subject to English law and the jurisdiction of the English courts, despite the transaction seemingly having little or nothing to do with England and Wales. The defendant companies argued that Article 3(3) was engaged so that the mandatory rules of Portuguese law, which provided defences to the claimant's claim, including that the swaps were prohibited gambles, which were not available under English law, applied.

In his detailed and careful analysis, which merits consideration, Blair J noted the priority to be given to the parties' freedom of choice and the absence of any European authority on Article 3(3). He explained that because Article 3(3) permitted an incursion into parties' choice of law, and, therefore, into the agreed rights and obligations, the provision needed to be interpreted strictly.[19] Blair J went on to explain his opinion that the purpose of the rule was to prevent the parties from avoiding any mandatory rules in a purely domestic case, and there was no need to show evasiveness or bad faith, so the relevant question was whether the transaction was a purely domestic one.[20] He further explained: "the court is not concerned to determine the applicable law – there is already a valid choice of law. The question is whether the choice takes effect subject to non-derogable provisions in domestic law".[21] The conclusion reached by the court was that:[22]

> For the purposes of article 3.3 of the Rome Convention, in determining whether, choice of law aside, all the other elements relevant to the situation are connected with one country only, the inquiry is not limited to elements that are local to another country, but includes elements that point directly from a purely domestic to an international situation. In financial transactions, the use of ISDA or other standard documentation used internationally may be relevant.

The essence of Blair J's decision was, therefore, that Article 3(3) would not apply if there was an internationalised agreement such that the transaction was not a purely domestic one.

In reaching this conclusion, Blair J rejected and departed from the reasoning and conclusions adopted by Walker J in the very similar case of *Dexia Crediop S.p.A v Comune di Prato* ("*Dexia*").[23] In this case, Walker J decided that the defendant would be entitled to rely upon relevant provisions of Italian law in defence of the claim, despite the contract between the parties providing for a choice of English law, in accordance with Article 3(3) of the Rome Convention.[24] Walker J proceeded on the basis that in order for a case to fall within Article 3(3) the defendant would need to show *no elements*

18 Ibid. [373].
19 Ibid. [367].
20 Ibid. [373].
21 Ibid. [394].
22 Ibid. [404].
23 [2015] EWHC 1746 (Comm).
24 Ibid. [212].

relevant to the situation at the time of the choice of law are connected with a country different from Italy.[25] He concluded that despite the agreement between the parties being in international standard form, everything else relevant happened in Italy.[26]

The essence of Walker J's decision was, therefore, that in order for Article 3(3) not to apply in respect of an agreement, there needed to be elements of the transaction that pointed to another jurisdiction and the fact of there being an international agreement did not appear to be enough, particularly where the main elements of the transaction were associated with Italy. It could be said that this was a wider interpretation of Article 3(3) with a greater incursion into the principle of party autonomy.

The defendant companies in *Banco Santander* appealed the decision of Blair J, and the Court of Appeal of England and Wales considered the matter.[27] The relevant ground of appeal was that:[28]

> the Judge was wrong to hold that, in determining whether, choice of law aside, all other elements relevant to the situation are connected with one country only for the purposes of Article 3(3), the enquiry is not limited to elements that are local to another country but include elements that point directly away from a purely domestic to an international situation.

In support of this ground of appeal, it was argued on behalf of the defendant companies that the purpose of Article 3(3) "was to ensure that contracts which are not objectively international in a conflict of laws sense, and fall within the Rome Convention only because of a choice of law by the parties, remain subject to the mandatory rules of what is objectively the proper law" and they relied upon the analysis of Walker J in *Dexia*.[29]

The Court of Appeal disagreed with the criticism of Blair J's approach and rejected the appeal. The Court of Appeal reasoned that the "primary rule, or fundamental principle, is the parties' autonomy to choose the applicable law";[30] "Article 3(3) is properly to be approached as a limited exception to the policy or principle or starting point of party autonomy and, as such, it is to be construed narrowly";[31] the defendants' "interpretation of Article 3(3) provides a much wider exception to the fundamental principle of party autonomy";[32] and:[33]

> If it had been intended that "elements relevant to the situation" in Article 3(3) should be confined to factors of a kind which connect the contract to a particular country for the purpose of identifying the proper law in the absence of an express choice, the drafter could have used the familiar and simple conflict of laws language of "close connection", which one finds in Article 4. The marked difference between the language of Article 3(3) and of Article 4(1) is striking and supports an interpretation of Article 3(3) in accordance with the natural and ordinary meaning of its words.

---

25 Ibid. [209].
26 Ibid. [211].
27 *Banco Santander Totta SA v Companhia Carris de Ferro de Lisboa SA* [2016] EWCA Civ 1267.
28 Ibid. [25].
29 Ibid. [35]–[37].
30 Ibid. [44].
31 Ibid. [46].
32 Ibid. [51].
33 Ibid. [53].

The Court of Appeal went on to hold that[34]

> the enquiry under Article 3(3) includes elements that point directly from a purely domestic to an international situation. Expressing the same point in a different way, I accept Mr Rabinowitz's submission, that the only question under Article 3(3), so far as relevant to this part of the appeal, is whether the situation is purely domestic.

Prior to the judgment of the Court of Appeal in *Banco Santander* being delivered, the claimant in *Dexia* appealed against the decision of Walker J and, in a judgment delivered after *Banco Santander*, the Court of Appeal upheld the appeal in respect of Walker J's application of Article 3(3).[35] On this point, it was explained in the court's judgment that the critical question was whether, apart from the law and jurisdiction clause, all other elements relevant to the situation were connected with one country only.[36] It was noted that Walker J had considered that "the phrase 'elements in the situation' had to be elements connected to a country other than Italy"[37] but that in the Court of Appeal's decision in *Banco Santander*, it had rejected the argument that Blair J was wrong in deciding that the "elements relevant to the situation" could include factors of an international kind which did not point to another country.[38]

The Court of Appeal in *Dexia* decided that it was bound by the Court of Appeal decision in *Banco Santander* and, therefore, given there was standard international documentation which governed the relationship between the parties, namely the IDSA Master Agreement, and the fact back-to-back contracts had been concluded with banks outside of Italy, that this[39]

> was enough on its own to demonstrate an international and relevant element in the situation such that it is impossible to say that "all elements (other than the choice of law) relevant to the situation" are located in a country other than England such as (in this case) Italy. The international dimension precludes any such assertion. The use of the IDSA Master Agreement is self-evidently not connected with any particular country and is used precisely because it is not intended to be associated exclusively with any such country.

It was further stated that "[o]nce an international element comes into the picture, Article 3(3) with its reference to mandatory rules should have no application".[40] The defendants sought permission to appeal to the Supreme Court but such permission was refused. This approach was followed in a number of subsequent cases including *Dexia Crediop SpA v Provincia di Pesaro e Urbino*[41] and *Banca Intesa Sanpaolo SpA and another v Comune di Venezia*.[42]

What one can see from this analysis is that a strict interpretation is applied in respect of Article 3(3) which is consistent with upholding the parties' choice of law and their autonomy in making such a decision which, as stated in Rome I, is a cornerstone of

34 Ibid. [57].
35 *Dexia Crediop S.p.A v Comune di Prato* [2017] EWCA Civ 428.
36 Ibid. [121].
37 Ibid. [125].
38 Ibid. [126].
39 Ibid. [134].
40 Ibid. [137].
41 [2022] EWHC 2410 (Comm) [78]–[80].
42 [2022] EWHC 2586 (Comm) [338]–[342].

the conflict of law rules. It is only where a transaction is purely domestic, that Article 3(3) will be engaged and a court will be required to apply the mandatory rules of the relevant state. It is also important to note that where Article 3(3) is engaged, it does not mean that the choice of law is wholly invalidated. Rather, the choice of law is upheld but subject to the mandatory rules of the other state, which cannot be derogated from. Therefore, even in the narrow and limited circumstances in which Article 3(3) applies, the choice of law is only restricted to a certain degree. This strikes a careful balance between upholding the principle of party autonomy and preventing the principle from being abused by parties to avoid particular and important rules of law which would otherwise apply but for the choice of law.

B Public Policy

Whilst there is broad freedom for parties to select the law governing their agreement, virtually all jurisdictions retain an ability to refuse to enforce a choice of law that conflicts with any mandatory domestic law or public policy.

Article 7(2) of the Rome Convention provides that "[n]othing in this Convention shall restrict the application of the rules of the law of the forum in a situation where they are mandatory irrespective of the law otherwise applicable to the contract". In respect of this provision, it was explained in the Giuliano and Lagarde Report that "[t]he principle that national courts can give effect under certain conditions to mandatory provisions other than those applicable to the contract by virtue of the choice of the parties or by virtue of a subsidiary connecting factor, has been recognized for several years"[43] and further that "[t]he origin of this paragraph is found in the concern of certain delegations to safeguard the rules of the law of the forum".[44]

This principle was also included in Rome I. Article 9 of the Regulation provides that:

> (1) Overriding mandatory provisions are provisions the respect for which is regarded as crucial by a country for safeguarding its public interests, such as its political, social or economic organisation, to such an extent that they are applicable to any situation falling within their scope, irrespective of the law otherwise applicable to the contract under this Regulation.
> (2) Nothing in this Regulation shall restrict the application of the overriding mandatory provisions of the law of the forum.
> (3) Effect may be given to the overriding mandatory provisions of the law of the country where the obligations arising out of the contract have to be or have been performed, in so far as those overriding mandatory provisions render the performance of the contract unlawful. In considering whether to give effect to those provisions, regard shall be had to their nature and purpose and to the consequences of their application or non-application.

43 Giuliano and Lagarde Report, note 9, 26.
44 Ibid., 28.

In addition, Article 21 of Rome I provides that "[t]he application of a provision of the law of any country specified by this Regulation may be refused only if such application is manifestly incompatible with the public policy (ordre public) of the forum". Recital 37 of Rome I provides interpretative guidance in respect of the aforementioned limiting provisions. It states that "[c]onsiderations of public interest justify giving the courts of Member States the possibility, in *exceptional circumstances*, of applying exceptions based on public policy and overriding mandatory provisions" [emphasis added].

A similar provision is included in the Mexico Convention with Article 11 of the Convention providing that "[n]otwithstanding the provisions of the preceding articles, the provisions of the law of the forum shall necessarily be applied when they are mandatory requirements". This is also reflected in the Hague Principles; Article 11(1) provides that "[t]hese Principles shall not prevent a court from applying overriding mandatory provisions of the law of the forum which apply irrespective of the law chosen by the parties", and Article 11(3) provides that

> [a] court may exclude application of a provision of the law chosen by the parties only if and to the extent that the result of such application would be manifestly incompatible with fundamental notions of public policy (ordre public) of the forum.

The existence of these provisions reflects the retention of control by nation-states against party autonomy; as has been argued by Girsberger et al., the principle of *ordre public* "is based upon the sovereignty and autonomy of each State, and appears to be an overarching condition for the functioning of any system of private international law. Otherwise, difficult tensions would arise with any jurisdiction's domestic law"; furthermore, it is explained that both overriding mandatory provisions and *ordre public* place a limit on party autonomy.[45]

The question, however, is to what extent these principles limit the parties' freedom of choice of law and/or the application of it. It is first noted that the commentary on the Hague Principles explains that:

> [t]he law chosen by the parties may only be excluded "to the extent" that its application would be incompatible with the forum's public policy. Thus, as in the case of overriding mandatory provisions, the existence of an incompatibility of this kind does not deprive the parties' choice of law of any effect. Instead, the chosen law must be applied to the greater possible extent consistently with the public policy of the forum.

This suggests that the choice of law is not overturned by any mandatory provisions or on public policy grounds. Rather, the extent of applying the choice of law may be limited in some respects and in limited circumstances. Again, this represents a careful balancing between upholding party autonomy and protecting key state interests. It is further necessary to consider how the courts have approached these provisions.

In the case of *Deutsche Schachtbau- und Tiefbohrgesellschaft mbH v R'as al-Khaimah National Oil Co*, although not dealing with such provisions expressly, it was said by the Court of Appeal that "[c]onsiderations of public policy . . . should be approached with extreme caution".[46]

45 Girsberger, note 2, 112.
46 [1987] 3 WLR 1023, [1035d].

In *United Antwerp Maritime Agencies (Unamar) NV v Navigation Maritime Bulgare*, it was explained by the Court of Justice of the European Union (CJEU) that *ordre public* legislation "applies to national provisions compliance with which has been deemed to be so crucial for the protection of the political, social and economic order in the Member State concerned".[47] Moreover, given the cornerstone of party autonomy and the choice of law in the Rome Convention and Rome I, "the plea relating to the existence of a 'mandatory rule' within the meaning of legislation of the Member State concerned . . . must be interpreted strictly".[48]

In the case of *Republik Griechenland v Grigorios Nikiforidis*, the Grand Chamber of the CJEU emphasised that Article 9 of Rome I must be "interpreted strictly", and it held that courts were only entitled to restrict the choice of law of parties in respect of the application of overriding mandatory provisions of those states identified expressly within Article 9.[49]

What one can see from the prevailing, albeit limited, case law on the topic is that whilst there is a balance struck between the protection of party autonomy and state interests, the balance is much more in favour of upholding and enhancing party autonomy with mandatory rules only be applicable in clearly defined and exceptional circumstances. Therefore, whilst public policy and mandatory provisions do impose some limitations on the application of the choice of law, in reality, the limitations are very limited.

C Non-state Law

The third section of this chapter briefly considers the question of the choice of non-state law. Non-state law is, as it suggests, rules, norms and principles, other than as created by states, that seek and intend to govern the relationship between commercial entities. It may be a set of rules or principles established by an international organisation, a group of experts, or a specialist entity. These may be promoted as an alternative or complementary to state law.

An example of such non-state law is the UNIDROIT Principles of International Commercial Contracts.[50] These are a detailed set of rules and principles governing contractual relationships, and they include articles relating to the formation of contracts (Section 1), agency (Section 2), validity (Chapter 3), and interpretation (Chapter 4). The question is whether such non-state law could be a choice of law within the jurisdiction of national courts.

At present, it is generally understood and accepted in the vast majority of jurisdictions that parties do not have the option of making a choice of non-state law in order to govern their rights and duties established in a commercial contract if any disputes arising out of the contract are to be litigated in the courts of a state,

47 C-184/12, *United Antwerp Maritime Agencies (Unamar) NV v Navigation Maritime Bulgare* ECLI:EU:C:2013:663, para 47.
48 Ibid. [48].
49 C-135/15, *Republik Griechenland v Grigorios Nikiforidis* ECLI:EU:C:2016:774, paras 44–55.
50 UNIDROIT Principles of International Commercial Contracts (4th Edn, 2016). www.unidroit.org/wp-content/uploads/2021/06/Unidroit-Principles-2016-English-bl.pdf, last accessed 18 December 2023.

as opposed to being resolved in some private forum, such as arbitration, where the scope for the use of non-state law is much wider. It appears that only a few nation-states provide for the ability to select non-state law: Venezuela, Argentina,[51] Paraguay, Bahrain, Ukraine, and Qatar.[52]

In many states, however, it is possible for parties to incorporate the chosen non-state law as part of the terms of the contractual agreement such that the non-state law may regulate the relations between the parties. However, the contract as a whole would still be subject to the law of the state.

Using non-state law would represent a significant challenge to the state-based global order. It would arguably divest states of a substantial level of control and governance over contractual relationships between parties and represent a further step in privatising the commercial sphere. The use of non-state law would represent a significant extension of party autonomy.

The use of non-state law is a central and important feature of the Hague Principles. Article 3 of the Principles provides: "[t]he law chosen by the parties may be rules of law that are generally accepted on an international, supranational or regional level as a neutral and balanced set of rules, unless the law of the forum provides otherwise". The commentary to the Principles states that the rules "must have garnered general recognition beyond a national level", which is the emancipation of choice of law from the state, and that they must be a set of rules which implies the need for comprehensiveness akin to what one would find at the domestic level. The notes to the Principles recognise that the extent of non-state law is at present limited but growing given the "dynamic and evolving nature of international commercial law". It will be remembered, of course, that the Hague Principles are not binding but rather are guidance that seek to advance the principle of party autonomy.

The role of non-state law is given express consideration in Rome I. It had been suggested during the negotiating stages of the Regulation that non-state law should be permitted as a choice of law. However, it was not adopted in the final version of the Regulation.[53] The Regulation does provide at recital 13, however, that it "does not preclude parties from incorporating by reference into their contract a non-State body of law or an international convention", and it thereby provides for some role for non-state law. Recital 14 further provides that "[s]hould the Community adopt, in an appropriate legal instrument, rules of substantive contract law, including standard terms and conditions, such instrument may provide that the parties may choose to apply those rules", which recognises the potential for the future development of non-state law.

While the idea of using non-state law enhances the application of party autonomy superficially, its practical relevance is perhaps somewhat limited. This is because of the limited non-state law frameworks that are available for choosing by parties and

51 Born and Kalelioglu, note 1, 86.

52 Girsberger, note 2, 46.

53 Commission of the European Communities, Proposal for a Regulation of the European Parliament and the Council on the law applicable to contractual obligations (Rome I) (15 December 2005) Doc. COM/2005, 650 Final https://eur-lex.europa.eu/LexUriServ/LexUriServ.do?uri=COM:2005:0650:FIN:EN:PDF, last accessed 18 December 2023.

the limited depth of those existing rules. Whilst it is possible for an organisation to develop a detailed set of rules that could govern a contractual relationship between parties, there will always be a dearth of interpretative principles and decisions which help guide the application of the rules, such as we find in domestic law. This may not be so much of an issue regarding very simple and straightforward contracts and disputes, but non-state law is unlikely to be equipped to deal with complex, transnational commercial relationships. This creates substantial unpredictability in respect of how a contract would be interpreted and how disputes would likely be resolved, which creates uncertainty and risk for parties. Therefore, parties may ask themselves what is the point of using non-state law, at least at the present time.

It can, therefore, be concluded that whilst the inability of parties to choose non-state law as the law governing their transaction and any disputes arising out of it does represent a substantial limitation on choice of law, the limitation is more theoretical than a reality. As stated, it is not really feasible for parties to choose to use non-state law at present given the limited legal frameworks that could be adopted and given that those frameworks do not come equipped with the often vast background of case law that critically assists in the interpretation and the application of rules, as there is in domestic legal systems.

IV Conclusion

In summary, what one can learn from this chapter is that there is a wide and well-established consensus around the world as to the importance of the choice of law for parties to international commercial transactions, which is firmly underpinned by the cornerstone principle of party autonomy. Whilst there are limits to the choice of law and, more particularly, the application of the choice of law, the circumstances in which such limitations are engaged are narrow and they do not substantially or unjustifiably impinge on the principle of party autonomy in the choice of law.

CHAPTER 14

Methodological Variations in Determining Applicable Laws in International Commercial Arbitration

A Comprehensive Analysis

*Patricia Živković**

I Introduction

International commercial arbitration does not exist in a legal vacuum but functions in a different legal environment from national courts. Unlike national courts, arbitral tribunals are not automatically subject (at least not entirely) to the laws of the jurisdiction where the arbitration is seated, including conflict of laws provisions. In my previous work, I focused on the issue of limited court review, a cornerstone of arbitration that has undergone certain adjustments in the past few decades.[1] These adjustments have consisted of widening the scope of public policy grounds during the annulment/enforcement stage and interventionist attitudes of national courts in cases when the parties claim to be "taken by surprise" by arbitrators' choice or application of the law.[2] This chapter builds on that work by discussing the primary question of the methodology applied by arbitral tribunals when determining the applicable law in arbitration.

The central thesis of this chapter is that there is a need to preserve a proper understanding of the methodological differences between national courts and arbitral tribunals in their determination of the applicable law in arbitration to achieve procedural efficiency and retain the legitimacy of arbitration as a dispute resolution method. To support this argument, the methodology for choosing the following applicable laws will be analysed:

- the law, or the relevant legal rules, governing merits, i.e. the substantive issues in dispute;
- the law governing the arbitration agreement;
- the law governing the effects of bankruptcy of one of the parties to an ongoing arbitration;
- the law governing the allocation of costs in arbitration.

* **Senior lecturer in International Dispute Resolution (University of Aberdeen, School of Law); Associate Director of the Centre for Private International Law (University of Aberdeen); Member of the Centre for Commercial Law (University of Aberdeen).** I am grateful to my friend and colleague Dr Euan West for reading an earlier draft of this chapter and providing invaluable comments and suggestions.

1 Patricia Živković, "International Commercial Arbitration: Law Applicable to Merits and 'Creeping' Judicial Substantive Review" in Justin Borg-Barthet, Katarina Trimmings, Burcu Yüksel Ripley, Patricia Zivkovic (eds), *From Theory to Practice in Private International Law* (Bloomsbury 2024) (Živković).

2 Ibid.

DOI: 10.4324/9781032726243-17

The determination of these laws developed, to varying degrees, through legislation, arbitral practice, and doctrine and has reflected different tendencies in the localisation and transnationalisation of arbitration law.

The transnational approach is the starting point for modern arbitration when determining applicable laws. The transnational and international theories of international arbitration contributed to the more widespread use of arbitration, especially in the second half of the 20th century after adopting the Convention on the Recognition and Enforcement of Foreign Arbitral Awards in 1958 (New York Convention). These theories also served as a baseline for a more liberal approach to determining the applicable laws, as this chapter will show.

Due to this starting point, as a general rule, arbitrators have fewer mandatory conflict of laws rules to follow than national courts and more discretion in determining and applying the applicable substantive laws.[3] However, this chapter argues that, with time, the harmonisation of approaches in determining applicable law throughout different jurisdictions led to perceptible localisation (i.e. territorialisation) of international arbitration. This claim cannot be made for all applicable laws in arbitration. Still, it is submitted that it is borne out as regards the law applicable to merits in arbitration and that applicable to an arbitration agreement (Section II). In this regard, the chapter argues that the methodology for determining applicable law in international arbitration scholarship developed through and together with the progressive development of arbitral practice, which in some cases even led to codification. This chapter also argues that further arbitral practice and jurisprudence may lead to similar results for some other applicable laws in arbitration.

However, the significance of methodological differences between arbitral tribunals and national courts as to how they determine and apply applicable laws is preserved precisely because the legal framework of arbitration allows a more liberal approach to determining applicable laws. For example, such harmonisation and localisation of methodology for determining the applicable law are not yet present when it comes to the law governing the effects of bankruptcy of one of the parties to a pending arbitration (Section III) and the law governing the allocation of costs (Section IV). The former still reflects a fragmented, localised, and non-uniform approach to determining applicable laws. In contrast, the methodology for determining the law applicable to allocating costs transcends national laws and presents a proper transnational legal solution. This chapter contends that practitioners and academics should acknowledge the differences in approach to foster an appropriate understanding of methodology, which is crucial for preventing a loss of predictability in the future but also for preserving the flexibility inherent in international arbitration: one of its most important advantages.

II Harmonisation and Localisation of Methodologies for Determining Applicable Substantive Laws in Arbitration

The methodology for determination of the law applicable to an arbitration agreement and that applicable to the merits developed to the point of providing a solid framework

3 Ibid.

for arbitrators and courts. Due to its harmonisation and localisation tendencies, this developed framework challenges the starting point of arbitral tribunals not belonging to a particular legal system of conflict of laws rules. It is argued in this section that, despite the welcome predictability and harmonisation that characterises the determination of such applicable laws, the methodology for such determination departs from that of national courts. The distinction is crucial and stems from theoretical and legislative frameworks of international arbitration. It serves the essential purpose of allowing for more flexibility in arbitration, and a proper understanding of it preserves procedural efficiency.

As mentioned earlier, the methodology for determining these two applicable laws was designed following the transnational (delocalised) theories of arbitration, according to which the legitimacy of arbitration is rooted in a transnational legal order and not in a national legal system.[4] In this context, it means that arbitrators are, to some extent, sometimes even completely, detached from the conflict of laws rules of the seat and rely heavily on procedural regulations chosen by the parties and/or on their discretion in determining the law.[5]

Despite these transnational roots of methodologies for determining applicable law to merits and an arbitration agreement, the arbitral practice and doctrine eventually led to a more territorial and systemised approach. This will now be addressed in greater detail.

A Critical Assessment of the Need for the Localisation of the Methodology for Determining Applicable Law to Merits

When it comes to the determination of applicable law to merits in arbitration, two aspects need to be observed:

1 who determines the applicable law;
2 the potential scope of the applicable rules that might be determined applicable.[6]

As to who determines the applicable law, party autonomy is recognised as the cornerstone of international arbitral practice. The parties' choice of the law applicable to the merits is the primary source for determining the governing law.[7] Without such a choice, the usual practice recognised in arbitration laws and rules is that the arbitral tribunal will determine the governing law.[8]

Regarding the arbitrator's determination, the first main difference between national courts and arbitral tribunals' respective stances comes to light. The latter are not embedded entirely in the legal system of any jurisdiction, which means that the conflict of laws and rules of the seat are not directly applicable in international

4 Emmanuel Gaillard, *Legal Theory of International Arbitration* (Brill 2012) 15–24 (Gaillard).
5 Živković, note 1, 183.
6 Ibid.
7 English Arbitration Act 1996, s 46(1); French Arbitration Act, art 1511; 2008 UNCITRAL Model Law on International Commercial Arbitration, art 28(1); 2021 ICC Rules, art 21(1); 2020 LCIA Rules, art 22.3; 2021 UNCITRAL Arbitration Rules, art 35(1).
8 English Arbitration Act 1996, s 46(3); French Arbitration Act, art 1511; 2008 UNCITRAL Model Law, art 28(2); 2021 ICC Rules, art 21(1); 2020 LCIA Rules, art 22(3); 2021 UNCITRAL Arbitration Rules, art 35(1).

arbitrations taking place within that jurisdiction.[9] This, however, does not mean that no laws of the seat shall apply. The application of the arbitration law or act of the seat is, in most cases, not contested. These laws, to varying degrees depending on the drafting history, address the methodology for determining the substantive law in international arbitration. Still, they are usually not of a mandatory nature and do not always follow the usual composition of a conflict of laws rule. Therefore, when determining the governing law, arbitral tribunals are to follow the guidance provided by the applicable arbitration rule (contained in the parties' agreements or arbitration rules) or the arbitration law of the seat in the absence of the former. The methods for determination of the governing law in these sources can have a looser or tighter connection to conflict of laws rules:

1 An arbitral tribunal determines the governing law by the conflict of laws rules which it considers applicable.[10]
2 An arbitral tribunal determines the governing law without any reference to conflict of laws rules, but instead, it directly chooses the applicable law it deems appropriate.[11]

In other words, the relevant arbitration rules or arbitration laws will determine to what extent arbitrators are bound to justify their decisions based on the governing law; but even in cases where the rules or the law require them to refer to conflict of laws rules, they do not usually identify the conflict of laws rules of a particular jurisdiction. This is a logical consequence of the lack of a holistic forum for arbitrators as decision-makers.

The first of the methods mentioned earlier is, to some extent, a reflection of the localised theory of arbitration and will usually find its place in national arbitration laws rather than in institutional arbitration rules, given that national legislators are more interested in anchoring arbitral tribunals to the jurisdiction than are independent arbitral institutions. This theory echoes the stance that the legitimacy of the arbitration process stems from the seat, as the national courts have the ultimate power to decide whether an arbitral award is to be set aside.[12]

As a counterweight to this theory stands the transnational theory or the theory of arbitral order, which claims, as mentioned earlier, that "the juridicity of arbitration is rooted in a distinct, transnational order . . . and not in a national legal system".[13] This is a more acceptable approach for independent arbitral institutions, which, in principle, allow arbitral tribunals to determine the governing law without indicating any specific private international law rule but by simply finding such a law "appropriate" in the circumstances.

Figure 14.1 visualises the parties' and arbitrators' methods to determine the governing law. Understanding this methodology and considering inherent features of arbitration, such as the absence of a holistic forum in a conventional sense (which

9 M Petsche, "The Application of Mandatory Rules by Arbitral Tribunals – Three Salient Issues" (2020) 1 ELTE Law Journal 69, 72 (Petsche).

10 English Arbitration Act 1996, s 46(3); French Arbitration Act, art 1511; 2008 UNCITRAL Model Law, art 28(2).

11 French Arbitration Act, art 1511; 2021 ICC Rules, art 21(1); 2020 LCIA Rules, art 22(3); 2021 UNCITRAL Arbitration Rules, art 35(1).

12 Gaillard, note 4, 15–24.

13 Ibid. 35.

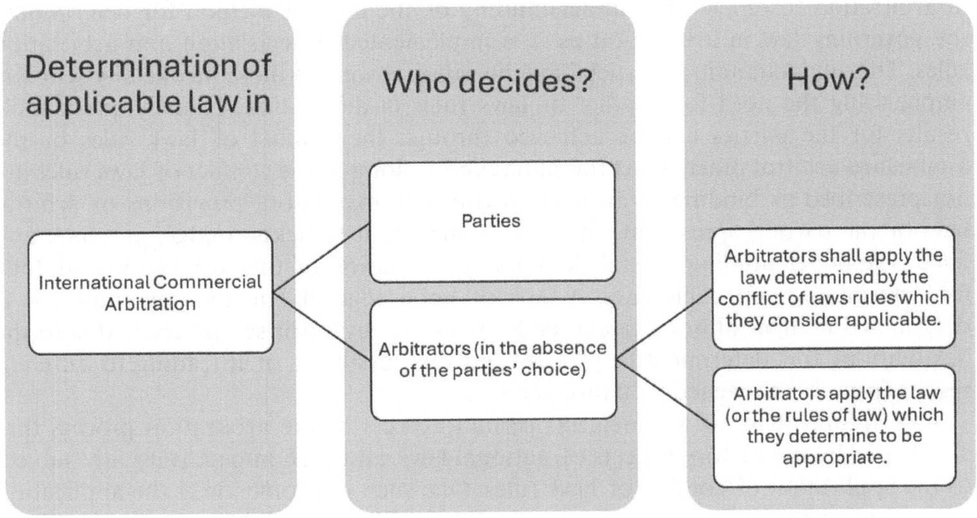

Figure 14.1 Methodology for determining the law applicable to merits in arbitration.

leads to the lack of concrete conflict of laws rules), gives arbitrators and arbitration users more flexibility and control over the decision-making procedure.

This approach regarding arbitrators' methodology for determining the governing law is supported, criticised, and sometimes even reinvented by scholarship. For example, some authors argue that

> whenever the basic provisions were insufficient to decide the case, and the parties did not specify which rules to apply, arbitrators themselves must select the applicable rules [and] [r]ather than applying some national law, they should look for "non-national" or generally accepted rules.[14]

The same authors state that "whenever the other approaches do not work, as ultimate backstop or guide, commercial arbitrators must refer" to the conflict of laws rules of the arbitral *lex fori*.[15] Furthermore, other scholars are calling for the recognition of the usefulness of the application of conflict of laws rules by arbitrators, even when not prompted by legislation, especially in terms of providing predictable results for the parties and improving the effectiveness of arbitration when it comes to preserving an arbitral award amidst the potentially applicable mandatory rules.[16]

This chapter does not argue against the aforementioned scholarly points of view. Instead, it invites scholars, legislators, policymakers, and other stakeholders

14 Hans van Houtte, "Chapter 11: Julian Lew and the Applicable Law in International Courts and Tribunals" in Stavros Brekoulakis, Romesh Weeramantry, Lilit Nagapetyan (eds), *Achieving the Arbitration Dream: Liber Amicorum for Professor Julian DM Lew KC* (Kluwer Law International 2023) 120.

15 Ibid. 122.

16 Giuditta Cordero-Moss, "Why Arbitration Needs Conflict of Laws Rules" (*Kluwer Arbitration Blog*, 17 October 2018) https://arbitrationblog.kluwerarbitration.com/2018/10/17/why-arbitration-needs-conflict-of-laws-rules/, accessed 18 March 2024.

in arbitration to renew their understanding of the current method for determining the governing law in arbitration as it is implemented in legislation and arbitration rules. This understanding is crucial for the same reasons as those invoked by scholars emphasising the need for conflict of laws rules in arbitration. Namely, predictable results for the parties can be achieved through the conflict of laws rules or the established arbitral practice. At the same time, as long as the conflict of laws rules are not prescribed as binding in arbitration (through mandatory provisions of arbitral laws or the parties' agreement), it is more important to acknowledge, preserve, and foster the understanding of stakeholders in arbitration of the current methodology for determining applicable laws. A lack of knowledge of *how* the governing law is determined in arbitral practice can take the parties by surprise[17] precisely due to the flexibility of this determinative process and the possibility of it leading to different results from those reached by national courts.

This argument in no way neglects certain aspects of the arbitration process that are shaped by mandatory aspects of national laws, and such impact is usually subject to the application of conflict of laws rules. One such phenomenon is the application of overriding mandatory rules in arbitration, which are an inherent part of private international law and applicable as a matter of comity by national courts. There is, however, no such duty of comity for international arbitrators.[18] Still, by not applying the mandatory rules, they might jeopardise the enforceability of their arbitral award, so a proper understanding of the issue is needed.

Overriding mandatory rules are rules passed to protect a state's public interest.[19] To give a few examples, these rules usually deal with legal situations stemming from consumer protection, currency control, environmental protection, trade sanctions, competition law matters, and similar issues involving strong public interests.[20]

When national courts resolve the dispute, these norms are meant to replace applicable substantive law and override party autonomy or the law chosen by the forum court.[21] International arbitration has no uniform stance regarding whether arbitrators should consider overriding mandatory rules.[22] It can be concluded that the observation and application of overriding mandatory rules by international arbitrators are still very much decided on a case-by-case basis. Such arbitrators have discretion whether to apply them or not. Unlike national courts, international arbitrators are not bound by legislation providing for the application of overriding mandatory norms and by the principle of comity.

In conclusion, it can be seen that international arbitrators are aware they are not operating in a legal vacuum and need to consult the legal systems that may threaten the validity of their award. However, this does not affect the methodology for determining

17 See more in Živković, note 1, 194–196.

18 Petsche, note 9, 81.

19 H Fazilatfar, *Overriding Mandatory Rules in International Commercial Arbitration* (Edward Elgar 2019) 1 (Fazilatfar).

20 Petsche, note 9, 70; Fazilatfar, note 19, 1.

21 Fazilatfar, note 19, 1.

22 See more in Petsche, note 9; Ibrahim Mohamed Nour Shehata, "Application of Overriding Mandatory Rules in International Commercial Arbitration: An Empirical Analysis" (2017) 11 World Arbitration and Mediation Review 36; Živković, note 1, 187–189.

the applicable law. Without legislative intervention or parties' choice on the matter, international commercial arbitrators enjoy broad discretion in this matter, which is, in some cases, more localised regarding requesting a reference to an applicable conflict of laws rule. These tendencies, however, do not diminish the arbitrators' discretion but strengthen it. In the end, there is a discussion about whether there is a need for bringing arbitration closer to the conventional methodology contained in conflict of laws rules to increase the predictability of results. At the moment, without legislative intervention, such discussion should not overshadow a proper understanding of the less conventional methodology inherent in the arbitration process.

B Harmonising Tendencies Towards the Localisation of the Law Applicable to an Arbitration Agreement

In international arbitration, the choice of law applicable to an arbitration agreement is significant, especially when considering the differing contexts of countries that adopted the UNCITRAL Model Law on International Commercial Arbitration 1985 (UNCITRAL Model Law or Model Law) and non–Model Law countries. The intricacies of this matter are best explored through the lenses of established legal principles and critical cases.

In jurisdictions that adopted the UNCITRAL Model Law, the determination of the law applicable to an arbitration agreement is guided by Article 34. This article stipulates that an arbitral award may be set aside only under specific circumstances. Among other grounds, it provides that the party seeking to set aside the award must provide evidence regarding the incapacity of a party involved or the validity of the arbitration agreement under the "law to which the parties have subjected it or, failing any indication thereon, under the law of [the state of the seat]". Though indirectly, this article provides a conflict of laws rule on determining the law applicable to the arbitration agreement. It gives priority to the parties' agreement, in the absence of which it determines the law of the seat as applicable to the validity of the arbitration agreement. This conflict of laws rule is aligned with the New York Convention that refers in Article V(1)(a) to the law "to which the parties have subjected [the arbitration agreement] or, failing any indication thereon, [to] the law of the country where the award was made". This approach ensures a consistent framework for the determination of applicable law in international arbitration contexts and speaks in favour of the localisation of the law applicable to the arbitration agreement since both of these conflict of laws rules tie the arbitration agreement's validity to the law of the seat, in the absence of the parties' agreement.

Contrasting with UNCITRAL Model Law countries, one might expect that the approach(es) in non–Model Law countries differ from the Model Law solution. In fact, that was so for quite some time. For example, in England and Wales, in 2012, the *Sulamerica* case introduced a comprehensive three-pronged test for identifying the law governing an arbitration agreement.[23] This test considers whether the parties explicitly chose a governing law, made an implied choice, or identified the law with the closest

23 *Sulamerica CIA Nacional De Seguros SA & Ors v Enesa Engenharia SA & Ors* [2012] EWCA Civ 638 (EWCA (Civ)), [2013] 1 WLR 102.

and most real connection to the agreement in the absence of both. Since then, the *Enka v Chubb* case deviated to an extent from the Sulamerica test by deeming the law of the seat to enjoy a strong presumption as an implied choice:[24]

(1) The AA law is to be determined by applying the three stage test required by English common law conflict of laws rules, namely (i) is there an express choice of law? (ii) if not, is there an implied choice of law? (iii) if not, with what system of law does the arbitration agreement have its closest and most real connection?
(2) Where there is an express choice of law in the main contract it may amount to an express choice of the AA law. Whether it does so will be a matter of construction of the whole contract, including the arbitration agreement, applying the principles of construction of the main contract law if different from English law.
(3) *In all other cases there is a strong presumption that the parties have impliedly chosen the curial law as the AA law*. This is the general rule, but may yield to another system of law governing the arbitration agreement where there are powerful countervailing factors in the relationship between the parties or the circumstances of the case [emphasis added].

In 2022 and 2023, building upon this case law while conducting consultation concerning the Arbitration Act 1996, the Law Commission sought responses to address the proposal "that the law of the arbitration agreement is the law of the seat unless the parties expressly agree otherwise in the arbitration agreement itself".[25] Most respondents to the consultation supported this reform, which was introduced in the Arbitration Bill in September 2023.[26] In other words, the localisation of the law applicable to the arbitration agreement, which developed to a certain extent through arbitral practice in England and Wales, might lead to the localisation of this governing law through legislation.

England and Wales is not the only non–Model Law jurisdiction that follows the steps of the Model Law Article 34 solution. The Swedish Arbitration Act,[27] another non–Model Law arbitration law, in s 48 provides that for an arbitration agreement that "has an international connection, the agreement shall be governed by the law agreed upon by the parties", and "[i]f the parties have not reached such an agreement, the arbitration agreement shall be governed by the law of the country where, by the parties' agreement, the arbitration had or shall have its seat". Moreover, Switzerland provides for the *in favorem validitatis* conflict of laws rule in Swiss Private International Law (Swiss PIL), according to which arbitration agreements are deemed valid if they conform to the law chosen by the parties, the law governing the subject matter of the dispute or Swiss law.[28] Interestingly, the Swiss PIL does not recognise the primacy of

24 *Enka Insaat Ve Sanayi AS v OOO Insurance Company Chubb* [2020] UKSC 38, [2020] 1 WLR 4117; *Enka Insaat Ve Sanayi AS v OOO Insurance Company Chubb & Ors* [2020] EWCA Civ 574 (EWCA (Civ)), [2020] 3 All ER 577.

25 Law Commission of England and Wales, "Review of the Arbitration Act 1996". https://lawcom.gov.uk/project/review-of-the-arbitration-act-1996/, accessed 18 March 2024.

26 Ibid.

27 SFS (2018:1954).

28 Emmanuel Gaillard and John Savage (eds), *Fouchard, Gaillard, Goldman on International Commercial Arbitration* (1999) 237–238.

party autonomy. Instead, this conflict of laws rule is localised through the national legislation of the seat. Yet, it allows for more discretion and favours the effectiveness of arbitration agreements, which is, in essence, an argument in favour of recognising the international framework.

Representing the other end of the spectrum, i.e. a purely transnational approach, French law considers arbitration agreements to be governed by supranational rules. The argument is that these agreements derive their existence, validity, and effectiveness

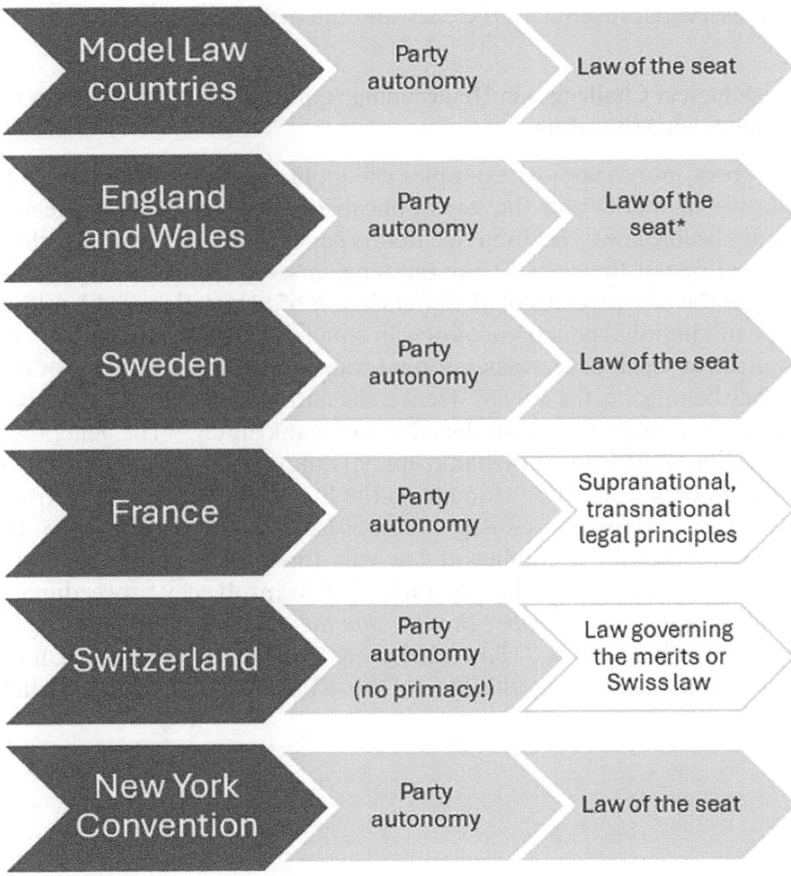

Figure 14.2 Harmonising tendencies towards the localisation of law applicable to an arbitration agreement.

* At the time of writing, the Arbitration Bill proposes the law of the seat in England and Wales as a legislative solution. Under case law, the law of the seat currently enjoys a strong presumption as an implied choice, which can be overruled depending on the circumstances of the case. In this respect, England and Wales is a jurisdiction that showcases the localisation trend.

from supranational law, thereby rendering the need for reference to national law unnecessary.[29]

As Figure 14.2 shows, comparing the example jurisdictions mentioned, it becomes clear that determining the law applicable to an arbitration agreement does not have a globally accepted methodology but is shaped by legal frameworks, cases, and scholarship. While UNCITRAL Model Law countries, non–Model Law countries, and varying national perspectives contribute to the complexity of this issue, there is some perceptible harmonisation of the issue on the horizon. While the harmonisation of these conflict of laws rules through arbitration legislation progresses further, it is even more critical to preserve the knowledge of all available methodologies and the scope of arbitrators' discretion on the determination of applicable law matters, yet again for preserving procedural efficiency and the overall legitimacy of arbitration.

III Methodological Challenges in Determining Applicable Laws to the Effects of Bankruptcy on Arbitration

Departing from more classical examples of applicable laws – the law and rules of law applicable to merits and the law applicable to the arbitration agreement – the following applicable law to be discussed in this paper is the law governing the effects of bankruptcy of one of the parties to an ongoing cross-border arbitration. This analysis will showcase the complexities of the intersection of arbitration and bankruptcy that arbitrators and national courts encounter in some cross-border arbitration disputes.

As discussed in previous sections, national courts are bound by the law of the country to which they belong, i.e. the *lex fori*. Hence, the national and cross-border bankruptcy laws provide the applicable law on the effects of bankruptcy.[30] The generally accepted law which governs the impact of bankruptcy is the *lex fori concursus* (the law of the bankruptcy proceedings).[31] For example, in the European Union (EU), Article 7(1) of the Recast European Insolvency Regulation 2015/848[32] (Recast European Insolvency Regulation) provides for a conflict of law rule for the law applicable to the effects of bankruptcy. It states that "the law applicable to insolvency proceedings and their effects shall be that *of the Member State within the territory of which such proceedings are opened*" [emphasis added].[33] Hence, the general rule under the European Insolvency Regulation is that the law applicable to the effects of bankruptcy is the *lex fori*

29 Ibid., 228–236.

30 Simon Vorburger, *International Arbitration and Cross-Border Insolvency: Comparative Perspectives* (Kluwer Law International 2014) 83–84 (Vorburger).

31 Ibid., 86.

32 Regulation (EU) 2015/848 of the European Parliament and of the Council of 20 May 2015 on insolvency proceedings (recast) [2015] OJ L 141, pp. 19–72. In force as of 26 June 2015, with amendments in 2017, 2018, and 2021.

33 The original Council Regulation (EC) No 1346/2000 of 29 May 2000 on insolvency proceedings [2020] OJ L 160, pp 1–18 provided for the same rule in art 4(1).

concursus.[34] Such conflict of laws rules follow the prevailing principle of universalism, favouring applying the law of the "main" insolvency proceedings.[35]

Although based on the idea of more effective bankruptcy laws through their broader reach in the international market, the principle of universalism is not unlimited.[36] There are certain exceptions to it in the European Insolvency Regulation as well. For example, the Recast European Insolvency Regulation provides in Article 18 that[37]

> The effects of insolvency proceedings on a pending lawsuit or pending arbitral proceedings concerning an asset or a right which forms part of a debtor's insolvency estate shall be governed solely by *the law of the Member State in which that lawsuit is pending or in which the arbitral tribunal has its seat.* [emphasis added]

However, applying these conflict of laws rules will be preceded by characterising a legal issue. A so-called Vivendi saga of courts' decisions on the relation between bankruptcy and arbitration exemplifies the importance of characterising the legal category. The Vivendi saga was discussed before two different sets of national courts – the English courts and the Swiss court – and the courts came to different conclusions due to differences in characterisation and different applicable laws.[38] In both cases, one of the parties, a Polish company called Elektrim, went bankrupt in the course of arbitration, and this led to the possible application of Article 142 of the Polish Law on Bankruptcy and Reorganization (Polish LBR), which provides that:

> [a]ny arbitration clause concluded by the bankrupt shall lose its legal effect as at the date bankruptcy is declared and any pending arbitration proceedings shall be discontinued.

The provision was, however, applied only by the Swiss court and not by the English court(s). Namely, the English courts resolved the issue by applying Article 18 of the European Insolvency Regulation Recast. They found English law applicable as "the law of the Member State in which that lawsuit [was] pending". Since English law contained no legal provisions that would require the discontinuance of the arbitration, the courts did not set aside the arbitral award.

The Swiss Federal Supreme Court did not apply the Recast European Insolvency Regulation for obvious reasons. It characterised the issue of a bankrupt Polish party as one regarding legal capacity and applied Swiss PIL to determine the governing law.

---

34 Vorburger, note 30, 86.

35 Jay Lawrence Westbrook, "International Arbitration and Multinational Insolvency" (2010) 29 Penn State International Law Review 635, 643.

36 Ibid.

37 The original Council Regulation (EC) No 1346/2000 of 29 May 2000 on insolvency proceedings [2020] OJ L 160, pp 1–18 was less clear regarding the application of this provision on arbitration proceedings since it provided the following: "The effects of insolvency proceedings on a lawsuit pending concerning an asset or a right of which the debtor has been divested shall be governed solely by the law of the Member State in which that lawsuit is pending". Still, national courts within the EU have decided that the phrase "lawsuit pending" covers arbitration proceedings. See Gabriel S Moss, Ian F Fletcher and Stuart Isaacs (eds), *The EC Regulation on Insolvency Proceedings: A Commentary and Annotated Guide* (2nd ed, OUP 2009) 281–282.

38 *Syska v Vivendi Universal SA* (2008) EWHC 2155 (Comm) 244 (Clarke J), [2009] 1 All ER (Comm); *Syska v Vivendi Universal SA* [2009] EWCA Civ 677, [2009] 2 All ER (Comm) 891; Swiss Federal Supreme Court, Mar 31, 2009, docket no 4A_428/2008 31; Gabrielle Nater-Bass and Olivier Mosimann, "Effects of Foreign Bankruptcy on International Arbitration" [2011] Austrian Yearbook on International Arbitration 163.

Legal capacity under Swiss PIL was to be governed by the law of the place of a party's incorporation, which was Polish law. The Swiss Court consequently applied Article 142 of the Polish LBR and found that the Polish party had lost its legal capacity to conclude an arbitration agreement once it went bankrupt.

In 2015, a bankrupt party once again invoked this Polish provision before the Svea Court of Appeal in a case between Advadis S.A. and Mr. AB (Advadis) and Royal Unibrew A/S (Royal Unibrew).[39] Royal Unibrew commenced the arbitration in 2011 before the Arbitration Institute of the Stockholm Chamber of Commerce, and on 29 May 2013, the final award was rendered: Advadis and Mr. AB were liable jointly and severally to compensate Royal Unibrew.

Advadis, a company incorporated in Poland, had been declared bankrupt in 2012. In the proceedings regarding setting aside, Advadis submitted that Polish law should apply to the effects of bankruptcy on arbitration. Royal Unibrew submitted that Swedish law was applicable. The Svea Court of Appeal stated that the agreement provides "that the substantive laws of Poland shall govern the parties' agreement but does not explicitly provide that the parties' arbitration agreement shall be governed by Polish law".[40] It concluded that the choice of Stockholm as the place of arbitration indicated that Swedish law applied to the arbitration agreement. Consequently, the Svea Court of Appeal found no provision under which the arbitration agreement should cease in the given circumstances and found the agreement valid.

Interestingly, though an EU Member State national court, the Svea Court of Appeal did not follow the English court's approach. It circumvented the application of the Recast European Insolvency Regulation by characterising the legal category of this dispute as an issue concerning the validity of the arbitration agreement.[41]

This decision raises the question of whether the purpose of Article 18 of the Recast European Insolvency Regulation was violated by such non-application of the regulation. Since the party invoked Article 142 of the Polish LBR, which governs not only the validity of the arbitration clause but also the effects of bankruptcy on pending arbitration, the issue before the Svea Court of Appeal should probably have been characterised as one under Article 18 of the Recast European Insolvency Regulation. Hence, the question is whether the law governing an arbitration agreement

39 *Advadis SA v Royal Unibrew A/S* [2015] Svea Court of Appeal Case No. T 8043–13. Case No. T 8043–13, translation available at www.arbitration.sccinstitute.com/swedish-arbitration-portal (*Advadis S.A. v Royal Unibrew A/S)*; see also in Patricia Živković, "The Effects of Bankruptcy on Arbitration: An Unresolved Issue of Characterization and Applicable Law" (*Kluwer Arbitration Blog*, 14 September 2015). https://arbitrationblog.kluwerarbitration.com/2015/09/14/the-effects-of-bankruptcy-on-arbitration-an-unresolved-issue-of-characterization-and-applicable-law/, accessed 18 March 2024.

40 *Advadis S.A. v Royal Unibrew A/S*, note 39.

41 It needs to be pointed out that the application of art 15 of the European Insolvency Regulation in this particular case would again lead to the application of Swedish law since it would be "the law of the Member State in which [the] lawsuit was pending". Nevertheless, the conclusion that the law applicable to the arbitration agreement supersedes art 15 may lead to undesirable results in cases where this law is different from the law of the state where the arbitral tribunal has its seat. Finally, it is interesting to note that the arbitral tribunal that rendered the award, which was challenged in this case, also found Swedish law to apply to this issue. Still, it based its decision on art 15 of the European Insolvency Regulation. See *Royal Unibrew A/S v Advadis S.A. and Adam Brodowski, Partial Award on Jurisdiction*, Arbitration No. 87/2011, 1 June 2012, paras 140–141, 150.

should supersede the Recast European Insolvency Regulation application. Also, one might ask whether the parties' choice of the law applicable specifically to the effects of bankruptcy should prevail over the conflict of laws rules in the Recast European Insolvency Regulation. Although such a choice of law would reflect party autonomy, it was argued that there is no possibility of such a choice under the Recast European Insolvency Regulation or in other national legal systems.[42]

It is important to note that, in 2016, after the Vivendi saga, Poland amended its insolvency laws, so this type of dispute should not arise again under that applicable law.[43] There are, however, still examples in European jurisdictions that contain similar provisions either in the insolvency or arbitration laws.[44]

What is necessary for present purposes is that this brief analysis of the determination of the law applicable to the effects of bankruptcy on arbitration shows a lack of harmonisation. The national courts in three different jurisdictions characterised the same issue in three different ways: (1) as a matter of the effects of bankruptcy on arbitration, (2) as a matter of legal capacity, and (3) as a matter of the validity of an arbitration agreement. This led to the application of different conflict of laws rules and ultimately to different decisions regarding the applicable law and different ultimate conclusions. Hence, it can be concluded that a conflict of laws rule regarding the law applicable to the effects of bankruptcy is needed at the international level. However, the examples of the two EU courts show that this problem will not be adequately solved until a consensus regarding the the meaning of the category of the "effects of bankruptcy" is also reached.

Since this analysis focused on the national courts' decision-making, which was shaped by characterisation and conflict of laws rules of the forum, it requires investigation from the arbitrators' side. In all three cases mentioned, arbitrators rendered an arbitral award, which implies their stances on the validity of the arbitration agreement, each party's legal capacity, and the lack of effects of bankruptcy on the arbitration dispute before them. These cases, nevertheless, raise the following questions for arbitral tribunals confronted with similar legal arguments made by a bankrupt party:

1. characterisation/categorisation of the legal issue;
2. method of determination of applicable law;
3. binding effect of national laws that are to be considered applicable by national courts (arbitration law and other national legal acts);
4. binding effect of overriding mandatory rules (if any) in light of the public policy objection under the New York Convention or national laws on setting aside arbitral awards.

42 Vorburger, note 30, 86–87.

43 Fernando Mantilla-Serrano, "Chapter 8: Arbitration and Insolvency: Important Aspects for Tribunals to Consider" in W Michael Reisman and Nigel Blackaby (eds), *Arbitration Beyond Borders: Essays in Memory of Guillermo Aguilar Álvarez* (Kluwer Law International 2023) 152 (Mantilla-Serrano); Marcin Orecki, "Does the Polish Arbitration Law Finally Move toward International Standards?" (*Kluwer Arbitration Blog*, 27 May 2015), https://arbitrationblog.kluwerarbitration.com/2015/05/27/12526/, accessed 18 March 2024.

44 For a broader overview of the topic see Patricia Živković, "Bankruptcy and International Arbitration: Some Comparative Snapshots" (2015) IV Slovenian Arbitration Review 6ff (Živković Bankruptcy); see also examples in Mantilla-Serrano, note 23, 152.

The norms of conflict of laws will not bind arbitrators confronted with these legal issues as national courts, so the divergence of the results is further multiplied. Convergence of methodology in these situations might be desirable given the significance of the public interest in bankruptcy proceedings. However, this is far from claiming that national courts' approaches are binding arbitral tribunals.[45] To an extent, this is comparable to the progressive development of arbitral practice on the arbitrability of antitrust claims in arbitration. Since the *Mitsubishi* case,[46] the second-look doctrine has been accepted in the United States and Europe, according to which national courts are to scrutinise arbitrators' application of competition law at a later stage of annulment or enforcement of the arbitral award.[47] The second-look doctrine presupposes that a national court "believes that arbitrators will be able to decide antitrust cases but, simultaneously, requires arbitrators to decide the case in a way that will ensure that the [national court] will be satisfied with the outcome".[48]

Similarly, trust is placed again on arbitral tribunals to characterise the issue arising from the status of a bankrupt party, use the appropriate method for determining the applicable law, and decide on the effect the relevant law should have on the pending arbitration proceeding. It is still incumbent on national courts to scrutinise this three-stage decision-making process under their public policy. The question here would be whether their *lex fori* provisions on methodology and applicable law form a part of overriding mandatory rules to be followed by arbitral tribunals.

In conclusion, whereas the harmonisation or even uniformity of conflict of laws rules that would be imposed on arbitral tribunals might be a desirable outcome, it is currently subject to the lack of interstate coordination on the matter: that is, there is still a lack of harmonised practice among national courts, so at the moment arbitrators' discretion is a potential corrective tool that can be used to render an enforceable arbitral award. The future looks promising for these issues as Working Group V at UNCITRAL has been working on a project dedicated to the applicable law in insolvency proceedings for several years.[49] In the meantime, the localisation tendencies of national courts, evident from the second-look doctrine, are, somewhat paradoxically, best addressed through arbitrators' discretion and flexibility in approaching these legal issues.

IV A Transnational Methodological Framework for Allocating Costs in Arbitration

The last applicable law analysed in this chapter is an example of a transnational substantive rule created by international arbitral tribunals. This is the law governing

45 See more in Živković Bankruptcy, note 44.

46 *Mitsubishi Motors Corp v Soler Chrysler-Plymouth, Inc,* 105 S Ct 3346 (1985).

47 Emanuela Lecchi and Michael Cover, "Arbitrating Competition Law Cases" (2008) 74 Arbitration: The International Journal of Arbitration, Mediation and Dispute Management 65, 65.

48 Ibid., 68.

49 "Working Group V: Insolvency Law | United Nations Commission on International Trade Law". https://uncitral.un.org/en/content/working-group-v-insolvency-law, accessed 18 March 2024; Manuel Penades, "The Law Applicable to the Effects of Insolvency in Arbitration: UNCITRAL's Work in Progress" (*Kluwer Arbitration Blog*, 13 December 2023). https://arbitrationblog.kluwerarbitration.com/2023/12/13/the-law-applicable-to-the-effects-of-insolvency-in-arbitration-uncitrals-work-in-progress/, accessed 18 March 2024.

the allocation of costs in arbitration. As shown herein, this law required no reference to any of the conflict of laws rules; on the contrary, the substantive rule on the allocation of costs in arbitration is a creation of international arbitration tribunals.

The debate regarding the rules of allocation of costs revolved around two diametrically opposite approaches initially developed in litigation: the American Rule, under which each party bears its own costs, and the "costs follow the event" rule, under which, roughly speaking, the losing party pays all the costs.[50] The dichotomy of these two approaches made it difficult to achieve uniform treatment of costs in the last/global award to be completed in the arbitration community. Hence, the regulation of the allocation of costs was left to national legislators and arbitration institutions, which opted for the arbitral tribunal to have discretion on the matter. Consequently, the arbitral practice has developed a harmonised approach to the moderated "costs follow the event" rule.[51] This is an example of how progressive arbitral practice can lead to predictable results in determining the applicable law by creating a transnational substantive rule.

This prevailing approach, which is applicable under the arbitration rules, is the "costs follow the event" rule, but never in its strict form: the "event" is no longer only the case's outcome, as other circumstances are also considered. Therefore, one may say that the "event" is no longer subject only to determining a "winner" and a "loser". A shift in terminology is suggested by some other authors as well; for example, Colin and O'Reilly recognise that there is a clear tendency towards a "moderated costs follow the event" approach.[52] Under the moderated version of this approach, "the principle that costs follow the event is merely the starting point and may be adjusted or even eclipsed by other factors . . . [and] the recoverable costs are subject to a test of reasonableness and possibly proportionality also".[53]

The notion of the "event", i.e. factors to be taken into account under the "costs follow the event" principle, was identified in arbitral practice, and some of the most often used are analysed below.

A Who Is the Winner?

The first "event" that comes to mind is the case's outcome. However, as mentioned earlier, according to the arbitration rules, this approach is no longer to be applied in its strict version, as other circumstances also need to be considered. Arbitral practice, nevertheless, sometimes shows an opposite development by considering the outcome, even if it is not set as the starting point. Under the 1998 ICC Rules, the tribunals had broad discretion regarding allocating costs. Article 31(3) provided that "[t]he final

50 Patricia Zivkovic, "Determination, payment and allocation of costs in international commercial arbitration" (Central European University 2016) 233–241. www.etd.ceu.edu/2016/zivkovic_patricia.htm, accessed 18 March 2024.

51 Colin Ong and Michael O'Reilly, *Costs in International Arbitration* (LexisNexis 2013) 20.

52 Ibid.

53 Ibid.

Award shall fix the costs of the arbitration and decide which of the parties shall bear them or in what proportion they shall be borne by the parties".

The ICC tribunal in Case No 11509 read this rule in such a way as to impose all costs on the "loser", as long as there were no "factors to the contrary".[54] In another ICC case, No. 13756, a sole arbitrator stated:[55]

> [u]nder . . . the ICC Rules, I have discretion as to the allocation of cost. Agent has won on all its major claims. It is thus the winning party in this arbitration. Against this background I find that the arbitration costs are to be paid by Principal. . . . Principal must also bear the costs of the arbitration, as fixed by the ICC Court.

In both cases, the first issue the arbitral panel and the sole arbitrator addressed was the determination of a "winner". In the former case, the tribunal concluded that the claimant was a winner simply by stating that it "succeeded in recovering almost the entire amount of its claim".[56] No further explanation was given in the last award. Similarly, the sole arbitrator in the latter case stated that the "[a]gent won on all its major claims".

Measuring a party's success in arbitration and calculating the costs to be shifted following success can be difficult and complex. The ICC ADR Commission's Report on Decisions on Costs in International Arbitration listed three approaches so far made by arbitral tribunals. They could (1) conclude that a party succeeded in all its claims (or most of them) and order the other party to pay all of the successful party's costs; (2) award costs in proportion to the degree of success; or (3) apportion the costs according to the relative success and failure of the parties.[57]

The circumstances of a case that the tribunal considers can benefit a party that is unsuccessful with its claims. On the other hand, they usually disadvantage a party that was entirely or almost entirely successful in a case. The overview of tribunals' decisions on costs, which follows in this section, will show that multiple circumstances can be considered. It will also showcase how broad tribunals' discretion is in that regard.

B The Success of Procedural Requests Made by the Parties and Procedural Conduct in General

Some tribunals consider both success in the case's merits and the parties' conduct during procedural matters when deciding cost allocation. For instance, in ICC Case No 14630, the sole arbitrator ordered the claimant to cover two-thirds of arbitration costs due to partial success and denied procedural requests.[58] Similarly, in ICC Case No 15248, the respondent was responsible for all costs due to non-compliance with tribunal orders.[59]

---

54 *Company A (Singapore) v Company B (Austria), Final Award,* ICC Case No 11509.

55 Ibid.

56 Ibid., 13.

57 "ICC Arbitration and ADR Commission Report – Decisions on Costs in International Arbitration", [2015] ICC Dispute Resolution Bulletin 20.

58 *Consortium member (Italy) v Consortium leader (Netherlands), Final Award,* ICC Case No. 14630.

59 *Final Award,* ICC Case No 13730, para 163.

Party behaviour influences cost allocation in various legal systems, like failure to appear on time, document production delays, or baseless objections. The IBA 2013 Guidelines on Party Representation in International Arbitration (Guideline 26(c)) mentions that misconduct by a Party Representative can affect cost distribution:

> [i]f the Arbitral Tribunal, after giving the Parties notice and a reasonable opportunity to be heard, finds that a Party Representative has committed Misconduct, the Arbitral Tribunal, as appropriate, may . . . consider the Party Representative's Misconduct in apportioning the costs of the arbitration, indicating, if appropriate, how and in what amount the Party Representative's Misconduct leads the Tribunal to a different apportionment of costs.

While the ICC Techniques for Controlling Time and Costs in Arbitration (ICC Techniques) and IBA Guidelines tackle "unreasonable behavior" and "misconduct", respectively, both address similar actions. These are unreasonable and bad faith conduct, delays, and dilatory tactics, such as those named in the ICC Techniques: excessive document requests, excessive legal argument, excessive cross-examination, exaggerated claims, failure to comply with procedural orders, unjustified interim applications, and unjustified failure to comply with the procedural calendar.[60]

In conclusion, arbitral tribunals consider the case outcome and the parties' procedural behaviour when allocating costs. Predicting the specifics of such behaviour can be challenging due to the broad range of possible conduct. Nevertheless, emphasising early notice of such considerations, as suggested by the IBA Guidelines and ICC Techniques, is a step in the right direction.

C Necessity of the Costs

In ICC Case No 12877, the tribunal observed that even though the respondent was granted five-eighths of the counterclaim costs, some arbitration costs were related to the claim regardless, and the claimant succeeded.[61] Therefore, the arbitrator decreased the respondent's reimbursement, considering that certain counterclaim costs were unnecessary for responding to the claim.

D Parties' Contribution to the Adoption of a Pathological Clause

In ICC Case No 14581, the tribunal, despite the respondent's success on the point of arbitral jurisdiction, allocated only some procedural and legal costs to the claimant due to a jointly drafted flawed arbitration clause, resulting in the claimant bearing only 32% of the claimed costs.[62] This instance illustrates a pre-arbitration factor influencing cost decisions with a substantive aspect. Debate arises over whether such factors should impact cost allocation. In this case, the respondent's role in the faulty arbitration

60 Ugo Draetta, *Counsel as Client's First Enemy in Arbitration?* (Juris 2014) 122–123.

61 *Seller (UK) v Buyer (Australia), Final Award,* ICC Case No. 12877.

62 *Lessor (Ireland) v (1) Ministry A (State X), (2) Ministry B (State X), (3) State Enterprise (State X), (4) State X, Final Award on Jurisdiction,* ICC Case No 14581.

clause led to unrecoverable jurisdictional stage costs. The interplay of substantive and procedural elements in costs is evident and aligned with the compensatory nature of costs. This mitigation aligns with the contributory fault principle, reducing compensation if a party's fault contributes to its own loss.[63] Such practices maintain legal certainty and predictability in international arbitration.

E Commencement of Arbitration Proceedings in Good Faith

In ICC Case No 13730, despite dismissing the claimant's unfounded claims, the tribunal acknowledged their good faith in initiating arbitration due to uncertainties in Japanese law and the respondent's conduct ambiguities.[64] This led to an equal allocation of costs. Similarly, in SCC Case No 73/2011, the tribunal assigned the claimant's procedural and legal costs to the respondent, considering the claimant's obligation to begin arbitration to secure payments upon agreement termination.[65]

F Reasonableness and Proportionality Tests

Arbitration rules, such as those of the SCC, the ICC, the ICDR, the LCIA, and the Swiss Rules, incorporate the standard of reasonableness, necessity, or appropriateness for recovering party costs, mainly legal fees.[66] Arbitrator fees are predefined, ensuring presumed reasonableness. Party costs incurred during proceedings are not pre-set and vary, leading to debates on their reasonableness. This reasonableness standard, related

---

63 Sergey Ripinsky, "Assessing Damages in Investment Disputes: Practice in Search of Perfect" (Social Science Research Network 2009) SSRN Scholarly Paper ID 1547089 15. https://papers.ssrn.com/abstract=1547089, accessed 18 March 2024.

64 *Distributor (Poland) and Daughter Company of Distributor (Isle of Man) v Manufacturer (Japan) and Manufacturer Europe (European country), Final Award*, ICC Case No. 13730.

65 *Final Award*, SCC Case No. 73/2011, para 62.

66 The different approaches are as follows: Article 50 of the SCC Rules: "Unless otherwise agreed by the parties, the Arbitral Tribunal may in the final award, at the request of a party, order one party to pay any reasonable costs incurred by another party, including costs for legal representation, having regard to the outcome of the case, each party's contribution to the efficiency and expeditiousness of the arbitration and any other relevant circumstances". Article 38(1) of the 2021 ICC Rules: "The costs of the arbitration shall include the fees and expenses of the arbitrators and the ICC administrative expenses fixed by the Court, in accordance with the scale in force at the time of the commencement of the arbitration, as well as the fees and expenses of any experts appointed by the arbitral tribunal and the reasonable legal and other costs incurred by the parties for the arbitration". Article 37(d) of the ICDR Rules: "The arbitral tribunal shall fix the costs of arbitration in its award(s). The tribunal may allocate such costs among the parties if it determines that allocation is reasonable, taking into account the circumstances of the case. Such costs may include: . . . d. the reasonable legal and other costs incurred by the parties". Article 38(e) of the Swiss Rules: "The costs for legal representation and assistance, if such costs were claimed during the arbitral proceedings, and only to the extent that the arbitral tribunal determines that the amount of such costs is reasonable". Article 28.3 of the LCIA Rules: "The Arbitral Tribunal shall also have the power to decide by an award that all or part of the legal or other expenses incurred by a party (the 'Legal Costs') be paid by another party. The Arbitral Tribunal shall decide the amount of such Legal Costs on such reasonable basis as it thinks appropriate. The Arbitral Tribunal shall not be required to apply the rates or procedures for assessing such costs practised by any state court or other legal authority".

to cost proportionality, is frequently applied to party costs. Tribunals require detailed party cost breakdowns to assess their reasonableness, aiding fair allocation decisions. Encouraging detailed expense documentation from parties early in proceedings benefits both parties and tribunals, ensuring more predictable cost decisions.

These practices in allocating costs in international commercial arbitration are based on arbitral tribunals' discretion guaranteed through the international arbitration framework and their willingness to develop a transnational rule that surpasses national boundaries. Such an approach maintains fairness, transparency, and predictability in arbitration cost allocations. The stability of the arbitral practice in this matter speaks to the lack of a need for legislative reform. Still, it depends on arbitrators having a proper understanding of their discretion and on how well-informed parties in arbitration are. Without full transparency on the allocation of costs from the commencement of proceedings, it is difficult to argue in favour of such a transnational rule.

V Conclusion

This chapter has illustrated the methodological differences in determining applicable laws by arbitral tribunals and national courts, emphasising the evolving nature of this crucial issue. It argues that preserving a nuanced understanding of these disparities is imperative for practitioners and academics, as it acknowledges the current developments and anticipates future tendencies.

Section II explored the evolution of methodological approaches in determining the laws governing merits and arbitration agreements, and it showed that certain aspects of it have witnessed a harmonisation. However, even in these two applicable substantive laws, there is an ongoing interplay between transnationalisation and localisation tendencies. On the one hand, the laws applicable to arbitration agreements are evolving, with some notable exceptions, in the direction of recognising the importance of anchoring their validity in the jurisdiction of the seat. Conversely, arbitral institutions maintain their position, which affirms the authority of arbitrators directly to determine the applicable law without reliance on conflict of laws rules. This stance respects their autonomy from local legal systems to the utmost extent. Acknowledging this dynamic is essential for anticipating future shifts in applicable substantive laws.

Section III explored the law applicable to the effects of bankruptcy on arbitration, revealing a fragmented and non-uniform approach to determining applicable laws among national courts. The scattered nature of this framework transposes into arbitration and poses challenges for international arbitrators. This section showed that arbitrators are confronted with the same questions as national courts when deciding what effect the bankruptcy of one of the parties should have on arbitration proceedings. While there is a pressing need for continued examination and potential future harmonisation of this issue in national legal frameworks, in the meantime, arbitrators' discretion on conflict of laws matters serves as a corrective tool for the non-uniform approaches of national courts and supports the procedural efficiency and legitimacy of arbitration.

Finally, Section IV examined the law governing the allocation of costs, which presents a contrasting picture – a legal solution that transcends national boundaries. This section showed the adaptability of international arbitration and a methodological framework that fosters predictability and flexibility across diverse jurisdictions without any reliance on conflict of laws rules or substantive and procedural rules regarding cost allocation contained in national legal systems.

This chapter highlights the significance of understanding methodological disparities between arbitral tribunals and national courts in determining applicable laws. While certain aspects have witnessed harmonisation and localisation tendencies, as shown in Figure 14.3, preserving diversity and adequately understanding the methodology

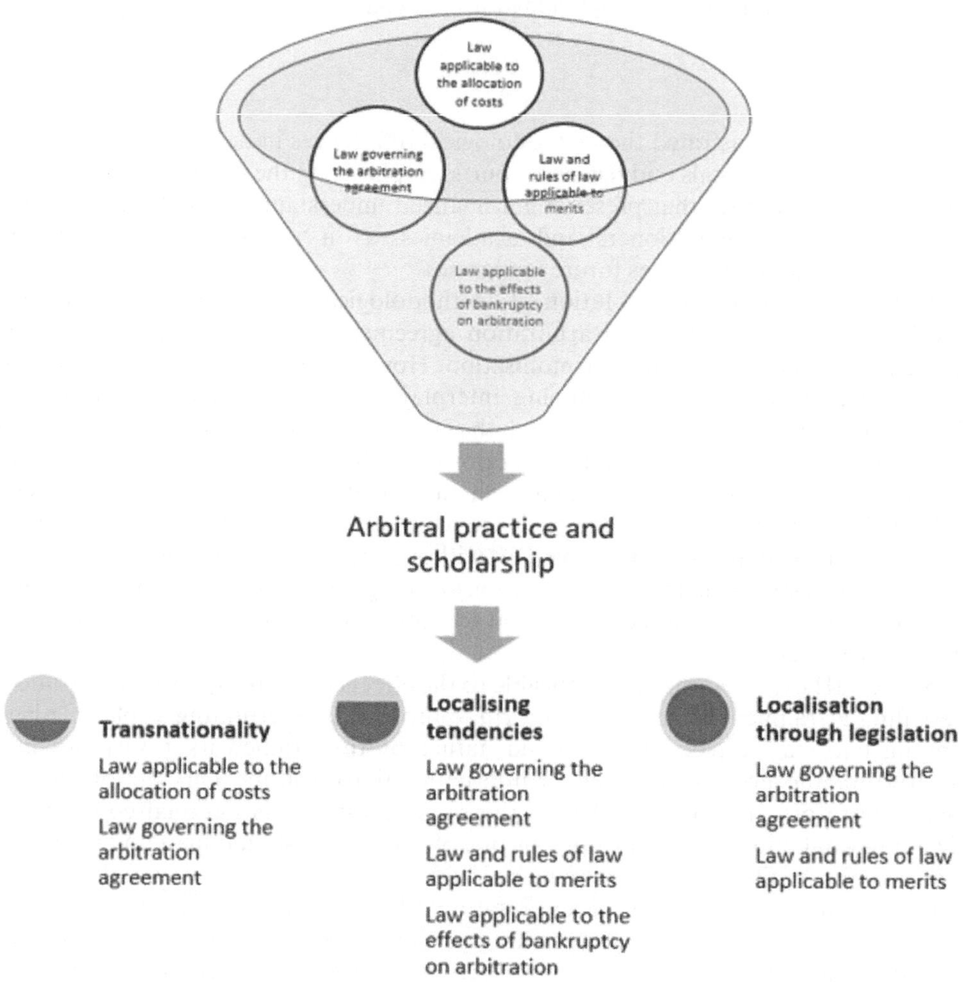

Figure 14.3 The co-existence of transnational and localisation tendencies in international commercial arbitration.

is crucial for upholding the inherent flexibility of international arbitration and its legitimacy. This figure showcases how localisation and transnationalisation can co-exist in international commercial arbitration and serve the same purpose. Practitioners and academics should acknowledge these differences and actively engage with them to ensure a comprehensive grasp of the evolving nature of the methodology for determining applicable laws. Embracing this diversity is not merely a scholarly pursuit but a pragmatic necessity for effectively navigating international commercial arbitration's complex and dynamic realm.

INDEX

Note: Page numbers in *italic* indicate a figure on the corresponding page.

For Product Safety Concerns and Information please contact our EU representative GPSR@taylorandfrancis.com Taylor & Francis Verlag GmbH, Kaufingerstraße 24, 80331 München, Germany